STUDIES IN IMPERIALISM

General Editor: Andrew S. Thompson

Founding Editor: John M. MacKenzie

When the 'Studies in Imperialism' series was founded by Professor John M. MacKenzie more than twenty-five years ago, emphasis was laid upon the conviction that 'imperialism as a cultural phenomenon had as significant an effect on the dominant as on the subordinate societies'. With well over a hundred titles now published, this remains the prime concern of the series. Cross-disciplinary work has indeed appeared covering the full spectrum of cultural phenomena, as well as examining aspects of gender and sex, frontiers and law, science and the environment, language and literature, migration and patriotic societies, and much else. Moreover, the series has always wished to present comparative work on European and American imperialism, and particularly welcomes the submission of books in these areas. The fascination with imperialism, in all its aspects, shows no sign of abating, and this series will continue to lead the way in encouraging the widest possible range of studies in the field. 'Studies in Imperialism' is fully organic in its development, always seeking to be at the cutting edge, responding to the latest interests of scholars and the needs of this ever-expanding area of scholarship.

The suppression of the Atlantic slave trade

D1590332

MANCHESTER
1824

Manchester University Press

The suppression of the Atlantic slave trade

BRITISH POLICIES, PRACTICES AND REPRESENTATIONS OF NAVAL COERCION

Edited by
Robert Burroughs and Richard Huzzey

MANCHESTER UNIVERSITY PRESS

Published by MANCHESTER UNIVERSITY PRESS
ALTRINCHAM STREET, MANCHESTER M1 7JA, UK
www.manchesteruniversitypress.co.uk

British Library Cataloguing-in-Publication Data
A catalogue record for this book is available from the British Library

Library of Congress Cataloging-in-Publication Data applied for

ISBN 978 0 7190 8511 6 *hardback*

ISBN 978 1 5261 2288 9 *paperback*

First published in hardback 2015

First published in paperback 2018

Typeset in Trump Medieval by
Koinonia, Manchester

CONTENTS

LIST OF FIGURES AND TABLES

Figures

Table

LIST OF CONTRIBUTORS

Robert Burroughs is Senior Lecturer in English Literature at Leeds Beckett University. He is the author of a number of works on empire, humanitarianism and Africa in the nineteenth century, including *Travel Writing and Atrocities* (New York: Routledge, 2011).

Emma Christopher is on the faculty at the University of Technology, Sydney, and is in charge of research for Anti-Slavery Australia. Her works include *A Merciless Place: The Fate of Britain's Convicts after the American Revolution* (Oxford: Oxford University Press, 2011) and *Slave Ship Sailors and their Captive Cargoes, 1760–1807* (Cambridge: Cambridge University Press, 2006).

Richard Huzzey is Senior Lecturer in History at the University of Liverpool and Co-Director of the Centre for the Study of International Slavery, a joint research initiative of his university and the International Slavery Museum. He is the author of *Freedom Burning: Anti-Slavery and Empire in Victorian Britain* (Ithaca: Cornell University Press, 2012) and a series of articles in scholarly journals.

David Lambert is Reader in History at the University of Warwick and former Director of the Yesu Persaud Centre for Caribbean Studies. He is the author of *Mastering the Niger: James MacQueen's African Geography and the Struggle over Atlantic Slavery* (Chicago: Chicago University Press, 2013), *White Creole Culture, Politics and Identity during the Age of Abolition* (Cambridge: Cambridge University Press, 2005), and a wide variety of other works.

John McAleer is Lecturer in History at the University of Southampton. For six years, he was Curator of Imperial and Maritime History at the National Maritime Museum, Greenwich. He is the author of *Representing Africa: Landscape, Exploration and Empire in Southern Africa, 1780–1870* (Manchester: Manchester University Press, 2010) and (with H. V. Bowen and Robert J. Blyth) *Monsoon Traders: The Maritime World of the East India Company* (London: Scala, 2011).

John Rankin is Assistant Professor in the Department of History at East Tennessee State University. His interests lie in the overlapping themes of imperialism, transnational and global studies, issues of race and racism and the social history of medicine. His forthcoming monograph (University of Missouri Press) examines the intersection of health, race and empire in British West Africa, 1800–60.

Mary Wills completed her thesis 'The Royal Navy and the suppression of the Atlantic slave trade: anti-slavery, empire and identity' in 2012, following an AHRC collaborative doctoral award held at the University of Hull's Wilberforce Institute for the Study of Slavery and Emancipation and the National Maritime Museum.

ACKNOWLEDGEMENTS

This book was formed from conversations at a series of conferences surrounding the bicentenary of British abolition of the slave trade. Working on British slave-trade suppression, in different disciplines, we agreed that a new academic history of this campaign was overdue. In the subsequent years, we recruited specialists to meet our aims for a volume that incorporated African experiences, metropolitan literature and cultural histories of suppression. The quality of their contributions exceeded our greatest hopes, and we have enjoyed working with them all. We remain indebted to organisers of a conference at the National Museum of the Royal Navy in 2007 and an AHRC-funded workshop at the National Maritime Museum in 2009 for the ideas they provoked us to pursue.

We are particularly grateful to Douglas Hamilton and John Oldfield and colleagues in our current and past universities for encouragement as we prepared the chapters. Robert Burroughs would like to acknowledge the support of a Leverhulme Trust Early Career Fellowship in enabling the research on which his contributions to this volume are based. He also received the support of a Promising Researcher Fellowship at Leeds Beckett University while writing parts of this volume, and Richard Huzzey benefited from research funding and an early career international networking award from Plymouth University and support from the Department of History at the University of Liverpool. We would also like to thank the Picture Library of Royal Museums Greenwich for kind assistance in preparing this volume.

Emma Brennan at Manchester University Press and our series editors, John MacKenzie and Andrew Thompson, have been outstandingly patient and supportive. We are both grateful to our families and, most of all, our wives Antoinette Burroughs and Irene Middleton for their tolerance of weekends tweaking the format of references and evenings responding to each other's editorial queries. We very much appreciate Irene's work preparing the index and proofreading.

CHAPTER ONE

Suppression of the Atlantic slave trade: abolition from ship to shore

Robert Burroughs

This study provides fresh perspectives on critical aspects of the British Royal Navy's suppression of the Atlantic slave trade. It is divided into three sections. The first, Policies, presents a new interpretation of the political framework under which slave-trade suppression was executed. Part II, Practices, examines details of the work of the navy's West Africa Squadron which have been passed over in earlier narrative accounts. Part III, Representations, provides the first sustained discussion of the squadron's wider, cultural significance, and its role in the shaping of geographical knowledge of West Africa. One of our objectives in looking across these three areas – a view from shore to ship and back again – is to understand better how they overlap. Our authors study the interconnections between political and legal decision-making, practical implementation, and cultural production and reception in an anti-slavery pursuit undertaken far from the metropolitan centres in which it was first conceived. Such an approach promises new insights into what the anti-slave-trade patrols meant to Britain and what the campaign of 'liberation' meant for those enslaved Africans and naval personnel, including black sailors, whose lives were most closely entangled in it.

The following chapters reassess the policies, practices and representations of slave-trade suppression by building upon developments in research in political, legal and humanitarian history; naval, imperial and maritime history; medical history; race relations and migration; abolitionist literature and art; nineteenth-century geography; nautical literature and art and representations of Africa. Topics that this book encompass are accordingly varied and include: the origins and implementation of the suppression policy; the rise of 'anti-coercionist' challenges to naval deployment in West Africa in the mid-nineteenth century and the failure of those challenges; responses to Britain's abolitionist policy from outside Britain; Britain's imperial belligerence in enforcing the anti-slave-trade patrols; emotional responses of officers and sailors to this task; race relations in the West Africa Squadron; health histories; the transition of liberated Africans into apprenticeship in the colonies; images of officers, sailors, slaves and slave traders in representations of slave-trade suppression; and the impact of this endeavour upon British perceptions of West Africa.

A scholarly reassessment of the long-running coercive crusade against the trafficking of enslaved Africans to the Americas is overdue. In the years since Eric Williams's *Capitalism and Slavery* (1944) fundamentally challenged self-satisfied and complacent histories of Britain's anti-slavery movement, and ignited scholarly inquiry into the slave trade and slavery in the Atlantic world, slave-trade suppression has been valuably examined in several studies.[1] These works mainly focus upon the economic and political shaping of all or certain parts of the Atlantic world, often with particular attention paid to questions of international diplomacy and law.[2] Discussions by maritime and slave-trade historians, centred on the policies and practices of arresting the commerce, have hitherto tended to fall back on accounts by the naval historians Christopher Lloyd (1949) and W. E. F. Ward (1969),[3] while the cultural significance of slave-trade suppression in nineteenth-century Britain has received little attention despite the increase in studies of this dimension of slavery and abolition.[4] Lloyd's and Ward's accounts contain much useful anecdotal information, and both are particularly strong in detailing the suffering of naval crews chasing 'slavers' in West Africa. However, both are written in admiring tones which assume humanitarian motives for naval suppression as much as they presume patriotic pride on behalf of the reader. They encourage the understanding of slave-trade suppression as an end-point, a self-satisfied conclusion in triumphalist narratives of Britain's emergence as a leading anti-slavery nation. As many commentators note, official and popular commentaries on British history traditionally linger on the presumed beneficence of abolition of slave trading and/or slavery, rather than other parts of that history such as Britons' leading role in trafficking and exploitation. This was notoriously the case with many of the events in 2007 that marked the bicentennial commemorations of the Abolition Act. Slave-trade suppression featured then primarily in specialist (military) events which at times echoed the laudatory tone of the historical sources that they drew upon. Richard Huzzey and John MacAleer explore these recent representations in chapter 8 of this volume.

Another by-product of the 2007 remembrances, Siân Rees's history of slave-trade suppression, *Sweet Water and Bitter: The Ships that Stopped the Slave Trade* (2008), significantly improves upon its forebears by retelling the rich anecdotal history of the West Africa Squadron in newly clear, chronological form. Rees makes particularly good use of the *Sierra Leone Gazette* in shedding new light on the early years of the pursuit, and pays much-required attention to African perspectives and life-stories. Even so, Rees at times repeats Lloyd's and Ward's moralistic interpretation of events in which support for and service in the squadron is interpreted as an innate response to the violence of slavery, or an act of personal or national atonement.[5] By reassessing the policies, practices and representations of slave-trade suppression, our contributors seek to address the thornier questions raised by a campaign apparently founded on national atonement and altruism in an age of empire and aggrandisement, on vast financial and military commitment in an age of colonial retrenchment, and on the universalist rhetoric of the anti-slavery movement in an age of nationalism and competing views on racial difference. The remainder of this chapter offers supporting information on the Atlantic slave trade in the nineteenth century and the efforts of the navy to eliminate it and introduces the following chapters. Along the way I explain further our objectives for this volume by comparing our concerns and emphases to those of previous histories of slave-trade suppression.

The Atlantic slave trade entered a new and uncertain phase after the British government passed the Abolition Act (1807) to outlaw British participation in the industry as of January 1808. The act led to a sharp decrease in the volume of slave trading, as only a small number of British merchants and captains continued illicitly in the trade, running the risk of confiscation of their ship and a fine of £100 for every slave found in their possession. Domestic laws were reinforced to extinguish the embers of the British traffic. From 1811 Britons' slave trading was punishable by fourteen years' transportation; three years later Britons' lending of capital to non-British slave merchants was prohibited. These laws brought a swift end to British merchants' open participation in the slave trade. Yet the traffic persisted, and rapidly regenerated, as slave traders from throughout the Atlantic world filled the vacuum created by British withdrawal by operating under the colours of other nations that had yet to enforce meaningful anti-slave-trade laws. By the 1820s, the volume of Atlantic slave trading was nearly as great as it had been in its all-time peak decades, the 1780s and 1790s.[6] Illegality makes it harder to find written records, but British support for and involvement in the slave trade probably also recovered over time as merchants sought loopholes and conspiracies to continue profiting.[7]

The decline in British slave dealing was nonetheless momentous because of the scale of the nation's participation in the trade prior to 1808. According to the important research of the 'Transatlantic Slave

Trade Voyages' project, an estimated 12.5 million enslaved Africans were entered into the Atlantic slave traffic. (Of those embarked, approximately 10.7 million arrived in the Americas. Most of the remaining 1.8 million persons were killed at sea.[8]) More than a quarter of the total number travelled on English or British ships. Portugal was the most active slave-trading nation over the long history of the slave trade, but David Eltis and David Richardson calculate that Britons dominated the slave trade in eight of the thirteen decades between 1681 and 1807. The peak years of British slave trading were those immediately prior to the Abolition Act. In the 1780s and 1790s, Britons took away roughly 45% of all enslaved Africans bound for the Americas.[9]

As it became apparent that the trade would continue in the hands of other nations, the British government set about enforcing abolition by means of what Serge Daget describes as a 'supranational policy' of legal and diplomatic pressure, naval patrolling and confiscation of slave ships and their human cargoes at courts of mixed commission.[10] While Britain remained at war, its navy seized slave ships sailing under the flags of its enemies France, Holland and Spain, taking their human cargoes as contraband, as it had done throughout the Napoleonic Wars in accordance with wartime belligerent rights. Despite not possessing the legal authority, the navy also detained slave ships sailing under the US and Danish flags on the premise that it acted on behalf of these nations, which had illegalised the trade. After the Strangford Treaty of 1810, which outlawed Portuguese slave trading outside of its own dominions and fixed import taxes on British goods entering Brazil, Portuguese (including Brazilian) ships also were intercepted unless they could prove that they were travelling between Portuguese ports. There is little question that during the war the navy operated on the fringes of, and sometimes outside, international law.[11]

Almost immediately after the Napoleonic Wars, the seizure of the French ship *Louis* by HMS *Queen Charlotte* caused a legal controversy that tested and defeated Britain's right to search suspected (and actual) slave traders. It then became imperative that government officials (in particular the Foreign Secretaries Castlereagh and Canning) and abolitionist leaders intensify their campaign 'to coax or coerce' the other maritime powers in the Atlantic, plus the slave-trading states of Africa, to sign anti-slave-trade treaties with Britain, impose their own abolition laws, establish their own anti-slave-trade squadrons, participate in courts of mixed commission, and grant the British navy rights to help enforce their legislation.[12] By 1819, the navy had installed a permanent squadron off the west coast of Africa. It would remain in place until 1870. At its peak in the mid- to late 1840s, Britain's West Africa Squadron annually comprised in excess of 36 vessels and 4,000 personnel. These figures represent roughly 15% of warships then in commission, and one-tenth of the naval workforce.[13]

Statistics only tell us so much about the extent of the British government's commitment to these patrols. Lord Palmerston's famous comment that '[i]f there was a particularly old slow-going tub in the Navy she was sure to be sent to the coast of Africa to try and catch the fast sailing American clippers' needs to be read in context as a hyperbolic complaint to Russell about the Admiralty's frustration of his plans.[14] Naval historians have nevertheless agreed that the navy was for the most part ill-provisioned to perform its task. In most years, the squadron that patrolled the West African coast was too small, and its ships too old or low-rating, to offer a major threat to illegal slave trading. And yet the military inadequacy of the force does not negate the surprising cost and commitment to suppression throughout a period of fiscal retrenchment.[15] In the first part of this book, Richard Huzzey traces the political debates which framed legal and diplomatic policies for the British state's waning but unbroken commitment to slave-trade suppression. He considers the popularity of this campaign and assesses the motives of subsequent generations of politicians who maintained, and occasionally challenged, the anti-slave-trade patrols.

One of the main aims of this volume is to come to a more nuanced understanding of the motivations behind Britain's anti-slave-trade policies and actions. This entails studying the work of slave-trade suppression with awareness of its political motivations and repercussions, its practical difficulties and the impact of these on enslaved peoples, former slaves, and naval sailors and the broader cultural and ideological framework of the political and practical considerations of the campaign. Far from discounting morality as a motivating factor, we seek to examine how moral motives might figure in this context. Lloyd's view that the squadron was launched out of 'purely philanthropic motives' understates the complexity and the momentousness of Britain's transition from leading poacher to gamekeeper of the slave trade, for the nation as a whole (or at least its vocal minority) and for the navy as an institution.[16] Prior to 1807, the navy had looked favourably upon the slave trade as a 'nursery' for seamen helping to preserve naval supremacy, especially at times of war. Naval members of the House of Commons voted against abolition,[17] Nelson famously spoke out against Wilberforce, while naval commanders turned a blind eye to the illegal trade between the West Indies and the USA. Most naval protection of the British slave trade had of course been undertaken in the straightforward preservation of the nation's mercantile trade. Even the last British ships legally to carry slaves from Africa did so, in October 1807, under escort of a naval frigate to guard against attacks by enemy navies.[18] Points such as this remind us that the Africa Squadron was the product of an unlikely union between the navy and the anti-slavery society, two institutions with different conceptualisations of freedom. Many of its policies and practices bear the mark of this ambiguity, as do representations of them.

To understand morality as one contingent and conditional factor among several others, including less savoury incentives such as prize monies, is to treat the human agents of Britain's anti-slave-trade initiatives as three-dimensional beings acting in a moment of complicated historical change. If at times the humans seem less than humane, then they seem no less human for it. Indeed, the moralistic interpretation of events tends to represent naval personnel assigned to anti-slave-trade policing as unreflexive and, in more ways than one, selfless agents of imperial power founded on humanitarian convictions. Rees, for example, characterises sailors in this context as guided by an unconscious humanitarianism – 'inflexibly xenophobic, unthinkingly racist yet dying in their thousands to save individuals with whom they had nothing in common but humanity'.[19] While the debate continues as to the severity of conditions of service in the eighteenth- and early-nineteenth-century navy, it is unsafe to assume that sailors did or did not recognise shared humanity with enslaved Africans. Life at sea might have desensitised sailors to this point.[20] Alongside Rees's interpretation we might place the fictional tars (including press-gang victims) in Captain Marryat's *Peter Simple* (1834), who, when petitioned to donate wages to the anti-slavery movement by a West Indian missionary, curtly reply, '[t]he nigger's better off [than] we'.[21]

Domestic debates and calculations such as the sailors' rights movement were framed by the international context of suppression. The British forces were joined sporadically by squadrons from the navies of France, Portugal and the USA – although only during the brief Paine–Tucker accord of 1840 did any of these squadrons (those of Britain and the USA) work co-dependently with one another.[22] The Royal Navy's campaigns generated more hostility than amity with foreign nations. Most of the Atlantic powers were unwilling or unable to enforce meaningful measures against their merchants' trade in slaves. They had not experienced the same levels of abolitionist sentiment as had Britain, their navies were weaker than Britain's, in part because of war, and so too were their economies more dependent on slavery. The resistance of other governments to Britain's campaign posed an insurmountable difficulty for ships on the anti-slave-trade patrols: as long as one nation refused to enter into effectual bilateral agreements with Britain, slave traders could continue to operate by raising that nation's flag if approached by naval patrollers. If boarded, they could show forged documentation of the ship's place of origin. Slave-ship captains travelled with more than one set of papers and flags and evaded capture by employing these appropriately according to geographical location and current legislation. As foreign ministers worked to close the loopholes, anti-slave-trade officers were charged with navigating a labyrinthine, and ever-shifting, network of treaties. For naval captains this meant continuing economic risk in capturing slave ships. They were forced to weigh the pecuniary incentives of seizing slave-ship prizes against the threat of personal liability for the compensation of merchants who could prove – legitimately or otherwise – that their ship had been illegally condemned.

Taking into consideration the various practical problems of naval suppression in her chapter in Part II of this volume, Mary Wills considers the responses of officers serving on the squadron, exploring how far faith, profits and honour shaped their responses to the assignment. Much of the disquiet among sailors and the Admiralty came from the fearful mortality rates on British naval vessels assigned to West Africa. The morale-sapping effects of death – be it in the infrequent but fierce battles against slave-ship crews or, as was more likely, through infection by tropical diseases – profoundly determined naval sailors' attitudes to the squadron. John Rankin's chapter in Part II further delineates the health of sailors of European and African descent, finding that the latter were deemed more suited to the unhealthy climate and consequently given more unenviable tasks and more aggressive medical treatments. Although they are frequently overlooked in previous historical studies, black seamen were crucial to the day-to-day practices of slave-trade suppression.

Given the costs for Britain in blood and coin, it is hardly surprising that some of the sailors who worked in it, as well as the taxpayers who financed it, viewed the campaign uncharitably. While many commentators of the nineteenth century saw in it cause for benign celebration of British far-sightedness, others questioned its effectiveness. As several contemporary observers noted, as long as it could not stop the trade, the navy may have exacerbated the suffering of the enslaved on Atlantic crossings by forcing the once legitimate trade into the hands of individuals who adopted ever more mercenary and hazardous tactics to ship the largest possible quantities of Africans to the Americas. This realisation raised questions about the value of suppression as a moral act that are not straightforwardly settled by pointing to the squadron's successes. Those periods in which the navy appeared to be making the greatest in-roads by capturing large numbers of slave traders, thanks in part to changes in treaty obligations and naval strategies, for example, often reflect proportionate increases in slave-trading activity. As Eltis notes, while the squadron may have checked the growth of the slave trade, only when the British government imposed its self-perceived moral authority upon the governments of other nations, in particular Portugal and Brazil, could it effect change in regions and markets beyond its formal control.[23] Aside from British insults to the sovereignty of Portugal and Brazil, recent research by Robin Law suggests that anti-slave-trade agreements made in West Africa laid the groundwork for British presumption and colonial expansion by discriminating against the sovereign rights of 'uncivilised' peoples.[24] Even then the navy could not fully stop the supply so long as demand for slaves and legal protection for slave traders existed in the Americas.[25]

And yet in spite of the various complications, between 1808 and 1867 the navy intercepted more than 1,600 slave ships carrying approximately 160,000 slaves bound for the Americas.[26] Naval suppression further proved a deterrent to the trade by increasing costs and risks. In most likely curbing the growth of the industry, it effectively prevented hundreds of thousands of Africans' undergoing the trauma of the Atlantic crossing and enslavement in the Americas.[27] This is not necessarily to say that these same Africans won freedom thanks to the work of the West Africa Squadron. The liberty afforded to the individuals who entered as apprentices into the fledging colonial society of Sierra Leone or were shipped as 'free emigrants' to the West Indies cannot be clearly distinguished from the bonded labour awaiting them had their enslavers completed the voyage to the Americas. As Emma Christopher shows in chapter 4 of this volume, the British authorities showed contempt for the abilities and liberties of those individuals it tellingly labelled as 'recaptives' and 'freed slaves'. Christopher centres her enquiry on early records from Freetown, Sierra Leone, the hub of anti-slave-trade activity.

J. R. Oldfield comments that one of the most striking aspects of the history of Atlantic slavery 'is its silencing of African perspectives, and, in particular, the suffering of the millions who were sold into slavery'.[28] Histories of slave-trade suppression tend to bear out this observation. Another main aim of this volume is to highlight the impact of anti-slave-trade measures upon enslaved and formerly enslaved Africans, and the lack of attention paid to African perspectives in earlier (including contemporaneous) writings about the subject. As noted before, the books by Lloyd and Ward not only prioritise white perspectives but also white suffering on the preventive patrols, though Rees's book already has done much valuable work in drawing upon West African historiography to fill in the noticeable gap in African experiences.[29] New research in this volume on the handling of 'recaptives' in Sierra Leone, and the racialised medical treatment on naval vessels, adds to our understanding of the African experience of anti-slave-trade patrols. In particular, this research makes clear that the lack of African perspectives consulted in contemporary discussions, and in subsequent histories and memorialisation of the West Africa Squadron, should not be assumed to denote a lack of agency on the part of enslaved peoples or other Africans involved in suppression. Just as historians have recovered histories of resistance to the slave trade and slavery, so one of the most pressing tasks for researchers of slave-trade suppression is to recall the variety of black experiences of and roles in it and the trade it sought to curb.[30]

The experiences of sailors and Africans ashore and on ship often stand in contrast to contemporaneous representations of naval suppression. Robert Burroughs considers the ambiguities of British writers' representations of the West Africa Squadron in his chapter in Part III. As with political debate, literary representations contested the meanings of the campaign, and ideas and impressions about the slave trade, its victims, perpetrators and prosecutors further informed the ways Britons imagined themselves in relation to other peoples and places. Perhaps above all other territories, this is the case with West Africa. Eltis writes that '[d]espite occasional redeployment of cruisers from West Africa to Brazil and the Caribbean, the centre of suppression was always on the west coast of Africa'. More than 85% of all slave-ship captures took place there.[31] On top of the legal and diplomatic implications of suppression policies for the future of British imperialism in Africa, the naval campaigns played an important part in framing images of the continent and, in particular, its west coast. In his chapter for Part III David Lambert examines how the suppression campaign forged geographical knowledge and expert prejudices in the metropole.

As I mentioned at the start of this chapter, a further aim of this volume is to identify the cross-fertilisation of ideas and understandings of the anti-slave-trade squadron among its metropolitan architects, critics, and other interested parties, and those who experienced it at the coal-face. Generally speaking, Lloyd understands this flow of information to be one-way: from ship to shore. As naval captains witnessed horrors of the slave trade, they were converted to the anti-slavery cause, supplying the evidence that persuaded far-seeing politicians such as Russell to push home the measures required to eliminate the trade. In contrast, Williams and his followers focus on the flow of information from shore to ship: economic and political considerations in the metropolitan centres of empire forced the government's hand in pursuing its anti-slave-trade agenda, no matter the various hardships it inflicted upon sailors, recaptives and enslaved Africans. Taken together, the following chapters identify a complex, transformative negotiation of knowledge and understanding of the Africa Squadron, one in which the ship, and the maritime world more broadly, is found to help shape, and not just passively reflect, the cultural, political and other spheres of nineteenth-century Britain. One of the main examples of this is the literal disillusionment that takes place as naval personnel contemplated philanthropic ideals amid the complicated reality of patrolling the African coast. While working to suppress the subsidiary trade in the southern Indian Ocean of slaves bound for the Americas, for example, Lt. F. L. Barnard criticised 'Englishmen, who annihilate the slave-dealers and civilize Africa by their own comfortable firesides, little thinking of the hardships and privations their countrymen are undergoing to carry out their impossible theories'.[32] Although the straightforwardness of this view from the fireside is upheld in the writings of some eyewitnesses, sobering appraisals such as Barnard's would also feed back into metropolitan discussions, changing home-grown expectations and priorities in the process. This understanding of the ship and its environs as units of cultural exchange that inform 'the centre' has the effect, advised by Paul Gilroy, of challenging 'the unthinking assumption that cultures always flow into patterns congruent with the borders of essentially homogeneous nation states'.[33]

The image of slave-trade suppression has changed not only in different spheres but also over time. Our final chapter considers how the nineteenth-century suppression of the slave trade has survived in British public memory, tracing early commemorations through to the museums and political debates of our own times. Huzzey and John McAleer examine how those with divergent agendas have appropriated the history of suppression to recover different uses of the past for the present.

The British navy's campaign to suppress the Atlantic slave trade ran for more than half a century, and in that time it directly impacted upon several nations and peoples of Africa, Europe and the Americas. It is a history of hemispheric proportions. Far from attempting comprehensive coverage, the present study works toward the objectives that I have outlined above through detailed discussion of particular issues, regions and time-frames. We have focused almost exclusively on British naval operations, and much of our discussion is centred on activities in and around the West African coast, which was the centre-ground of preventive action. Further research may profitably look at the anti-slave-trade squadrons despatched by the navies of other nations, both in terms of their direct engagements with the slave trade and in their interrelationship with the dominant, British presence, and at the work of other British squadrons beyond West Africa.[34] In view of the danger of 'maritimisation' of the history of transatlantic slavery, which in truth stemmed from and shaped industrial centres far removed from the ports of the Atlantic world, researchers need also to trace deeper lying metropolitan connections to the post-1808 traffic.[35] This is not to mention the 'many middle passages' and other anti-slave-trade activities beyond the Atlantic world, including (but not limited to) the campaigns against the Indian Ocean slave trade, the Swahili–Arab slave traffic across the Sahara to North Africa, the Ottoman Empire and India, and the trafficking of indentured labourers from the Pacific Islands to Queensland, Australia.[36] The subject is practically inexhaustible, and doubtless future studies of anti-slave-trade operations at different historical junctures and geographical loci – the many ships, ports and courts that comprise this history – will complicate as well as corroborate the arguments advanced here. We submit this collaborative venture as a new history of slave-trade suppression, not the final one, and a collective intervention in an important episode in the histories of slavery, empire and nineteenth-century Britain.

Notes

1 'The unwearied, unostentatious, and inglorious crusade of England against slavery may probably be regarded as among the three or four perfectly virtuous acts recorded in the history of nations', wrote the historian W. H. Lecky. Qtd in Christopher Lloyd, *The Navy and the Slave Trade* [1949] (London: Frank Cass, 1968), p. xiii. See Eric Williams, *Capitalism and Slavery* [1944] (London: André Deutsch, 1964).
2 Important studies include Leslie Bethell, 'The Mixed Commissions for the Suppression of the Transatlantic Slave Trade in the Nineteenth Century', *Journal of African Historical Studies* 7 (1966), 79–93; Johnson U. J. Asiegbu, *Slavery and the Politics of Liberation, 1787–1861: A Study of Liberated African Emigration and British Anti-Slavery Policy* (London: Longmans, 1969); Bethell, *The Abolition of the Brazilian Slave Trade: Britain, Brazil and the Slave Trade Question, 1807–1869* (Cambridge: Cambridge University Press, 1970); David R. Murray, *Odious Commerce: Britain, Spain, and the Abolition of the Cuban Slave Trade* (Cambridge: Cambridge University Press, 1980); David Eltis, *Economic Growth and the Ending of the Transatlantic Slave Trade* (Oxford: Oxford University Press, 1987); Robin Law (ed.), *From Slave Trade to 'Legitimate Commerce': The Commercial Transition in Nineteenth-Century West Africa* (Cambridge: Cambridge University Press, 1995); Paul Michael Kielstra, *The Politics of Slave Trade Suppression in Britain and France, 1814–48* (New York: St. Martin's Press, 2000); Joseph C. Dorsey, *Slave Traffic in the Age of Abolition: Puerto Rico, West Africa, and the Non-Hispanic Caribbean, 1815–59* (Gainesville, FL: University Press of Florida, 2003); Holger Lutz Kern, 'Strategies of Legal Change: Great Britain, International Law, and the Abolition of the Transatlantic Slave Trade', *Journal of the History of International Law* 6 (2004), 233–58; Wayne Ackerson, *The African Institution (1807–1827) and the Antislavery Movement in Great Britain* (Lewiston, NY: Edwin Mellen Press, 2005); Jean Allain, 'Nineteenth Century Law of the Sea and the British Abolition of the Slave Trade', *British Yearbook of International Law* 78 (2008), 342–88; Mark C. Hunter, *Policing the Seas: Anglo-American Relations and the Equatorial Atlantic, 1819–1865* (St. John's, Newfoundland: International Maritime Economic History Association, 2008); Keith Hamilton and Patrick Salmon (eds), *Slavery, Diplomacy and Empire:*

Britain and the Suppression of the Slave Trade, 1807–1915 (Eastbourne: Sussex Academic Press, 2009). For further references see Peter C. Hogg, *The African Slave Trade and Its Suppression: A Classified and Annotated Bibliography* (Frank Cass: Abingdon, 1973).

3 Lloyd, *Navy and the Slave Trade*; W. E. F. Ward, *The Royal Navy and the Slavers* (London: George Allen and Unwin, 1969). Among histories of the slave trade, see for example Daniel P. Mannix and Malcolm Cowley, *Black Cargoes: A History of the Atlantic Slave Trade* [1962] (London: Longmans, 1963), pp. 191–265; Hugh Thomas, *The Slave Trade: The History of the Atlantic Slave Trade, 1440–1870* (London: Picador, 1997), pp. 559–785. Among naval historians, see Anthony Preston and John Major, *Send a Gunboat: The Victorian Navy and Supremacy at Sea, 1854–1904* [1967] (London: Conway, 2007), pp. 91–97; Peter Padfield, *Rule Britannia: The Victorian and Edwardian Navy* [1981] (London: Pimlico, 2002), pp. 109–25.

4 The fullest discussions are in Philip D. Curtin, *The Image of Africa: British Ideas and Actions, 1780–1850* (Madison, WI: University of Wisconsin Press, 1964), pp. 318, 341; David Turley, *The Culture of English Antislavery, 1780–1860* (London: Routledge, 1991), p. 47.

5 In accounting for Lt Joseph Denman's aggressive assault on slave-holders of the Gallinas River, for example, Rees's comment that this naval officer 'had already served on the African coast as lieutenant and been converted to active abolitionism by the horrors he had seen there', echoes Lloyd's assertion that '[s]uch an initiation into the horrors of the trade bit deep into the young man's mind … The ruthless methods he subsequently adopted clearly owe their origin to that experience.' Siân Rees, *Sweet Water and Bitter: The Ships that Stopped the Slave Trade* (London: Chatto and Windus, 2008), p. 202; Lloyd, *Navy and the Slave Trade*, p. 93. I pursue representations of this kind in chapter 6 of this study.

6 David Eltis and David Richardson, 'A New Assessment of the Transatlantic Slave Trade', in Eltis and Richardson (eds), *Extending the Frontiers: Essays on the New Transatlantic Slave Trade Database* (New Haven, CT: Yale University Press, 2008), pp. 1–60, at pp. 40–41, Table 1.6.

7 For speculation on continuing British capitalist complicity, see Marika Sherwood, *After Abolition: Britain and the Slave Trade Since 1807* (London: I. B. Tauris, 2007). Richard Huzzey discusses the stubborn problem of Britons' indirect benefitting from the slave trade in his chapter for this volume.

8 Eltis and Richardson, 'New Assessment', pp. 37, 45.

9 Eltis and Richardson, 'New Assessment', p. 39; 'Voyages: The Transatlantic Slave Trade Voyages Database', Emory University, www.slavevoyages.org. Accessed 29 December 2013.

10 Serge Daget, 'France, Suppression of the Illegal Trade, and England, 1817–1850', in David Eltis and James Walvin (eds), *The Abolition of the Atlantic Slave Trade: Origins and Effects in Europe, Africa, and the Americas* (Madison, WI: University of Wisconsin Press, 1981), pp. 193–217, at p. 202.

11 Eltis, *Economic Growth*, pp. 104–5; Allain, 'Nineteenth-Century Law'.

12 Bethell, *Abolition of the Brazilian Slave Trade*, p. x

13 Eltis, *Economic Growth*, p. 92 (table 2), p. 94. In chapter 2 of this book Richard Huzzey considers national expenditure on the squadron.

14 Qtd in Bethell, *Abolition of the Brazilian Slave Trade*, p. 124.

15 Examining the campaign as humanitarian intervention, the social scientists Kaufman and Pape nominate it as, in relative terms, the costliest moral action in modern history. Chaim D. Kaufmann and Robert A. Pape, 'Explaining Costly International Moral Action: Britain's Sixty-Year Campaign against the Atlantic Slave Trade', *International Organization* 53 (1999), 631–68.

16 Lloyd, *Navy and the Slave Trade*, p. xiii.

17 Ralph A. Austen and Woodruff D. Smith, 'Images of African and British Slave-Trade Abolition: The Transition to an Imperialist Ideology, 1787–1807', *African Historical Studies* 2 (1969), 69–83, at p. 74.

18 Rees, *Salt Water and Bitter*, p. 8.

19 Rees, *Salt Water and Bitter*, p. 6.
20 On shipboard interrelations in the eighteenth-century slave trade, see Emma Christopher, *Slave Ship Sailors and Their Captive Cargoes, 1730–1807* (Cambridge: Cambridge University Press, 2006).
21 Captain Frederick Marryat, *Peter Simple* [1834], 2 vols (London: Macmillan, 1904), pp. i: 69. The Marryat family were compensated for the emancipation of slaves in the British West Indies. See Catherine Hall et al.'s 'Legacies of British Slave-Ownership' database, UCL, http://www.ucl.ac.uk/lbs/. Accessed 20 February 2014.
22 Lloyd, *Navy and the Slave Trade*, pp. 53–54.
23 Eltis, *Economic Growth*, pp. 102–122. See also Bethell, *Abolition of the Brazilian Slave Trade*.
24 Robin Law, 'Abolition and Imperialism: International Law and the British Suppression of the Atlantic Slave Trade', in Derek Peterson (ed.), *Abolition and Imperialism in Britain, Africa, and the Atlantic* (Ohio, OH: Ohio University Press, 2010), pp. 150–74.
25 Eltis, *Economic Growth*, p. 219.
26 E. P. LeVeen, *British Slave Trade Suppression Policies, 1821–1868*. (New York: Arno, 1977), p. 78 (table 11).
27 LeVeen calculates that 660,000 Africans were spared the Atlantic crossing because of the anti-slave-trade patrols. *British Slave Trade Suppression Policies*, p. 60. But see also LeVeen's evaluation of this figure on pp. 58–60. Eltis gives the figure of 213,000 for the period after 1830 in 'Volume and Structure', p. 43, table 7.
28 J. R. Oldfield, *'Chords of Freedom': Commemoration, Ritual and British Transatlantic Slavery* (Manchester: Manchester University Press, 2007), p. 2
29 On the propensity of white writers about Atlantic slavery to appropriate suffering in the forging of narratives of guilt and redemption, see Marcus Wood, *Slavery, Empathy, and Pornography* (Oxford: Oxford University Press, 2002).
30 On the range of journeys undertaken by black oceanic travellers in the eighteenth and early nineteenth century, see Philip D. Morgan, 'Black Experiences in Britain's Maritime World', in David Cannadine (ed.), *Empire, the Sea and Global History: Britain's Maritime World, c.1760–c.1840* (Basingstoke: Palgrave Macmillan, 2007), pp. 105–33.
31 Eltis, *Economic Growth*, pp. 91, 100; see also Bethell, *Abolition of the Brazilian Slave Trade*, p. 84.
32 F. L. Barnard, *A Three Years Cruise in the Mozambique Channel* [1848] (London: Dawsons, 1969), p. 232.
33 Paul Gilroy, *The Black Atlantic: Modernity and Double Consciousness* (Cambridge, MA: Harvard University Press, 1993), p. 5.
34 Daget, 'Suppression of the Illegal Trade'; Donald L. Canney, *Africa Squadron: The US Navy and the Slave Trade* (Dulles, VA: Potomac Books, 2006).
35 J. G. Beech, 'The Marketing of Slavery Heritage in the United Kingdom.' *International Journal of Hospitality and Tourism Administration* 2, 3/4 (2001), 85–105.
36 Emma Christopher, Cassandra Pybus and Marcus Rediker (eds), *Many Middle Passages: Forced Migration and the Making of the Modern World* (Berkeley, CA: University of California Press, 2007); Lloyd, *Navy and the Slave Trade*, pp. 290–1; Moses D. E. Nwulia, *Britain and Slavery in East Africa* (Washington, DC: Three Continents Press, 1975); Abdul Sheriff, *Slaves, Spices and Ivory in Zanzibar* (London: James Currey, 1987); Raymond C. Howell, *The Royal Navy and the Slave Trade* (Beckenham, Kent: Croom Helm, 1987); Gwyn Campbell (ed.), *Abolition and its Aftermath in the Indian Ocean, Africa and Asia* (Abingdon, Oxon: Routledge, 2005); Miers, *Britain and the Ending of the Slave Trade*, pp. 55–85; John Wright, *The Trans-Saharan Slave Trade* (New York: Routledge, 2007).

PART I

Policies

CHAPTER TWO

The politics of slave-trade suppression

Richard Huzzey

British suppression of the transatlantic slave trade rested on the threat of violent force. However, the use and exertion of naval power was shaped or constrained by political calculation. In considering the national and international politics of the maritime campaign, this chapter seeks to understand how the two interacted and, in particular, whether the stubborn survival of suppression is best explained by impersonal material forces, the individual quirk of high politics, or growing social pressure for responsive government. Other chapters in this volume consider the ways that authors represented the anti-slave-trade campaign in popular culture or the lived experiences of those participating in the cruises. Attention to those less-studied aspects of the West Africa Squadron's history should provoke a reconsideration of older assumptions about nineteenth-century anti-slavery policies. By casting the politics of suppression in the wider context of Victorian society, diplomacy and empire, it is possible to test how far 'public opinion', economic self-interest or strategic realpolitik directed the fate of the naval campaign. The following sections will examine the periods of British abolition and the West Indian emancipations of 1834–38, the early Victorian crisis of suppression, and the era of the American Civil War, tracing across time the development of priorities, motives and traditions.

Born of war (1807–30)

On a practical level, the Royal Navy's interception of transatlantic slave traders preceded Britain's abolition of the slave trade. As valuable cargo, enslaved Africans were frequently taken as prizes during European wars, like other enemy commerce or property captured on the high seas. In particular, the War of Jenkins' Ear and the French revolutionary wars saw a flurry of British captures; France's slave trade was largely destroyed after 1794.[1] Preying indiscriminately on enemy shipping, the navy's purpose was not suppression of the slave trade but rather war by economic means. However, the conflict with Napoleon created opportunities for abolitionism. James Stephen, the dynamic young lawyer who served as secretary of the Anti-Slavery Society, worked hard to promote slave-trade suppression as a war measure.[2] He drafted the orders-in-council, issued by Pitt the Younger's ministry in 1805, which prohibited the supply of slaves to people in newly captured colonies. The 1806 Foreign Slave Trade Act extended this principle to a ban on British slavers supplying planters in foreign countries. Although some mercantilist rhetoric surrounded these measures, they also reflected growing abolitionist sympathies across parliament.[3] It seems unlikely that many politicians or observers amongst the public shared Stephen's direct expectations of salvation, made in his 1807 book *Dangers of the Country*, where he declared that the scourge of war was God's vengeance for European sins as slave traders, which British abolition and suppression might appease.[4] What growing numbers of MPs shared, however, was an expectation that, despite the short-term costs, the slave trade should be rejected as un-English and improvident. If a decline in West Indian profits does not explain the rise of abolitionism, then the answer lies in shifting metropolitan attitudes to colonial prosperity and exploitation.[5]

The Abolition Act of 1807 and its attendant legislation sanctified the Navy's role as moral guardian of Africa rather than sly buccaneer preying on French commerce. While the closure of British and US markets for slaves saw their price collapse by half after 1807–08, illegal exports and foreign slave traders continued unabated.[6] The peace proposals of 1814 looked set to allow the new French regime to benefit from a safe revival of their slave trade, suppressed as a consequence of war.[7] As allies of Britain against the French Empire, slave traders from Portugal and the restored Spanish monarchy did not suffer British interdiction in the final years of the conflict. The concert of Europe, establishing a new order of continental harmony, was thus conducted against the background of a resurgent, recovering slave trade. International suppression, directing the Royal Navy to guard against illegal slave trading by foreigners, was not the irresistible or logical result of the 1807 Act. Rather, the politics of naval suppression deserve attention precisely because the British state's commitment was quixotic, contingent and tremulous. In analysing the birth of the suppression system it is impossible to ignore the question of economic advantage and British strategic calculation.[8]

Having abolished their own slave trade, suppression of foreign activity might have been a base material interest for Britons, especially if – as Seymour Drescher suggests – slave-labour production appeared to enjoy growing, not declining, prospects for the future.[9] It is easy to see why foreign powers, both at the end of the Napoleonic Wars and much later, assumed that suppression was part of a canny economic strategy to support British dominance. However, in 1814 British statesmen expressed little interest in spreading British abolitionism abroad and the government was not predisposed to dictate anti-slavery conditions as part of the peace negotiations. It was Wilberforce and his abolitionist allies who objected, raising fearsome new petitions against a resurrection of this branch of the Atlantic slave trade.[10] Popular demands for a regime of international abolition shaped government policy far more clearly and directly than the muted public involvement surrounding the passage of the 1807 Abolition Act itself.[11] The uproar of 1814, fearing the omission of abolition from the Treaty of Paris, produced 1,370 petitions with hundreds of thousands of signatures; one-fifth to one-third of adult men signed.[12]

Indeed, both Foreign Secretary Lord Castlereagh and Britain's lead negotiator at the Congress of Vienna, the Duke of Wellington, expressed surprise at the eruption of public pressure and reluctantly bowed to the petitioning campaign. Although popular discussion of the peace process in Britain presented slave-trade abolition as a fair and honourable spoil of victory after their wartime sacrifices, few campaigners touted the measure as economic reparation.[13] If abolitionists had believed their own claims, before 1807, that slavery without the slave trade would become more productive and less wasteful, then international suppression would be a boon to the West Indians' rivals. However, this aspect of anti-slave-trade campaigning had been marked more by confidence in the providential results of self-restraint than rational details about the imperial advantages promised.

Even if some individual abolitionists, including Sierra Leone's former governor, Zachary Macaulay, subsequently made personal fortunes as agents of Royal Naval officers who captured slavers' ships as prizes in the early years of the suppression campaign, the question of national economic advantage was far less clear.[14] Petitioning Britons were far more likely to fear the guilty responsibility of re-founding the French slave trade by acquiescing in a pro-slavery peace treaty than fear the competition from a slave-trafficking colonial rival.[15] The exception to this rule may lie among 30,000 signatures from Liverpool, where merchants and planters joined in the clamour against foreign slaving. John Gladstone, a Demerara slave-owner and the father of a future prime minister, encouraged the suppression of labour to rival French colonies. Still, even if some Britons spied private commercial advantages, they reacted to the initiative of the petitioning masses and bemused statesmen. Gladstone rallied slaveholders' support for the Liverpool petition, but he failed in a vote on whether to amend the text to include his self-interested arguments.[16] The government's speedy adoption of the national outcry was far easier in the absence of entrenched economic opposition, but national concerns about grace and honour forced politicians to act.

When Napoleon escaped from Elba and launched his Hundred Days campaign, he sought to forestall opposition with the promise of slave-trade abolition, attempting to seduce the British public by undercutting the compromise offered by the restored Bourbon King Louis XVIII.[17] His gambit failed, but the scale of the post-war campaign impressed Britain's rulers as mightily as the deposed Emperor of France. While suppression of the slave trade would be an important element in British foreign and imperial policy for decades to come, the petitioning of 1814–15 secured a more direct consultative role for abolitionist leaders than they would enjoy in later decades. The abolitionist radical Thomas Clarkson developed a surprisingly good working relationship with the Duke of Wellington during the peace process of 1814–15 and at the Congress of Aix-la-Chapelle in 1818, offering expert advice to British negotiators. Wilberforce reflected that Clarkson 'may do eccentric things with less offence than you or I could'.[18]

By the 1820s, statesmen such as George Canning had taken notice of 'the notion, sedulously inculcated by other Powers having colonies, that self-interest now mingles with our humanity' and that 'we are only seeking to inflict upon the Colonial Possessions of our Rivals, a portion of the evils which the partial Abolition is alleged to have brought upon our own'. Making these observations to Wellington, an improbable but regular diplomat, Canning suggested (mistakenly or disingenuously) that British planters did not regret abolition. Succeeding as Foreign Secretary upon Castlereagh's suicide, Canning encouraged the Duke to tell the reluctant French that abolition was 'dictated by considerations of a higher Order than have usually guided the conduct of States' but had generated no ill effects anyway.[19] At the Congress of Verona, in 1822, the other 'Great Powers' remained sceptical of such claims.[20] In the same letter to Wellington, Canning had suggested that international abolition might be enforced by banning the importation of produce from colonies still receiving slaves.[21] While this might share equally any disadvantages of abolition, it did little to address suspicions that Britain would somehow benefit. The French, motivated as much by domestic opinion as calculated realpolitik, preferred another declaration of principle to the treaty mooted at Verona.[22]

The post-war congresses failed to agree any form of multilateral abolition. Thereafter ministers pursued individual commitments from the 'Great Powers' and, as a price of recognition, from the younger states of Latin America.[23] In the absence of a pan-European agreement, these positive laws seemed the only way to avoid messy, difficult legal cases, such as that arising in 1817 when the Royal Navy intercepted *Le Louis*, a French vessel, without any clear authority to do so.[24] While anti-slavery leaders would rarely muster such strong public support or unmediated control of government policy in the future, politicians still feared offending popular sensibilities. Maintaining a national suppression system – after the permissive experiment of wartime – would require a peacetime 'right of search', hitherto used by belligerent forces against neutral shipping in the midst of a conflict.[25] Although Aix-la-Chappelle and Verona were not the Foreign Office's final efforts to secure a universal declaration of slave trading as a form of piracy against the *a priori* law of nations, it marked a turn, as Alfred Rubin suggests, towards international agreements between consenting nations.[26]

At the forefront of global shipping and investment finance, British subjects were likely to become entangled in continuing slave-trading enterprises, whether as smugglers under false flags or as stealthy speculators. In 1811 Lord Brougham's Slave Trade Felony Act extended the abolition law to punish foreigners trafficking captives into British territories and imprison any British slavers (rather than merely confiscating their property).[27] Even the introduction of capital punishment for those convicted, operating from 1824 until 1837, did not provide a satisfactory solution.[28] The problem lay not with the punishments meted out by Britain's Vice-Admiralty Courts, trying slave traders as they had tried captured prizes intercepted during war time, but with restraints on the Royal Navy's activities. The declarations of France (1815), Spain and Portugal (both 1817) and Brazil (1826) – alongside the decision of the United States in 1808 – abolished a number of national slave trades. Frustrated by the navy's limited legal powers to enforce abolition, the Foreign Office turned to bilateral treaties to satisfy practical goals as much as any ideologies of international law.[29]

From 1817 onwards, successive governments sought to collect treaties exchanging the right of search, since this permitted the contracting partners to search each other's shipping. Courts of Mixed Commission, consisting of judges from both countries, could try the captured vessels.[30] After 1823, British diplomats sought, beginning with Spain and Portugal, to secure an 'equipment clause' in suppression treaties. This permitted the detention and conviction of ships equipped with the distinctive furniture or voluminous supplies needed to transport slaves, even if no Africans were found aboard.[31] This series of negotiations showed that the Foreign Office remained acutely aware of the difficulties of squaring national conscience with international diplomacy more than a decade after the petitioning campaign of 1814. The same could not be said for the abolitionists or their sympathisers amongst the British populace.

Having pointed the diplomatic apparatus of the British state on a path of international negotiation, campaigners turned their attention to conditions in the British West Indies, which abolition had failed to transform, even once the stream of fresh captives had been prohibited.[32] After a Slave Registration Act in 1815, designed to prevent the secret, silent introduction of smuggled slaves onto British planters' estates, the abolitionist elite changed their strategy and tactics. Eschewing popular appeals, they instead began low-key lobbying in favour of action to arrest the excesses and longevity of British slaveholding. The eruption of impatient radicalism, following Elizabeth Heyrick's 1824 pamphlet *Immediate Not Gradual Abolition*, only strengthened the turn of the elite and popular battalions of British anti-slavery towards emancipation, not forensic examination of the suppression regime.[33] Indeed, as British officials institutionalised the attack on the slave trade as an objective of national policy, the changing priorities (and membership) of Britain's abolitionist leadership led them to other topics and, in some cases, to ambivalence or hostility towards naval suppression as a tactic.

After emancipation (1834–50)

The victories of popular pressure and parliamentary intrigue seen in the abolition of slavery (1834) and the termination of apprenticeship (1838) in the British West Indies changed the character of the slave-trade suppression campaign. Having defeated the planters, abolitionist leaders might have stood in a position of strength from which to defend the naval campaign and convince West Indians that it served their interests as much as those of the broader empire. However, abolitionist organisations themselves were losing confidence in the role of naval suppression. The British and Foreign Anti-Slavery Society (BFASS), the leading organised group after 1839, was dominated by Quakers, including its founder Joseph Sturge. The Society adopted a policy of fighting slavery across the globe through persuading foreign govern-ments and peoples of the merits of abolition, but opposing the naval squadron as counterproductive militarism.[34] Meanwhile, the parlia-mentary champion of emancipation, Thomas Fowell Buxton, raised his own doubts about the efficacy of force. In a pair of pamphlets, the *Slave Trade* and *The Remedy*, he drew a sorry picture of the slave trade's vigour despite thirty years of naval suppression. Although he did not call for the withdrawal of the navy's ships from West Africa – as he would later be misquoted – Buxton diminished their role, preferring to puff his (ultimately disastrous) plans for an expedition up the River Niger to spread commerce, Christianity and civilisation.[35]

If anti-slavery champions outside government had fallen out of love with the naval suppression campaign, we may reasonably ask why it continued. It is tempting to look to high politics and individual whim, personified in the fervent and passionate Viscount Palmerston, a statesman, controversialist and, ultimately, premier during the first half of Queen Victoria's reign.[36] He had expended more effort than art in searching for a Quintuple Treaty between the great powers of Europe, as Paul Michael Kielstra's work on this period reveals. Efforts to see 'the maritime Powers of Christendom ... united in a League' for the multilateral right of search stumbled, not so much because of Russian, Austrian and Prussian lack of interest but because of broader Anglo–French distemper. Adolphe Thiers, briefly French premier in 1840, captured this danger in his resistance 'to make treaty upon treaty with people who have been very bad to us' over the crisis resulting from Mehmet Ali Pasha's revolt against Ottoman rule.[37] After resisting Palmerston's indecent hurry to sign the treaty before leaving office, François Guizot, the sympathetic French Foreign Minister, still agreed to the text in December 1841 and ordered his ambassador to sign. Guizot delayed in large part because Palmerston's undiplomatic electoral address in Tiverton had insulted France over its North African policies. While willing to conclude the pact with the new Tory Foreign Secretary, Lord Aberdeen, the French government had wrongly assumed equal magnanimity from their citizens. The imminent ratification of the Quintuple Treaty roused in France's port cities a popular rebellion akin to Britain's anti-slave-trade petitioning of 1814; taking elites by surprise, the press erupted in condemnation of an insult to French pride and a menace to French commerce, a sensitive issue given that the Royal Navy had recently seized the innocent ship *Marabout*.[38]

On leaving the Foreign Office in 1841 (for what would prove, in fact, to be a five-year break), Palmerston warmly assured a delegation from the BFASS that: 'I shall always consider it as one of my first duties as a public man, to do all that may lie in my power to promote the attainment of those great ends for the accomplishment of which your association has been formed.' Acknowledging his differences with the abolitionist campaigners on many points of policy, not least the use of naval power against the slave trade, he nevertheless basked in their praise and took the opportunity to expound his views about Britain's anti-slavery mission.[39] Over the next few years, he skilfully attacked his Tory successor, Lord Aberdeen, for alleged timidity over slave-trade suppression, in part because of France's failure to ratify a treaty conferring the right of search.[40] While that process had been delayed and complicated by Palmerston's own conduct in office, he was adept at harassing his Conservative opponents. As Guizot faced electoral punishment for signing the Quintuple Treaty, the US Ambassador to France, General Lewis Cass, made the new British ministry's job even harder. A veteran of the War of 1812, fuelled by Anglophobia and presidential ambition, Cass denounced British demands for the right of search as a conspiracy, unrelated to supposed anti-slave-trade operations.[41] When Aberdeen subsequently accepted, against the judgement of his cabinet colleagues, Palmerston and his friends in the press were ready to pin the blame on Tory indifference. Though Aberdeen was different in style to his predecessor and less populist, it is hard to reconcile Palmerston's caricature of him with reality.[42]

In a similar vein, Palmerston suggested that his successor had shamefully capitulated to the Americans when he agreed to the Webster–Ashburton Treaty, signed in Washington in 1843.[43] As part of a far broader agreement settling the vexatious border between Canada and the USA, British officials had hoped to include a mutual right of search. However, Lewis Cass's suspicion of British demands proved popular back in Washington. President John Tyler had despatched Duff Green, an eccentric southern agitator, as his personal agent in Europe, and he joined Cass's call with an article denouncing Britain's anti-slavery policies as 'a movement to compel the whole world to pay her tribute'.[44] Deferring to similar opinion amongst US electors, Daniel Webster and Lord Ashburton agreed article VIII of the treaty, committing both nations to maintaining their own slave-trade squadron to West Africa, rather than conceding a right of search to each other.[45] BFASS activists, including the elderly Thomas Clarkson, worried about whether the tenth clause of the treaty would allow fugitive slaves in Canada to be extradited back to the USA. Meanwhile, Palmerston attacked this compromise and forced Aberdeen to support the retention of a right to visit ships and ascertain if they really were American, in direct contradiction to the US interpretation of the law of nations. Wholly differing anxieties about the Treaty of Washington underlined a growing gulf between the statesmen's focus on maritime suppression in international waters and the radical abolitionists' focus on moral condemnation of the domestic institution of slavery within America.[46] In the short term, however, the failure to secure the rights of search from France or the USA helped forge Palmerston's lasting reputation as a devotee of anti-slavery policy against the dithering indifference of his Conservative opposite.

Since he directed British anti-slave-trade efforts as Foreign Secretary (1830–41, 1846–51) and later as Prime Minister (1855–58, 1859–65), any historical assessment of the politics behind naval suppression policies tends towards a comparison of Palmerston and his rivals. However, it would be wrong to consider support for the West Africa Squadron as the accidental result of an eccentric statesman's publicity seeking. Aberdeen and successors in both parties, such as the Lords Clarendon and Granville, approached the diplomatic challenges of naval suppression with greater caution and reserve; still, their fundamental commitment to the campaign as a national interest was similar. Palmerston, in 1839, introduced an Act of Parliament to allow the Royal Navy to stop and search Portuguese ships, on the tenuous basis that they remained legally committed to slave-trade suppression even after treaties for cooperation with Britain had expired. By contrast, Aberdeen agonised over introducing a similar act, in 1845, against Brazil; still he introduced it, and the difference in temperament and tone should not blind us to their similar goals. The moralising populism, using foreign policy for domestic political advantage, was an important element of Palmerstonian politics, but also that of his Conservative opponents. The question of balancing anti-slavery objectives with other British national interests was common to 'Pam' and his rivals, even if they differed in their respect for diplomatic niceties and international law.[47]

This governing consensus in favour of naval suppression, however dramatic the partisan wrangles over detail, was strengthened by a growing institutional commitment to slave-trade suppression within the Foreign Office.[48] In Europe and the Americas, British diplomats sought new agreements to support the suppression system as they saw fit, even going so far as to extract a guarantee of slave-trade abolition from landlocked Paraguay.[49] The growth of an 'anti-slavery state' quickly outstripped other branches of government bureaucracy.[50] Direct expenditure on the naval squadron peaked at half a million pounds per annum in 1850, at a time when the overall size of government spending was shrinking.[51] While both parties' leaders, in office, showed similar commitment to naval suppression, backbenchers on all sides of the House of Commons grew dissatisfied.

Political crisis (1845–50)

The expanding cost provoked the ire of Richard Cobden, John Bright and other radical proponents of *laissez-faire* economics. They clashed with Palmerston, in particular, given his appetite for military spending and bullying bellicosity. *Punch* magazine, persuaded by critics of suppression in the subsequent debate, portrayed the diminutive Whig–Liberal Prime Minister, Lord John Russell, as 'the infant Hercules', wresting the twin serpents of the national debt and the Atlantic slave trade

TABLEAU VIVANT.

LORD JOHN AS THE INFANT HERCULES.

Figure 2.1 'Lord John as the Infant Hercules', *Punch*,
20 March 1850, p. 125.

(Figure 2.1).[52] Many newspapers concluded that 'the pursuit of a constant, irritant, and so far unavailing piece-meal conflict with a mighty evil is to try the patience of even the most humane nation'.[53] Though keen to reduce the taxpayer's burdens, critics in the 'Manchester School' were not simply penny-pinching. Rather, they pursued a broader ideological commitment to private ties of commerce and amity rather than the stately intrigues of aristocrats and empire.[54] In July 1846, when parliament voted a grant of £20,000 for the support of liberated Africans, MP Joseph Hume attacked the entire suppression system along these lines as 'unnecessary, and … a waste of human life'.[55] By the following year, Gateshead representative William Hutt succeeded in commissioning a Commons inquiry into the coercive policy of naval suppression. Keen to avoid accusations of heartlessness and indifference, Hutt and his allies bridled when the Foreign Secretary accused them of amoral or immoral disinterest in the suffering of enslaved Africans.[56] As Hume insisted, 'no man looked back with more satisfaction than he did to the labours of Mr. Wilberforce', but 'the question was, whether, by maintaining an armed force on the coast of Africa, this country could prevent other nations from carrying on the trade?'[57]

Such critics suggested that unimpeded slave trading would produce such a glut of slaves that Brazilian and Cuban authorities would be forced to extinguish the trade from fear of the racial imbalance created.[58] The Palmerston and Aberdeen Acts, they argued, were the moral equivalent of Russia or the USA presuming to attack British smugglers off the coast of Brighton.[59] By contrast, Britain needed only to win over the support of the public in Cuba and Brazil by removing the odium of national insult and British imperialism from the policy of slave-trade abolition. Then, 'they will not import at all if you will only give to the law which prohibits importations the best, the wisest, and most powerful assistance which the law gathers in every land from the support of public opinion'.[60]

As chair of the Commons Select Committee, Hutt summoned witnesses who believed that the cruisers had driven the trade underground, making it 'a smuggling trade' which worsened conditions for the human cargo.[61] As in other questions of imperial policy, battles over the effects of British activities and the burdens of national duty hinged on a 'war of representation', with naval personnel, merchants, missionaries and others proffering their rival expertise, opinions and observations.[62] The details of slave-trade suppression policy and Britain's influence in West Africa met with unprecedented scrutiny. Political critics consistently argued that the cruisers' operations forced slavers to adopt ever more inhumane tactics.[63] 'Anti-coercionist' members of the inquiry – those in league with Hutt – keenly welcomed evidence from British consuls that smaller vessels, now required to outrun the cruisers, meant more slaves per square foot than had been common before the Royal Navy interfered.[64] One diplomatic source reported seeing a 21-ton boat that carried 97 slaves, packing each one into a fifteenth of the space allotted to each soldier in Britain's own transport service. Britons could not 'by any stretch of the imagination, conceive how the powers of human endurance could have supported 20 days in this floating hell'.[65] Even James Bandinel, recently retired head of the Slave Trade Department, conceded Hutt's proposition that either the triumph or failure of the naval strategy would be 'purchased by an endless series of sufferings and death'.[66]

As the diplomatic and military scope of Britain's suppression system grew, so did the ambition of some naval officers seeking excitement and tangible achievement rather than the boring sentry duty of cruising off the West African coast.[67] In particular, Lieutenant Joseph Denman advocated the destruction of slave depots (barracoons), having destroyed one in the Gallinas region in 1840. His subsequent legal difficulties, having destroyed the non-slave property of a Spaniard, Buron, in the course of his attack, gave him plenty of time on desk duty in London to describe his proposals to Palmerston and other sympathetic politicians, but left his fellow officers cautious about following his example.[68] Where European property was not at stake, the navy could be more liberal in twisting international law and diplomatic agreements to violate African sovereignty and wreak revenge on suspected slave traders.[69] This violence offended the pacific principles of Cobdenite radicals, especially when they heard reports that 2,000 slaves had recently been killed when, on reaching the coast, their captors found there was no barracoon to keep them in.[70] Warfare and turmoil, fanned by British violence, might stop the development of trade, agriculture and security in West Africa, which *laissez-faire* MPs trusted would do more to wean Africans off slave trading than brute force ever could.[71]

At the same time that a serving officer such as Joseph Denman demanded more action on the coast, others pointed to the medical dangers of this course. Lord John Hay, a member of the select committee and a retired officer, argued that no measure could do more to encourage illness and disease than landing to attack barracoons.[72] Having previously heard of the use of Kru mariners on naval vessels, the radical MP and former Sierra Leone Governor Thomas Perronet Thompson pursued the possibility of raising an entirely black navy for the purpose of patrolling the slave trade, precisely to avoid the deadly toil of tropical sickness amongst British tars. As chapter 5 in this volume shows, he had good reason to think that the very survival of the squadron was based on black labour – though this was rarely acknowledged.[73]

While a larger, ideological battle raged between advocates of pacific and muscular methods of encouraging legitimate commerce and suppressing the slave trade, there was plenty of scope for witnesses and politicians to debate the effectiveness of the squadron's tactics along these lines. A few naval men warned that they needed newer steam ships, though the naval officer Henry Matson was more subtle in arguing that the quantity of ships was more important than their method of propulsion and that more sail vessels than steamers could be afforded for the same cost.[74] Looking from the quarter deck to the courtroom, Commander Thomas Birch suggested that the crews of convicted slave ships should be hanged, rather than left to walk free after the condemnation of their vessel.[75] Members of Hutt's select committee were divided over whether to feel delight or disgust over reports that the navy regularly abandoned captured slave traders to die on the African coast.[76] The Admiralty denied such a practice happened, but Palmerston disavowed it only on the basis that slavers could easily return to their man-dealing ways once they found their way back to civilisation.[77]

Some thought effective suppression might require new trading posts in Africa as a possible alternative to the cruisers.[78] A merchant, John Duncan, suggested that 'as the natives became acquainted with the development of the resources of their own soil, it would show the native kings and chiefs an advantage of retaining the people in their own country for that purpose; and I think the slave trade would die a natural death'.[79] The resources spent on the cruisers might be transferred to promoting commerce in West Africa, an argument that appealed to British businesses trading there.[80] There was sympathy for this view beyond the ranks of doctrinaire free traders. The Peelite MP William Gladstone, previously supportive of Buxton's Niger expedition, proved a useful and unexpected ally.[81] In his infamous 'Occasional Discourse on the Negro Question' in 1849, Thomas Carlyle took a moment away from denigrating West Indian freed people to cast doubt on both the efficacy and necessity of keeping 'the whole word in a pother about this question'.[82] An 1851 article in Charles Dickens's journal *Household Words* insisted, 'History proves that commerce is the great means ordained by Providence for the improvement and advancement of the human race' and that 'physical force is but a weak antagonist to moral wrong'.[83]

British merchants of West Africa supported these suggestions by complaining that naval interdiction hampered legitimate trade. The industrialist MP William Jackson condemned the Royal Navy getting involved with Africans' complaints against palm oil traders, and interfering with lawful commerce in that way.[84] More personally, Thomas Berry berated the detention of his company's vessel, the *Lady Sale*, under the equipment clause. Because palm oil trading required storage similar to that used for slaves, it could fall foul of the law. He argued that his vessel had been victimised by the malicious Portuguese navy, under their bilateral treaty with Britain, because it carried large reserves of water and rice. The treaty system might give dubious foreigners power over British merchants and, as Berry articulated with some help from the friendly chairman, penalise merchants in pursuit of that commerce which was an antidote to slaving. 'What a door is here opened to the most vexatious impediments to the freedom of English commerce!', he exclaimed. Berry's claims that his company was persecuted for helping the British squadron stop slave traders is fanciful, and his reasons for carrying slaving equipment is questionable – particularly in respect to the shackles needed to detain delinquent crewmen or Africans.[85] However, the British merchants who profited directly or supplied illegal slave traders vested their anxieties in virtue, since earlier inquires had decided to draw a clear line between British trade goods and their end users in the continuing slave trade.[86]

Those who resented regulation of their legal or illegal businesses in Africa had a clear reason to oppose suppression. The same should be true of West Indian planters in defence of the squadron. Those cultivating sugar might have seen a clear in interest in the criminalisation and prosecution of their rivals' supply of enslaved labour. That they failed to do so is a reflection of their vindictive logic and betrayed pride, alongside the canny politics of free traders such as Hutt. Many West Indian proprietors and their supporters saw the cruisers debate as a chance to reopen their complaint against the Whigs' Sugar Duties Act of 1846.[87] Rather than demanding stronger and more effective harassment of the illegal slave trade across the Atlantic, colonial planters tended to expect that the withdrawal of naval forces would reveal the folly and error of inviting foreign, slave-grown produce to compete with their free-labour sugar in the British marketplace. Fighting a rearguard action for colonial preference, Lord George Bentinck charged that thousands of sailors and hundreds of guns were committed to repressing the slave trade at the very same time as Britain resolved 'to add to the profits and premiums of slavery' by admitting its fruits.[88]

Through an unholy alliance with Cobdenites, protectionists might save the old monopoly by stripping Whigs of their squadron and revealing the naked truth of free trade's consequences for the slave trade. As late as 1860, a decade after the crucial vote on the naval coercion, Thomas Love Peacock's characters Dr Opimian and Lord Curryfin condemned the direct encouragement of foreign slave labour, given by our friends of liberty under the pretext of free trade. It is a mockery to keep up a squadron for suppressing the slave trade on one hand, while, on the other had we encourage it to an extent that counteracts in a tenfold degree the apparent power of suppression. It is a clear case of false pretension.[89]

The apparent contradiction on the part of Russell and Palmerston allowed some protectionists to see the death of free trade in the abolition of suppression. This is particularly odd given that Hutt and his Cobdenite friends had targeted the expense of the squadron as part of a broader attack on state intervention, including protection for imperial produce.

A Jamaican effort to support the abolition of Cuban and Brazilian slave trading, coordinated by the abolitionist David Turnbull and leading black and white allies, proves this point. They advised Palmerston to continue 'promoting the enforcement of the slave-trade treaties, and the suppression of the slave trade', but they spent most of their time demanding the return of sugar protection. At public meetings, they showed little interest in 'the naval force, so unprofitably, so injuriously employed in the ineffectual blockade', and instead demanded suppression and a level playing field for sugar competition through other means.[90] There was little hope for the majority of planters to rally around naval suppression if it could not command the support of missionaries, officials and former slaves (amongst whom numbered Assemblyman G. W. Gordon, a future victim of Governor Eyre). In local meetings, Jamaican elites and the new black middle class could denounce the free trader Milner Gibson as 'the mouth-piece of the mammon of the present-day' for encouraging slave-grown sugar as a way to sell more Manchester goods to Brazil.[91] However, for the vast majority of them this did not translate into a spirited defence of the squadron. In the crucial vote of 1850, following the Select Committee

Table 2.1 Comparison of 1850 votes on suppression and free trade in sugar

MPs' votes in 1850	For free trade in sugar	Against free trade in sugar
For military suppression	155 (The Whig–Liberal whip)	45 (Protection and suppression)
Against military suppression	44 (Laissez-faire)	87 (Protection and pacifism)

Source: Refer to endnote 95.

inquiries, the scion of West Indian wealth Henry Baillie seconded Hutt's motion and summed up this twisted logic that 'he did not wish to see that interest protected circuitously, in a manner that they would not do openly'.[92]

Protectionists in Westminster proved even keener to marry their desire for tariffs with the radicals' critique of maritime violence. Support for withdrawal was not limited to those free-trade purists, but aided by opportunistic Tory protectionists and betrayed West Indian planters who swelled Hutt's ranks of support. When the 1847–48 Select Committee voted on details of its resolutions, supporters and opponents of the cruisers split on the effects of the 1846 Act.[93] Even great defenders of naval power, such as Bishop Samuel Wilberforce (son of William) and the Law Lord Thomas Denman (father of Joseph), offered their parliamentary support for Palmerston's policy in spite of, not because of, his support for free trade.[94] Of those MPs present for votes in 1850 to reinstate sugar protection and scrap the cruisers (Table 2.1), both defeated by the government, loyalties were muddled. Rather than pursue abstract consistency in favour of interventionism or *laissez-faire*, the overwhelming majority approached questions in the abstract.[95] The link between the questions of naval coercion and sugar protection was complex but crucial; beyond all else, support for the duties overrode West Indian planters' natural interest in hurting the supply of slaves to Brazilian and Cuban sugar barons. Twice as many votes for withdrawal came from protectionists as from the *laissez-faire* purists who had raised the idea.

There was another reason that West Indian sympathisers came to see the suppression of the slave trade as Whig humbug rather than a weapon of economic nationalism. Their principal anxiety in the 1840s was the cost of black wages in the larger islands of the Caribbean, such as Jamaica, where the labour market was working to the advantage of freed people. Indentured labour for the West Indies had often been regulated or banned because of its perceived inconsistency with Britain's military and diplomatic suppression system: Britons should be beyond reproach whilst cajoling other nations. Lord John Russell, though he later changed his mind, had initially dubbed this 'a new system of slavery'.[96] For economic radicals, a desire for freer trade in 'free' labour from and to the West Indies was all part of a connected system that required the maximum liberty in every sphere of commerce. But emigration was equally appealing to protectionists, who wished to see the West Indies thrive again and who imagined new labour was the key to that problem. Hutt had advocated this combination as early as 1845. Understood in these terms, protectionist and free trader alike could aim to 'sap the foundations of slavery, by underselling its productions' thanks to cheaper free labour in the British sugar colonies.[97] The planters could hence come to the same conclusions as Hutt's *laissez-faire* cabal, if for different reasons.[98]

Withdrawal of the cruisers was therefore attractive to many West Indians as part of a scheme that would permit them to recruit 'free labour' in Africa and India. A rather different strategy saw some opponents of naval coercion, such as the *Daily News*, propose British support for a similar system of free labour emigration to foreign colonies.[99] James Bandinel imagined that the Brazilians would accept abolition of the slave trade if a source of free labourers could be found, and foresaw Britain being permitted to inspect it against abuse in exchange for the withdrawal of the cruisers.[100] Quite how close such schemes came to accommodation with legalised slaving varied from case to case. At their worst, emigration schemes proposed as alternatives to suppression flirted with open slavery: Jose Cliffe, a Brazilian slave dealer, suggested that abolitionists could act as superintendents for a system of exported labour to his country, in place of the slave trade. Africans would be released from their labour as free men after ten years.[101]

While Russell's Whig–Liberals embraced indentured labour as a way of supporting planters' profits without reneging on free trade, they drew clear lines in law – though not always in reality – between Indian and African indenture and a supervised slave trade. A widespread, racist prejudice against black West Indians' high wages helped defeat the Whigs' first instincts for curbing indentured labour. If protectionists failed to stop free trade and anti-coercionists failed to withdraw the cruisers, then they did both succeed in reshaping domestic debates to support labour coercion in the sugar colonies and bonded migration to them.[102] Tory Prime Minister Sir Robert Peel, for example, was a staunch defender of the squadron and an advocate of new labour for the West Indies as early as 1845; he did not see the two as incompatible.[103] Regardless of partisans' stance upon the cruiser system, their arguments over suppression revealed a common intolerance for the free operation of wage markets when they favoured black labourers.[104]

However, it is hard to see this kind of raw economic calculation in rival expectations of how the slave trade influenced West Indian prosperity. Guiana planter John Gladstone, who had tried to adopt international slave-trade abolition as a cause for planter protection in 1814, was one of the principal pioneers of indentured migration; by the time he died in 1851, slave-trade suppression no longer appealed to colonial proprietors as an economic weapon. If the West India Committee in London or planters in Jamaica entertained naval suppression by mid-century, they did so only as a pretext for pleading about the sugar duties.[105] Meanwhile, there is little evidence of a consistent government belief that slave-trade suppression would increase the price of rival sugar exports; on the contrary, Russell's equalisation of the sugar duties was intended to reduce prices Britons paid. That was the point: suppression held little appeal to him and Palmerston as a back-door method of protectionism.[106] The survival of the naval squadron into the second half of the nineteenth century would be decided by ministerial will and parliamentary arithmetic rather than any particular economic interest. However, as the subsequent decade suggests, this did not mean that British wealth and power were divorced from calculations surrounding suppression. Rather, advocates of suppression, like its enemies, focused on the growth of new commerce and the civilising dominance of Britain.

Survival and coercion (1850–58)

The Whig–Liberals' majority, in that key 1850 vote, owed everything to the threats made by Russell that he would resign as prime minister if the measure failed. Deriding the pliant backbenchers as 'slaves, cowards, and place-hunters', the Chartist *Northern Star* concluded that these 'parliamentary "niggers"' had bowed to the inflexible pride of 'ministerial drivers'.[107] Though parliamentary whipping saved the government and the squadron, many Whig–Liberal MPs liked Hutt's arguments.[108] The opportunistic support of Tory protectionists may have saved the squadron by transforming an ideological dispute into a partisan wrangle. In part, this was a clash between Cobdenite and Palmerstonian versions of liberal foreign policy; the two strands of thought both embraced free trade, but differed on whether international relations were best conducted with credit or cannon.[109] Naval suppression did not survive thanks only to a sense of duty, tradition and honour. The eccentric Tory MP Sir Robert Inglis had attacked Hutt's plan on the basis that 'England will again sanction the slave trade', but this bombast was not enough.[110] In order to demonstrate efficacy alongside virtue, Palmerston adopted and adapted his enemy's appeals to commerce, rather than relying on obligation alone. He encouraged Russell to join him in emphasising the importance of the squadron to well-ordered trade.[111]

By this logic, the only chance for legitimate trade to work came through the harassing cruisers, whose vigilance artificially increased the cost of slaves and undermined the full economic value of slave labour.[112] When one of Hutt's allies posited that slave trading in parts of Africa had been extinguished by commerce, not the cruisers, Palmerston told him 'that nowhere on the coast of Africa has legitimate commerce gained upon the slave trade, except in consequence of the efforts of our cruisers'.[113] Commerce was an augmentation to 'the strong arm' of military power, not an alternative.[114] The philosophy behind Palmerston's support of the squadron is revealed in his common description of it as the 'police'.[115] For him the Royal Navy was a West African Leviathan, interposing in a natural order that would otherwise have seen the continent (and its trade) slip into violence, anarchy and oppression. Slave traders were cast as pirates, disrupting native efforts to trade with legitimate British merchants.[116] Un-policed slavers, from their barbarous nature, would turn to piracy against legitimate commerce, driving it away and leaving Africa 'a scene of violence, of murder, of every kind of atrocity'. Fear and violence inherent in trans-porting a ship of unwilling captives naturally conditioned slavers to abuse, his thesis went.[117] A missionary witness such as the Rev. Jones provided strong eyewitness testimony that continuing wars for slaves in the interior would check the necessary development of commerce. The cruisers would do their work before slave trading gave way to free-labour exports and Christian civilisation.[118]

It is striking, though, that coercionists and anti-coercionists could agree that Britain, other 'civilised' nations and Africans would all benefit from the ending of the slave trade. The parliamentary crisis of 1850 hinged on whether military violence would cauterize 'the wounds of Africa', as Buxton had dubbed them.[119] In part, politicians divided on the question of whose testimony – and perspective – to adopt as wisdom. There were good reasons why Palmerston doubted those British traders in West Africa who resented the cruisers' inter-ference with honest and dishonest business there. In 1841–42, R. R. Madden's investigation in West Africa had warned that British trade was bound up not only in the promotion of export production but also of slave trading. The subsequent Select Committee of inquiry had concluded that it was impossible to hold Britons to account for the end use of their manufactures and that the net effect of British trade was to encourage alternatives to the export of slaves.[120] In tracing the supply chains of slave-trade goods to West Africa and the bonds of capital to finance slave enterprises in Brazil, Britons and their government proved unimaginative and largely uninterested.[121] Whether with the help of naval suppression or not, both Hutt's and Palmerston's supporters in 1850 expected the informal diffusion of British power and influence to suppress the slave trade, 'improve' Africans, and benefit Britons.[122]

There was no grand plan for the colonisation of Africa behind deploy-ment of the naval squadron. Detractors and enthusiasts alike imagined the projection of power through minuscule or non-existent territorial possessions on the coast.[123] However, historians have found ample evidence that the logic of naval suppression provided the occasion for establishing early 'bridgeheads' of British conquest.[124] Suppression of the slave trade encouraged British contempt for African statecraft; if there was not an economic 'crisis of adaptation' then political crises of frustration encouraged violence and ultimately annexation.[125] The controversy surrounding Denman's tactics, razing barracoons in the Gallinas, did not prevent a succession of other assaults on African villages or trading posts where Europeans' property was uninvolved. While pictures of burning villages graced the pages of illustrated periodicals, naval officers, politicians and administrators-on-the-spot equated pro-slaving barbarism with opposition to their plans. Instructions to the squadron's officers suggested that violence 'may be exercised upon shore as well as at sea, and irrespectively of the consent of the native government', when Africans were involved.[126] As Robin Law suggests, casual disregard for the plentiful agreements of commerce and abolition signed with African nations had striking long-term consequences; undertakings with 'uncivilised' countries did not require Privy Council approval and marked them out as lesser obligations. Moreover, the 'law of nations' did not fully apply with 'barbarian powers', as anti-slavery jurist Stephen Lushington put it. Disrespect for African sovereignty and territoriality, combined with a civilisation hierarchy of diplomatic protocol, established the moral and legal basis for European expansion.[127]

In particular, the bombardment of Lagos in 1851 saw a new phase in British relations with West Africa. The up-river kingdom of Dahomey and its coastal ally Lagos had proved a menace to the people of Abeokuta, in modern Nigeria. Missionaries stationed with the Abeokutans raised fears that they would be invaded and massacred by the rival nations. Samuel Crowther Ajayi, a liberated African who would later be the first black Anglican bishop, went to London to persuade Queen Victoria, Prince Albert and Palmerston that Britain should prevent such a state of affairs. Ouidah, ruled by King Guezo and his Portuguese slave trader Viceroy Francisco Da Souza, was too far inland for British power to strike.[128] However, Palmerston told his consul to remind Kosoko of Lagos that 'Lagos is near to the sea, and that on the sea are the ships and cannon of England'.[129] In correspondence with Prime Minister Russell, Palmerston argued that they should 'wink at any violation' of international law necessary to stop the 'piratical resistance of two barbarous African chiefs' to suppressing the slave trade.[130] Though they had no special appetite for the state's support of individual Britons spreading the gospel beyond the empire's borders, Palmerston and Russell could assimilate the Abeokutan conflict into anger at Guezo and Kosoko's encouragement of the slave trade and continuing commercial frustrations in Lagos.[131]

The physical presence of the squadron in West Africa might, in such cases, provide the practical encouragement and opportunity for the promotion of free commerce to assume a colonial character. After installing a new ruler in Lagos, Britain ruled the city as an informal colony until annexing it in 1861.[132] Thereafter, Lagos joined Sierra Leone as an outpost for Vice-Admiralty Courts trying suspected European slave traders. However, the squadron facilitated British 'bridgeheads' of empire in other ways too. Some proselytisers were ambivalent about naval violence, but David Livingstone, for example, became one of its greatest supporters.[133] Besides direct interference with slave trading, the cruisers projected British power across the coast. As Livingstone's young protégé, Horace Waller wrote home to his parents in 1861, wishing 'those who complain of English Government come out here & see whether her navy is not a thing to be appreciated by the few English dotted about'.[134] In the previous decade, as Livingstone's tracts gathered popularity with missionary supporters back home, he eagerly used Palmerston's model of slave-trade suppression and civilisation to frame his own plans and the fundraising appeals to support them. The evangelist praised the cruisers in an 1857 letter to *The Times* and dedicated the narrative of his 1858–64 expedition to the Zambesi to the then Prime Minister. [135]

Livingstone's dedication to Palmerston suggested that success on the West Coast 'has most forcibly shown the need of some similar system on the opposite side of the continent'.[136] This simple logic encapsulates the direct, if complex, link between naval suppression of the Atlantic slave trade and British expansion into Central and Eastern Africa. Though the expansion of British protectorates and colonies accelerated during the European 'scramble for Africa', the desire for commercial and political influence was wrapped up in expectations of free-labour production and wealth once the slave trade was gone. While naval suppression survived in the Indian Ocean and the Gulf of Arabia into the twentieth century, territorial protectorates and annexations after 1880 claimed a similar purpose. Though it is beyond the scope of this chapter, the legacy of suppression might be traced in other ways that British politicians hoped they could teach, cajole or force Africans towards 'civilisation'. Even if the Select Committee on West Africa of 1865 looked forward to British withdrawal from expensive and pointless colonies, once the slave trade had been suppressed, this rested upon fantasy; resistance and complex responses to new commercial pressures all offered powerful reasons why Britons would believe they still knew better than Africans themselves.[137]

Livingstone and others saw a diminution in the slave trade as the triumph of Palmerston's commitment, because the old manipulator had created his own evidence of success. As political scepticism brewed in 1850, he had redoubled efforts to vindicate suppression. Without support from his Liberal allies, Palmerston did not push for a formal increase in the size of the South American Squadron or an official blockade of Cuba and Brazil. However, he used the Aberdeen Act's silence on its territorial limits to support naval interception within the coastal waters of Brazil. While Aberdeen had been keen to offer apologies or reparations for these violations, from April 1850 Palmerston encouraged naval interloping, apparently without reference to the government's lawyers.[138]

As Eltis notes, 'by 1851, the British were financing antislavery societies in Brazil, subsidising the majority of newspapers in the province of Rio de Janeiro and were able to use the Brazilian customs department as their own information service'. These efforts did not, in themselves, shift the Brazilian government into action, so much as popular hostility to the Portuguese-led slave trade and immediate government anxieties about rebellions.[139] However, the *apparent* causal link destroyed the growing popular doubt and parliamentary antipathy for naval suppression. Palmerston was largely successful in claiming vindication for his suppression policies in compelling 'that great delinquent Brazil practically to abandon its crime', as he told an enthusiastic crowd in Perth in 1853.[140] Some organs, such as the *Examiner*, doubted – like many later historians – that Palmerston's initiative had mattered so much as fluctuating sugar prices and domestic politics in Brazil.[141]

Civil war and the Cuban slave trade (1858–65)

While Brazilians effectively ended the slave trade to their country, a boom in Caribbean demand revived the scale of the transatlantic traffic. The prime destination, Cuba, was at 'the center of a subtle three-handed international card game', as Eltis puts it. Spain and Britain's governments feared US annexation, while the USA resented British visits to establish even the legitimacy of ships flying the stars and stripes.[142] The British government offered new pressure on Spain, in light of complaints in the press that Spaniards represented a 'race that has preserved only its vices' and 'remained barbarous in the presence of civilisation'.[143] However, the fear of US retaliation against Britain or invasion of Cuba, as much as Old World respect, restrained the boldness of even Palmerston. As the *Saturday Review* lamented in 1864, 'what we did to Brazil we did not dare to do to Spain'.[144] Tentative efforts to enforce the Anglo–Spanish right of search, which included a clause condemning vessels with equipment for the slave trade but no slaves, confirmed this suspicion. Some newspapers had been belligerent in denying that 'we allow parties of marauders to carry on their vile traffic, when we have at our disposal strength sufficient to force its abandonment'.[145]

By 1858, President Buchanan's administration entered into a major row with Great Britain when four gunboats challenged US vessels cruising to the north of Cuba.[146] Though war was unlikely – the disincentives for both sides were great – the presence of British warships close to Florida spurred a bitter war of words across the Atlantic. In Britain, newspapers debated how far their government should defer to US sensitivities, with some critics noting the explicit exclusion of a right of search from the Webster–Ashburton treaty.[147] Against this backdrop, Hutt led renewed, lonely attempts to withdraw the cruisers in 1858.[148] Even those who agreed with Palmerston's continued resistance disapproved of the Prime Minister's 'easy imputation of Atheism' when accusing Hutt and critics of doubting 'that the world is governed by a Divine Providence'.[149] While Hutt won almost four in ten votes cast in the Commons in 1850, his 1858 hurrah garnered fewer than one in ten (and the whips could probably have mustered more support if they thought Hutt had any chance of winning).[150] The prospect of war with the USA should have given new succour for pacifist opposition to naval suppression, but the 'evidence' of Palmerston's success seemed too persuasive.[151] By 1860, Hutt, Gladstone and Russell sat around Palmerston's cabinet table as ministers in his government; the naval squadron had triumphed and the Prime Minister refused to repeal the defunct Aberdeen Act, despite demands from Brazilians, the Anti-Slavery Society and his own party. It was a guarantee against Brazilian backsliding and, one suspects, a trophy of his belief that might had been proved right.[152]

A reconfirmation of parliamentary support for suppression only strengthened the government's desires, in 1860, to find a new front against the Cuban slave trade. In a fanciful plan, Prime Minister Palmerston had written to Russell in March suggesting a practical alternative to the ever-hated concession of the right of search. The US Navy could only act against US citizens, but if they fervently inspected ships under the Union flag, then they could leave it to the Royal Navy to deal with any found to be using fake papers and flying false colours. Intelligence sharing between the Queen's representatives in Havana and the US State Department, aided by lashings of off-the-books Secret Service payments to informants by Britain, might interdict the Cuban slave trade.[153] However, confidential discussions with Secretary of State Lewis Cass had convinced the British minister in Washington, Lord Lyons, that requests for a more serious naval commitment would prove counterproductive, let alone a treaty. Lyons told Russell that

President Buchanan was sympathetic but 'very touchy' since 'he is very little supported by public opinion, especially in his own party, and he is no doubt made irritable by thinking that he gets no credit from anybody on the subject'. A convention in London to re-open questions of suppression treaties would be impossible, given that moral condemnation of the slave trade went down poorly with the President's own supporters.[154]

Shortly thereafter the Foreign Secretary Lord John Russell returned to the tactic of increasing British deployment in the Gulf of Mexico, requesting this in a letter of 22 August. As First Lord of the Admiralty, the Duke of Somerset warned that this was foolhardy since it would simply lead to US objections and another humiliating withdrawal. He asked Russell to destroy this request and issue a duplicate letter, without the Cuban suggestion, since 'it might be awkward if this letter of the 22nd should hereafter be called for, and I do not wish to have any public letter written from [this] office stating objections to such a course of proceeding'.[155] This exchange in the autumn of 1860 reflected ongoing British hesitancy about how to reinforce the slave-trade campaign without alienating the USA. Indeed, while suppression was an objective of national policy, it did not eclipse other official concerns, such as peaceful and prosperous relations with America.[156]

The US secession crisis of 1860–61 therefore came during a restless period of frustration with suppression arrangements. Palmerston clearly hoped to unpick, by open or covert measures, the 1842 Treaty of Washington, which he opposed as a 'capitulation', because the agreement secured only an American squadron off the coast of Africa and not the more effectual prize of a mutual right of search.[157] A civil war over the future of slavery was not an auspicious opportunity for British diplomats to raise this query. As Don Fehrenbacher argues, the US federal government was the vehicle for pro-slavery foreign policy in the decades before the Civil War.[158] Even after secession, there was little reason for Britain to expect that the disrupted Union would prove any more accommodating – and early Republican diplomacy, not to mention Lincoln's soothing promises to the Border States, confirmed the shallowness of their anti-slavery pronouncements.[159]

The Confederate constitution banned the Atlantic slave trade, even though detractors would consistently condemn this in the British press as a temporary measure 'to pacify only slave-trading Virginia, and blind the eyes of England'.[160] While Palmerston's Liberal government famously showed puzzled and puzzling indifference to a new pro-slavery country, his ministry's energies were directed more towards the implications of slave-owners' secession for slave-trade suppression. By February 1861, the Admiralty asked Lord John Russell how they should treat any vessels flying the flags of South Carolina or other Southern states – a full month before the famous stars-and-bars banner of the Confederacy was first unfurled.[161] During the winter, British journals noted that 'commanders of the African squadron would deal more unceremoniously with the new palmetto flag than with the susceptible stars and stripes of the New York speculators in human flesh'.[162] However, at the same time, the capture of a New York ship plying the slave trade to Cuba seemed to confirm that Northern states remained the main obstruction to British suppression efforts in Cuba.[163]

In the court of public opinion, as well as the councils of Downing Street, the slave-trade suppression issue shaded assessments of the Northern and Southern combatants. In the March of 1861 Lord Palmerston, in the House of Commons, defended the Liberal government's failure to arrest Cuban slave trading by blaming the US government's intransigence. Press coverage took the cue and emphasised Franco–American perfidy, often condemning Lord Aberdeen for the Treaty of Washington two decades earlier.[164] The strange fact was that, even months after secession, the British public still identified the US government with decades of obstruction. *Punch* magazine imagined the US response to Palmerston's undiplomatic criticism in a portion of Southern prose: 'Wal, we air a great people, but our dander's easy riz, and it aint allys easy toe be acting the magnanimous. So I reckon as yar Premier has best keep hisself at home, and not come visiting the States, unless so be he haeve a taste for tar and feather.'[165] Even more curious than the affected Southern accent and local colour was the desire to tar the US government with policies. Palmerston announced his proposal for cooperation in the seas surrounding Cuba, rejected by the US government in 1860, as if it was the fault of the Lincoln administration, not its predecessor.

British detractors of the Confederacy were not shy to associate it with support for reopening the slave trade.[166] Some, such as the editor of the *Economist*, suggested that the time was ripe to secure an anti-slave-trade treaty from the USA, while making one from the Confederate States a condition of recognition.[167] The radical abolitionists of the British and Foreign Anti-Slavery Society, neutral due to their pacifist principles, suggested that suppression agreements must be a price of any recognition of the CSA.[168] Southern propagandists, acting through commercial partners in Liverpool, quickly moved to assure Britons that the 'South are, to almost a man, opposed to the revival of the slave trade' and the Northerners 'have for years been the supporters of the institution in Cuba, by fitting out ships and sending men and money to buy them. Few if any vessels have ever been sent from the Southern States.'[169]

Moreover, the withdrawal of Union vessels to join the blockade of the states in rebellion back home left efforts to suppress slave trading in West Africa in disarray and eliciting censure from both Britain's press and the country's ministers.[170] The US African Squadron was the fig leaf diplomatically and practically covering an embarrassing hole in the Royal Navy's legal powers of interception. Warm words from Seward did little to satisfy the occupants of Downing Street and the Foreign Office.[171] By September 1861, Palmerston expressed to Russell his testy exasperation with the Union, asking 'why should they not prove their abhorrence of slavery, by joining and helping us heartily in our operations against slave trade, by giving us facilities for putting it down when carried under United States flag'. He went on to note Lord Lyons's observation that Seward may contemplate a deal, perhaps allowing British cruisers the right to visit US vessels and hand over those with slaves to the US Navy for prosecution. The premier cheerfully observed that, then, 'we might take without leave the same liberty with any under the Confederate flag'.[172]

The autumn and winter of 1861–62 saw both British and US governments distracted by the bad-tempered threats surrounding the seizure of Confederate diplomats Mason and Slidell from the Royal Mail Ship *Trent*. In the wake of this low point in Anglo–American diplomacy, however, Secretary Seward was eager to exploit Britain's longstanding frustration over the right of search.[173] An article of 1933 by Taylor Milne skilfully traces his response to Lyon's requests, seeing an opportunity to please the Palmerston ministry and convince British voters that the North represented anti-slavery morality.[174] In March of 1862, Lyons reported that 'Mr. Seward is willing to propose to me to negotiate a Slave Trade Treaty, provided the proposal have the air of coming originally from the United States, instead of from us'.[175] This trickery was the only significant concession Seward required from Britain, and it allowed him to maintain support from congressional conservatives by presenting the initiative as a US demand.[176] The Senate unanimously ratified the treaty, thus reversing the capitulation of 1842 and finally strengthening the British suppression system.

As this news reached Britain, the *Blackburn Standard* was on sale with an article chastising 'the obstinate refusal of the United States' to let Britain suppress the Cuban slave trade by granting a right of search.[177] Pro-Union newspapers, such as the *Daily News* and the *Examiner*, could welcome that 'Mr. Lincoln has given a fresh proof' of 'sincerity' in 'hostility to slavery'.[178] *The Times*, sympathetic to the South, weakly complained in response that Northerners were the sponsors of the Cuban slave trade and the southerners more sincere in hating it.[179] The *Lancaster Gazette* sneered that 'adversity has done its usual chastening work, when we find Brother Jonathan coming down from his high horse' since '[b]etter manners and sounder sense now prevail'.[180]

In a letter to Russell, the Duke of Argyll reflected on the fact that 'the North has never proposed to fight for the abolition of slavery' and so 'I have always looked to the irresistible tendency of events, rather than to the *intentions* of the North, for the anti-slavery effects of the war'.[181] British confusion and division over Confederate independence is more explicable and less eccentric in the context of popular and official interest in US obstruction of slave-trade suppression. Renewed efforts by the US Navy and the withdrawal of US sailors from the slave trade to Cuba marked a symbolic, if unexpected, conclusion to the suppression campaign.[182] From around 11,000 Africans taken to Cuba in 1861–62, the total dropped by more than ten times by 1865, the year Palmerston died. This dramatic decline appeared to be a final victory for naval suppression.[183] The ships of Britain's West Africa squadron would end their campaign within four years of the last Confederate surrender, which took place, appropriately enough, in the River Mersey, where so many early slave-trade voyages had begun.[184]

Conclusion (1865–69)

Despite generating parliamentary crises, international conflict and incipient colonialism, the British campaign against the Atlantic slave trade died quietly, at the hands of an accountant scribbling in the budget ledger and Admiralty officials organising naval deployments. In Cuba, the Spanish authorities acted against the hiring out of liberated Africans to slaveholders, which had provided ideal cover for those buying newly arrived slaves from the traders who had not been intercepted, and enforced a series of new regulations culminating in an 1867 suppression law.[185] Despite the fanfare and political importance of the Lyons–Seward Treaty, the Mixed-Commission Courts between Britain and the USA never actually tried a single case. As Prime Minister, in 1870, William Gladstone – a prominent supporter of Hutt's mid-century attempts to abort the suppression campaign – abolished the courts, and reformed the squadron as part of a broader, victorious dismantling of Britain's suppression apparatus.[186]

The best analysis of the efficacy of Britain's suppression campaign remains the study undertaken by David Eltis in 1987. He concludes that 'even after doing violence to international law, the British could expect to detain at best one out of perhaps every three ships sent to Africa' by foreigners. When it came to traders' profits, 'they could induce a loss of only one venture in five in any long-run period'.

Meaningful progress came only when 'a government passed and rigorously enforced legislation on their own nationals'.[187] Brazilian citizens and their politicians had acted decisively against the slave trade after 1850, while in Cuba plummeting sugar prices sapped demand for slaves. In both cases, British harassment had made suppression attractive in foreign policy but, at crucial moments, perilously unpatriotic in domestic politics. British efforts did not suppress the transatlantic traffic, though Eltis suspects they did help accelerate or extenuate the incentives for nations to enforce their own bans.[188]

In Victorian Britain, however, the pivotal role of naval suppression became an important precedent for the power of moral force and imperial duty. This would have important implications, most notably in efforts to suppress the trans-Saharan slave trade to East Africa and the Indian Ocean.[189] The ambiguities of anti-slave-trade humanitarianism might be traced in later nineteenth-century British policies colonising large portions of Africa or tolerating 'traditional' forms of slavery within those colonies. Moreover, while keen to criticise French abuses in Reunion Island, for example, British governments showed little future concern for Indians travelling under contracts of indenture and did not prevent such practices until 1922, by which time 1.5 million emigrants had sailed within the British Empire.[190]

To assess the politics of Britain's diplomatic and naval campaigns for suppression means analysing a curious mixture of imperial bombast, calculated realpolitik, economic pressure and anti-slavery sincerity. It would be impossible to impose a clear typology on the varied opinions of ordinary Britons, public officials, and leading politicians; the strength of anti-slavery feeling meant, perhaps inevitably, a varied, diffuse pluralism of understandings of what it should mean in practice.[191] However, it is hard to find direct, consistent economic calculations behind British policies of slave-trade suppression. It is far easier to see clear financial interests in *laissez-faire* opposition to the squadron – often aligned with current and aspirational commercial ties to Brazil, for example – than in support of suppression; even amongst anti-coercionists, ideology created expectations of economic interests as much as reflecting them. Typical of public defences of the squadron's role, the *Liverpool Mercury* praised Russell in 1850 by insisting that '[t]here are some things in this world better than money: freedom is one of them and character is another'.[192]

Anti-slave-trade policies, though, reflected widespread expectations that British pre-eminence, global prosperity and civilisation, and the decline of slavery might all go together. This did not, by mid-century, take the form of divine providence directly. Even supporters of Palmerston's muscular policies found his theological comments on this topic heavy-handed and embarrassing. One friendly journalist noted that the 'inscrutable ways of GOD to man are not to be judged by the transient phenomena of earthly success or failure' and so it was 'enough for a nation, as for an individual, to persist with courage and with faith in that which is right and true – the reward of our labour is not to be made the criterion of the goodness of our cause'.[193] However, such selfless strictures betrayed broader, only semi-secular, faith in the progress of civilisation and the backwardness of slavery; hence, Britons of different persuasions might approach the politics of suppression with arrogant patriotism and zealous conviction combined. The attack on the Atlantic slave trade did not cloak some fundamental material interest, but it did feed from and into Britons' presumption of their superiority and the ultimate benevolence of their dominance of international commerce and international relations.

Notes

1 David Eltis, *Economic Growth and the Ending of the Slave Trade* (Oxford: Oxford University Press, 1987), p. 52.
2 James Stephen, *War in Disguise, or, the Frauds of Neutral Flags* (London: J. Hatchard, 1805).
3 Seymour Drescher, *Econocide: British Slavery in the Era of Abolition* [1977], 2nd edn (Chapel Hill, NC: University of North Carolina Press, 2010), pp. 100–3, 122–4.
4 James Stephen, *The Dangers of the Country* (London: J. Butterworth and J. Hatchard, 1807).
5 Drescher, *Econocide*, pp. 183–6; Richard Huzzey, 'The Moral Geography of British Anti-Slavery Responsibilities', *Transactions of the Royal Historical Society*, sixth series, 22 (2012), 111–39. For a recent restatement of the economic context to the timing of abolition, see David Beck Ryden, *West Indian Slavery and British Abolition, 1783–1807* (Cambridge: Cambridge University Press, 2010).
6 Eltis, *Economic Growth*, p. 41.
7 Maeve Ryan, 'The Price of Legitimacy in Humanitarian Intervention: Britain, the Right of Search, and the Abolition of the West Africa Slave Trade, 1807–1867', in Brendan Simms and D. J. B. Trim (eds), *Humanitarian Intervention: A History* (Cambridge: Cambridge University Press, 2011), pp. 231–56, at p. 235.
8 On wider questions, see the essays collected in Thomas Bender (ed.), *The Antislavery Debate: Capitalism and Abolitionism as a Problem of Historical Interpretation* (Berkeley: University of California Press, 1992). See also Seymour Drescher, 'Review of Thomas Bender (ed.), *The Antislavery Debate: Capitalism and Abolitionism as a Problem of Historical Interpretation* (Berkeley: University of California Press, 1992), *History and Theory* 32 (1993), 311–29 Seymour Drescher, 'Antislavery Debates: Tides of Historiography in Slavery and Antislavery', *European Review* 19 (2011), 131–48.
9 Seymour Drescher, *The Mighty Experiment: Free Labour versus Slavery in British Emancipation* (Oxford: Oxford University Press, 2004), pp. 138–43.
10 Paul Michael Kielstra, *The Politics of Slave Trade Suppression in Britain and France, 1814–48: Diplomacy, Morality and Economics* (Basingstoke: Routledge, 2000), pp. 25–33; Drescher, *Econocide*, pp. 152–61.
11 Seymour Drescher, 'Whose Abolition? Popular Pressure and the Ending of the British Slave Trade', *Past and Present* 143 (1994), 136–66, at 159–65.
12 Seymour Drescher, 'Public Opinion and Parliament in the Abolition of the British Slave Trade', in Stephen Farrell, Melanie Unwin and James Walvin (eds), *The British*

Slave Trade: Abolition, Parliament and People (Edinburgh: Edinburgh University Press, 2007), pp. 42–65, at p. 64; Kielstra, *Politics*, pp. 30–1.

13 Huzzey, 'Moral Geography', pp. 120–1.

14 Catherine Hall, *Macaulay and Son: Architects of Imperial Britain* (London: Yale University Press, 2012), pp. 69–71.

15 Huzzey, 'Moral Geography', pp. 119–20.

16 Seymour Drescher, 'The Slaving Capital of the World: Liverpool and National Opinion in the Age of Abolition', *Slavery & Abolition* 9 (1988), 128–43, at 139–40.

17 Holger Lutz Kern, 'Strategies of Legal Change: Great Britain, International Law and the Abolition of the Slave Trade', *Journal of the History of International Law* 6 (2004), 233–58, at 244; Kielstra, *Politics*, pp. 56–8.

18 Qtd in Betty Fladeland, 'Abolitionist Pressures on the Concert of Europe, 1814–1822', *Journal of Modern History* 38 (1966), 355–73, at 368.

19 Canning to the Duke of Wellington, 1 October 1822. Reprinted in extract in *British and Foreign State Papers* (London: HM Government, 1850), x, 90–4, at p. 91.

20 Alfred P. Rubin, *Ethics and Authority in International Law* (Cambridge: Cambridge University Press, 1997), pp. 118–21.

21 Canning to the Duke of Wellington, 1 October 1822, as reprinted in extract in *British and Foreign State Papers*, x, 90–4, at p. 94.

22 Ryan, 'Price of Legitimacy', p. 237.

23 Huzzey, 'Moral Geography', p. 121.

24 Jean Allain, 'The Nineteenth Century Law of the Sea and the British Abolition of the Slave Trade', *British Yearbook of International Law* 87 (2007), 342–88, at p. 354; Ryan, 'Price', pp. 237–8.

25 Rubin, *Ethics and Authority*, p. 103; Ryan, 'Price', pp. 234–5.

26 Rubin, *Ethics and Authority*, pp. 82–137.

27 *Hansard*, 5 March 1811, 3rd series, vol. xix, col. 239.

28 J. E. Eardley-Wilmot, *Lord Brougham's Acts and Bills, From 1811 to the Present Time* (London: Longman, 1857), p. 1.

29 Chaim D. Kaufmann and Robert A. Pape, 'Explaining Costly International Moral Action: Britain's Sixty-year Campaign against the Atlantic Slave Trade', *International Organisation* 53 (1999), 631–68, at p. 658.

30 Jenny S. Martinez, *The Slave Trade and the Origins of International Human Rights Law* (Oxford: Oxford University Press, 2012), pp. 30–7, 68–70, 78–9; Richard Huzzey, *Freedom Burning: Anti-Slavery and Empire in Victorian Britain* (Ithaca, NY: Cornell University Press, 2012), pp. 47–51; Farida Shaikh, 'Judicial Diplomacy: British Officials and the Mixed Commission Courts' in Keith Hamilton and Patrick Salmon (eds), *Slavery, Diplomacy and Empire: Britain and the Suppression of the Slave Trade, 1807–1975* (Eastbourne: Sussex Academic Press, 2009), pp. 42–64.

31 Leslie Bethell, 'The Mixed Commissions for the Suppression of the Transatlantic Slave Trade in the Nineteenth Century', *African History* 7 (1966), 79–93, at p. 86.

32 Sierra Leone and attempts to undermine the slave trade in Africa also loomed large. See Suzanne Schwarz, 'Commerce, Civilization and Christianity: The Development of the Sierra Leone Company', in David Richardson, Suzanne Schwarz and Anthony Tibbles (eds), *Liverpool and Transatlantic Slavery* (Liverpool: Liverpool University Press, 2007), pp. 255–76.

33 Elizabeth Heyrick, *Immediate Not Gradual Abolition* (London: Hatchard et al., 1824).

34 Huzzey, *Freedom Burning*, 14–16, 67–8; David Turley, 'Anti-slavery Activists and Officials: "Influence", Lobbying and the Slave Trade, 1807–1850' in Hamilton and Salmon (eds), *Slavery, Diplomacy and Empire*, pp. 81–92.

35 Thomas Fowell Buxton, *African Slave Trade and its Remedy*, 2nd edn (London: John Murray, 1840), pp. 268–70; Howard Temperley, *White Dreams, Black Africa: The Antislavery Expedition to the Niger, 1841–42* (New Haven, CT: Yale University Press, 1991). After his death, Buxton was often misquoted as favouring withdrawal, however. P[arliamentary] P[apers] 1847–48, vol. xxii (283), p. 70. See chapter 7 of this volume for the wider geographical context of the Buxton campaign.

36 David Brown, *Palmerston and the Politics of Foreign Policy, 1846–55* (Manchester: Manchester University Press, 2002), pp. 41–3.
37 Kielstra, *Politics*, pp. 202–5, quotations at pp. 203, 205.
38 Jasper Ridley, *Lord Palmerston* (London: Constable, 1970), pp. 279–82; Kielstra, *Politics*, pp. 206–15.
39 Rhodes House Library, Oxford, MSS. Brit.Emp.s.19 E2/19, BFASS memorials book, p. 59.
40 Kielstra, *Politics*, pp. 224–35.
41 W. C. Klunder, *Lewis Cass and the Politics of Moderation* (Kent, OH: Kent State University Press, 1996), pp. 105–11.
42 Huzzey, *Freedom Burning*, pp. 70–1.
43 See Steven Heath Mitton's forthcoming reinterpretation, delivered as '"The Ashburton Capitulation": The Convention of London, British Defeat, and the Americanization of the Atlantic, c. 1842', paper presented at the 2010 Meeting of the American Historical Association, San Diego, CA, 7 Jan. 2010. I am grateful to Mitton for sharing this unpublished paper with me.
44 Qtd in Don E. Fehrenbacher, *The Slaveholding Republic: An Account of the United States Government's Relations to Slavery* (Oxford: Oxford University Press, 2001), p. 168.
45 Howard Jones and Donald A. Rakestraw, *Prologue to Manifest Destiny: Anglo–American Relations in the 1840s* (Wilmington, NJ: Scholarly Resources, 1997), pp. 71–81, 138–42. The compromise did not stop Cass from raising objections on his return to the USA. Klunder, *Lewis Cass*, pp. 112–18.
46 Fehrenbacher, *Slaveholding Republic*, pp. 169–71; Huzzey, *Freedom Burning*, pp. 54–6.
47 Huzzey, *Freedom Burning*, p. 71. Personal correspondence with Peter Jones, and consultation of his unpublished article 'Palmerston and the Suppression of the Slave Trade', have been immensely valuable in forming the argument presented here.
48 Keith Hamilton, 'Zealots and Healots: The Slave Trade Department of the Nineteenth-century Foreign Office' in Hamilton and Salmon (eds), *Slavery, Diplomacy and Empire*, pp. 20–41.
49 James Ferguson King, 'The Latin-American Republics and the Suppression of the Slave Trade', *Hispanic American Historical Review* 24 (1944), 387–411, at pp. 409–10.
50 Huzzey, *Freedom Burning*, pp. 43–5.
51 Huzzey, *Freedom Burning*, p. 43; Eltis, *Economic Growth*, pp. 92–3.
52 *Punch*, 20 March 1850, p. 125.
53 *Caledonian Mercury*, 18 July 1850, p. 2.
54 Richard Huzzey, 'Gladstone and the Suppression of the Slave Trade' in Roland Quinault, Roger Swift and Ruth Clayton Windscheffel (eds), *William Gladstone: New Studies and Perspectives* (Farnham, Surrey: Ashgate, 2012), pp. 253–66.
55 *Hansard*, 3rd series, 1846, vol. lxxxvii, col. 1267.
56 *Parliamentary Papers* (hereafter *PP*) 1849, vol. xix (410), p. xxiv; *Hansard*, 3rd series, 1850, vol. cxv, cols 62–3.
57 *Hansard*, 3rd series, 1848, vol. xcvi, col. 1111; a similar argument was used by Milner the following year: *Hansard*, 3rd series, 1849, vol. civ, col. 758.
58 *PP* 1847–48, vol. xxii (283), pp. 20, 137.
59 *Hansard*, 3rd series, 1845, vol. lxxxi, col. 1166.
60 *Hansard*, 3rd series, 1845, vol. lxxxi, col. 1171.
61 *PP* 1847–48, vol. xxii (283), p.172.
62 The phrase 'war of representation' is from Catherine Hall, *Civilising Subjects: Metropole and Colony in the English Imagination, 1830–1867* (Oxford: Polity, 2002), pp. 107–9. On representations of suppression, see also Robert Burroughs, 'Eyes on the Prize: Journeys in Slave Ships Taken as Prizes by the Royal Navy', *Slavery & Abolition* 31 (2010), 99–115, and also chapter 6 in this volume.
63 Buxton, *African Slave Trade and its Remedy*, pp. 268–70. Buxton explicitly imagined his civilisation scheme operating as supplement to the cruisers, not as presented by Christopher Lloyd, *The Navy and Slave Trade: The Suppression of the African Slave*

Trade in the Nineteenth Century (London: Longman, 1949), p. 106.

64 For W. L. Mathieson's invention of the term 'anti-coercionists', see Patrick Harries, 'The Hobgoblins of the Middle Passage: the Cape and the Trans-Atlantic Slave Trade', in Ulrike Schmieder, Katja Füllberg-Stolberg and Michael Zeuske (eds), *The End of Slavery in Africa and the Americas: A Comparative Approach* (Berlin: LIT Verlag, 2011), pp. 27–50, at p. 44.

65 Cowper to Foreign Office, 1 January 1844, as reprinted in *PP 1847–48*, vol. xxii (1), pp. 251–3.

66 *PP 1847–48*, vol. xxii (1), p. 253–4.

67 On officers' sentiments, see Mary Wills's research in chapter 4 of this volume.

68 Amanda Perreau-Saussine, 'British Acts of State in English Courts', *British Yearbook of International Law* 78 (2007), 186–254, at pp. 218–27; Martinez, *Slave Trade*, pp. 97–8; Ward, *Royal Navy*, pp. 167–78, 194–5.

69 Robin Law, 'Abolition and Imperialism: International Law and the British Suppression of the Atlantic Slave Trade', in Derek R. Peterson (ed.), *Abolitionism and Imperialism in Britain, Africa, and the Atlantic* (Athens, OH: Ohio University Press, 2010), pp. 150–74; Huzzey, *Freedom Burning*, pp. 141–7.

70 *PP 1847–48*, vol. xxii (1), p. 43; *PP 1847–48*, vol. xxii (283), pp. 69–70.

71 Huzzey, 'Gladstone', pp. 259–63.

72 *PP 1847–48*, vol. xxii (283), p. 9. Thomas Thompson agreed: *PP 1847–48*, vol. xxii (283), p. 128.

73 *PP 1847–48*, vol. xxii (283), p. 128.

74 *PP 1847–48*, vol. xxii (1), p. 92.

75 *PP 1847–48*, vol. xxii (1), p. 164. Inglis later suggested this to another witness, who seemed queasy at the prospect. *PP 1847–48*, vol. xxii (283), p. 123.

76 *PP 1847–48*, vol. xxii (1), p. 164.

77 This is not to say that he supported the death penalty, but rather seemed to have better faith in the stigma of appearing in the Mixed-Commission Courts. *PP 1847–48*, vol. xxii (272), pp. 15–16.

78 *PP 1847–48*, vol. xxii (1), p.75; see also *PP 1847–48*, vol. xxii (1), pp. 128, 142, 173–4; *PP 1847–48*, vol. xxii (283), p. 6.

79 *PP 1847–48*, vol. xxii (283), p. 213. See also *PP 1847–48*, vol. xxii (283), p. 115.

80 *Chambers's Edinburgh Journal*, August 1848, pp. 120–1.

81 Huzzey, 'Gladstone'.

82 Thomas Carlyle, 'Occasional Discourse on the Negro Question', *Fraser's Magazine*, December 1849, pp. 670–9, at p. 678.

83 'Our Phantom Ship, Negro Land', *Household Words*, 18 January 1851, pp. 400–7, at p. 407.

84 *PP 1847–48*, vol. xxii (1), p. 98. Thomas Tobin, another merchant in West Africa and a former slave-owner, thought that by offering to intervene when African partners had let down British traders, the nation artificially encouraged its citizens to enter into risky ventures they would otherwise have seen as foolish. *PP 1847–48*, vol. xxii (467), p. 9.

85 *PP 1847–48*, vol. xxii (283), pp. 90, 95–8. See also *PP 1847–48*, vol. xxii (467), pp. 12–13.

86 See *PP 1842*, vol. xi (551).

87 See, for example, the evidence of Alexander Macgregor, *PP 1847–48*, vol. xxii (467), pp. 45–6.

88 *Hansard*, 3rd series, 1846, vol. lxxxviii, col. 45. See also *Hansard*, 3rd series, 1846, vol. lxxxviii, col. 503; *Hansard*, 3rd series, 1846, vol. lviii, col. 136–7.

89 Thomas Love Peacock, *Gryll Grange* (London: Parker, Son and Bourn, 1860), p. 165. Many thanks to Roland Quinault for directing to me to this example of mid-Victorian opinion.

90 David Turnbull (ed.), *The Jamaica Movement, for Promoting the Enforcement of the Slave–Trade Treaties, and the Suppression of the Slave Trade* (London: Gilpin, 1850), pp. 24–5, 29.

91 Turnbull, *Jamaica Movement*, p. 409. For sceptical views on the squadron and emphasis on sugar duties, see also pp. 85–6, 103, 181–4, 198–200, 286–7.

92 *Hansard*, 3rd series, 1850, vol. cix, col. 110.

93 *PP 1847–48*, vol. xxii (705), p. 21. They only disagreed about whether the increase made coercion more desirable or impossible.
94 Samuel Wilberforce, *Cheap Sugar Means Cheap Slaves* (London: Ridgway, 1848), p. 7; Joseph Denman, *Practical Remarks on The Slave Trade and on the Existing Treaties with Portugal* (London: Ridgway, 1839), p. 15.
95 This analysis is based on a comparison of divisions on the sugar duties and slave trade bills of 19 March 1850 (*Hansard*, 3rd series, 1850, vol. cix, cols 1184–6) and 31 May 1850 (*Hansard*, 3rd series, 1850, vol. cxi, cols 593–6), as presented in summary in Richard Huzzey, 'Free Trade, Free Labour, and Slave Sugar in Victorian Britain', *Historical Journal* 53 (2010), 359–79, at pp. 375–6.
96 On historiographical debate, see Hugh Tinker, *A New System of Slavery: The Export of Indian Labour Overseas, 1830–1920* (Oxford: Oxford University Press, 1974); David Northrup, *Indentured Labor in the Age of Imperialism, 1834–1922* (Cambridge: Cambridge University Press, 1995); Amit Kumar Mishra, 'Indian Indentured Labourers in Mauritius: Reassessing the "New System of Slavery" vs. Free Labor Debate', *Studies in History* 25 (2009), 229–51.
97 *Hansard*, 3rd series, 1845, vol. lxxxi, col. 1171.
98 Philip D. Curtin, *The Image of Africa: British Ideas and Action, 1780–1850* (London: University of Wisconsin, 1964), pp. 444–5.
99 Joseph Denman, *The Slave Trade, The African Squadron and Mr. Hutt's Committee* (London: J. Mortimer, 1849), p. 7.
100 *PP 1847–48*, vol. xxii (1), pp. 232, 256, 247–9. John King proposed a similar plan. *PP 1847–48*, vol. xxii (283), p. 31.
101 *PP 1847–48*, vol. xxii (283), p. 73.
102 Huzzey, *Freedom Burning*, pp. 178–83.
103 *Hansard*, 3rd series, 1845, vol. lxxxi, col. 1178.
104 See Richard Huzzey, 'Concepts of Liberty: Freedom, Laissez-faire and the State after Britain's Abolition of Slavery', in C. Hall, N. Draper and K. McClelland (eds), *Emancipation and the Remaking of the British Imperial World* (Manchester: Manchester University Press, 2014), pp. 149–71.
105 Andrew Colvile, *Memorandum by the Acting Committee of West India Planters and Merchants* (London: Macnin, Lewis and Böhm, 1853); see also David R. Murray, *Odious Commerce: Britain, Spain, and the Abolition of the Cuban Slave Trade* (Cambridge: Cambridge University Press, 1980), pp. 215–18.
106 Huzzey, *Freedom Burning*, pp. 99–110.
107 *Northern Star*, 23 March 1850, p. 4.The racial epithets and report of events take their lead from *The Times*'s coverage.
108 Huzzey, *Freedom Burning*, pp. 119–20.
109 Anthony Howe, 'Two Faces of British Power: Cobden Versus Palmerston', in David Brown and Miles Taylor (eds), *Palmerston Studies II* (Southampton: Hartley Institute, 2007), pp. 168–92.
110 *PP 1847–48*, vol. xxii (283), p. 85.
111 Huzzey, *Freedom Burning*, pp. 119–20. They were subsequently mocked for this shift of ground. See *Morning Chronicle*, 20 March 1850, p. 5.
112 *PP 1847–48*, vol. xxii (1), p. 14.
113 *PP 1847–48*, vol. xxii (1), pp. 18–19, 31.
114 The phrase comes from Denman's exchange with Stanley on this same subject: *PP 1847–48*, vol. xxii (1), pp. 26, 47, 50.
115 For examples of this term being used: *PP 1847–48*, vol. xxii (1), pp. 13, 17. Captain Denman made identical claims to the Commons committee, *PP 1847–48*, vol. xxii (1), p. 31. Comparisons to London's police were also used to rebut anti-coercionist claims. William Gore Ouseley, *Notes on the Slave Trade with Remarks on the Measure Adopted for its Suppression* (London: John Rodwell, 1850), p.2; and 'A Barrister', *Analysis of the Evidence Given Before The Select Committee on the Slave Trade* (London: Partridge and Oakey, 1850), p. 7.
116 *PP 1847–48*, vol. xxii (272), p. 123. See also *Hansard*, 3rd series, 1850, vol. cix, cols 1152–3.

117 *PP 1847–48*, vol. xxii (272), pp. 11–12. Sceptical of this claim, Bingham Baring engaged in a surreal argument over whether keepers of lunatic asylums were prone to becoming cruel, and Palmerston indulged this tangent with cases illustrating just that point.

118 *PP 1847–48*, vol. xxii (272), p. 123. See also Anon., *Free Trade in Negroes* (London: J. Ollivier, 1849), p. 1.

119 Buxton, *Slave Trade and its Remedy*, p. 530.

120 On Madden, see David R. Murray, 'Richard Robert Madden: His Career as a Slavery Abolitionist', *Studies: An Irish Quarterly Review* 61 (1972), 41–53; Gera Burton, 'Liberty's Call: Richard Robert Madden's Voice in the Anti-Slavery Movement', *Irish Migration Studies in Latin America* 5 (2007), 199–207 at pp. 204–5.

121 Such questions are posed by Howard Temperley, *British Anti-slavery 1833–1870* (Longman: London, 1972), pp. 175–6; Marika Sherwood, *After Abolition: Britain and the Slave Trade since 1807* (London: I. B. Tauris, 2007); Huzzey, 'Moral Geography'. See also forthcoming research by Joseph G. Kelly.

122 Eltis, *Economic Growth*, pp. 209–11.

123 Huzzey, *Freedom Burning*, p. 142.

124 For 'bridgeheads', see John Darwin, 'Imperialism and the Victorians: The Dynamics of Territorial Expansion', *English Historical Review* 112 (1997), 614–42.

125 On the complex 'adaptation' debate, see the essays compiled in Robin Law (ed.), *From Slave Trade to 'Legitimate' Commerce: The Commercial Transition in Nineteenth-Century West Africa* (Cambridge: Cambridge University Press, 1995).

126 Huzzey, *Freedom Burning*, pp. 141–7, quotation at p. 142.

127 Law, 'Abolition and Imperialism', pp. 150–74, quotations at p. 167.

128 Robin Law, *Ouidah: The Social History of a West African Slaving 'Port', 1727–1892* (Athens, OH: Ohio University Press, 2004), pp. 137, 155–230.

129 *PP 1851*, vol. lvi, part 2, p. 33: Palmerston to Beecroft, 21 February 1851.

130 Qtd in Huzzey, *Freedom Burning*, p. 145.

131 Huzzey, *Freedom Burning*, pp. 145–7.

132 Kristin Mann, *Slavery and the Birth of an African City: Lagos, 1760–1900* (Bloomington, IN: Indiana University Press, 2007), pp. 94–102.

133 *PP 1847–48*, vol. xxii (467), pp. 171, 201; on importance of 'anti-slavery' to missionaries' potential as 'bridgeheads', see Bronwen Everill, 'Bridgeheads of Empire? Liberated African Missionaries in West Africa', *Journal of Imperial and Commonwealth History* 45 (2012), 789–805.

134 Yale Divinity School, Horace Waller Papers, Record Group 72, Box 1, Folder 2: Waller to parents, 20 October–12 November 1861, fo. 6.

135 Huzzey, *Freedom Burning*, p. 137.

136 David Livingstone, *Narrative of an Expedition to the Zambesi and its Tributaries* (London: John Murray, 1865), p. iii.

137 Huzzey, *Freedom Burning*, pp. 134, 166–8.

138 Eltis, *Economic Growth*, pp. 213–14.

139 Eltis, *Economic Growth*, p. 215.

140 *Examiner*, 1 October 1853, p. 633.

141 *Examiner*, 8 July 1854, 422–3; *Examiner*, 14 March 1863, p. 164.

142 Eltis, *Economic Growth*, 210.

143 *Lloyd's Weekly Newspaper*, 11 July 1858, p. 6.

144 *Saturday Review*, 23 July 1864, p. 105. See also *Morning Post*, 6 August 1857, p. 5.

145 *The York Herald*, 24 October 1857, p. 8.

146 Eltis, *Economic Growth*, p. 211; R. R. Davis, 'James Buchanan and the Suppression of the Slave Trade, 1858–1861', *Pennsylvania History* 33 (1966), 446–59.

147 *Morning Post*, 4 June 1858, p. 4; See also *York Herald*, 26 June 1858, p. 8; *Leeds Mercury*, 22 June 1858, p. 2.

148 Hansard, 3rd series, 1858, vol. cli, cols 1286–7; see also *Leeds Mercury*, 17 July 1858, supplement, p. 1.

149 *Examiner*, 24 July 1858, p. 465.

150 *Saturday Review*, 17 July 1858, p. 53.

151 *Leeds Mercury*, 15 July 1858, p. 2.
152 *Anti-Slavery Reporter*, 1 April 1865, p. 86.
153 National Archives, Russell papers, PRO 30-22-21: Memo from Palmerston to Russell, 14 March 1860.
154 National Archives, Russell papers, PRO 30-22-34: Lyons to Russell, 23 January 1860. See also National Archives, Russell papers, PRO 30-22-34: Lyons to Russell, 5 March 1860; National Archives, Russell papers, PRO 30-22-34: Lyons to Russell, 10 April 1860.
155 National Archives, Russell papers, PRO 30-22-24: Somerset to Russell, 29 August 1860.
156 Eltis, *Economic Growth*, pp. 210–12.
157 See Hansard, 3rd series, 1843, vol. lxvii, col. 1291 for contemporary discussion. See also Muriel Chamberlain, *Pax Britannica? British Foreign Policy, 1789–1914* (London: Longman, 1988), p. 86.
158 Fehrenbacher, *Slaveholding Republic*, pp. 128–33.
159 Lawrence Goldman, '"A Total Misconception": Lincoln, the Civil War and the British, 1860–65', in Richard Carwardine and Jay Sexton (eds), *The Global Lincoln* (Oxford: Oxford University Press, 2011), pp. 107–22 at 112–14. The best general analyses of British opinion and the Civil War are Richard Blackett, *Divided Hearts: Britain and the American Civil War* (Baton Rouge, LA: Louisiana State University Press, 2001) and Duncan A. Campbell, *English Public Opinion and the American Civil War* (Woodbridge: Boydell, 2003).
160 *Daily News*, 16 April 1862, p. 5.
161 National Archives, Russell papers, PRO 30-22-24: Somerset to Russell, 7 February 1861.
162 *Glasgow Herald*, 19 December 1860, p. 3.
163 *Morning Post*, 28 December 1860, p. 2.
164 *Punch*, 16 March 1861; p. 115; *Bell's Life in London and Sporting Chronicle*, 3 March, 1861, p. 3.
165 *Punch*, 16 March 1861; p. 115.
166 *Glasgow Herald*, 2 January 1861, p. 3.
167 As discussed by *Morning Post*, 22 January 1861, p. 3.
168 BFASS, *Twenty-second annual report of the British and Foreign Anti–Slavery Society* (London: BFASS, 1861), p. 13.
169 *Morning Chronicle*, 31 January 1861, p. 6.
170 National Archives, Russell papers, PRO 30-22-24: Somerset to Russell, 13 September 1861; *Morning Post*, 18 April 1862, p. 4.
171 Fehrenbacher, *Slaveholding Republic*, pp. 189–90.
172 National Archives, Russell papers, PRO 30-22-24: Palmerston to Russell, 24 September 1861.
173 Howard Jones, *Abraham Lincoln and a New Birth of Freedom: The Union and Slavery in the Diplomacy of the Civil War* (Lincoln, NE: University of Nebraska Press, 1999), pp. 65–7; Howard Jones, *Blue and Gray Diplomacy: A History of Union and Confederate Foreign Relations* (Chapel Hill, NC: University of North Carolina Press, 2010), pp. 122–3; Fehrenbacher, *Slaveholding Republic*, p. 190.
174 A. Taylor Milne, 'The Lyons–Seward Treaty of 1862', *American Historical Review* 38 (1933), 511–25.
175 Quoted in Milne, 'Lyons–Seward Treaty', p. 519.
176 Amanda Foreman, *A World on Fire: An Epic History of Two Nations Divided* (London: Allen Lane, 2010), pp. 234–8.
177 *Blackburn Standard*, 23 April 1862, p. 4.
178 *Daily News*, 10 May 1862, p. 4; *Bradford Observer*, 15 May 1862, p. 3.
179 *Birmingham Daily Post*, 24 May 1862, p. 3.
180 *Lancaster Gazette*, 17 May 1862, supplement, p. 1.
181 National Archives, Russell papers, PRO 30-22-25: Argyll to Russell, 16 October 1862. Original emphasis by underlining.
182 Eltis, *Economic Growth*, pp. 210–11; Ward, *Royal Navy*, p. 226; Seymour Drescher,

'Emperors of the World: British Abolitionism and Imperialism', in D. R. Peterson (ed.), *Abolitionism and Imperialism in Britain, Africa, and the Atlantic* (Athens, OH: Ohio University Press, 2010), pp. 129–49, at p. 143.

183 Milne, 'Lyons–Seward Treaty', p. 516.

184 Joseph McKenna, *British Ships in the Confederate Navy* (Jefferson, NC: McFarland, 2010), p. 202; Warren E. Wilson and Gary L. McKay, *James D. Bullock: Secret Agent and Mastermind of the Confederate Navy* (Jefferson, NC: McFarland, 2012), pp. 204–9.

185 Ward, *Royal Navy*, p. 226; Eltis, *Economic Growth*, pp. 219, 245.

186 Eltis, *Economic Growth*, p. 219. On Gladstone's views, see Huzzey, 'Gladstone'.

187 Eltis, *Economic Growth*, p. 101.

188 Eltis, *Economic Growth*, p. 219.

189 Recent works include Lindsay Doulton, 'The Royal Navy's Anti-Slavery Campaign in the Western Indian Ocean, c. 1860-1890: Race, Empire and Identity' (PhD dissertation, University of Hull, 2010); and essays in Robert Harms, Bernard K. Freamon, and David W. Blight (eds), *Indian Ocean Slavery in the Age of Abolition* (New Haven, CT: Yale University Press, 2013). See also Suzanne Miers, *Britain and the Ending of the Slave Trade* (New York: Africana Publishing, 1975).

190 Alessandro Stanziani, 'Beyond Colonialism: Servants, Wage Earners and Indentured Migrants in Rural France and on Reunion Island (c. 1750–1900)', *Labor History* 54 (2013), pp. 64–87; Huzzey, *Freedom Burning*, p. 181.

191 Huzzey, *Freedom Burning*, pp. 202–13.

192 *Liverpool Mercury*, 22 March 1850, p. 19.

193 *Saturday Review*, 17 July 1858, p. 53. For Palmerston's views, see John Wolffe, 'Lord Palmerston and Religion: A Reappraisal', *English Historical Review* 120 (2005), 907–36.

PART II

Practices

CHAPTER THREE

'Tis enough that we give them liberty'? Liberated Africans at Sierra Leone in the early era of slave-trade suppression

Emma Christopher

After slaves were freed from ships they arrived at points of disembarkation, such as Sierra Leone, in a wretched state. First-hand accounts of slave vessels captured in the earliest days of abolition are few and far between but Frederick Harrison Rankin, who went aboard a captured slave vessel in 1834, left a vivid description:

> Before us, lying in a heap, huddled together at the foot of the foremast, on the bare and filthy deck, lay several human beings in the last stage of emaciation – dying. The ship fore and aft was thronged with men, women and children, all entirely naked, and disgusting with disease. The stench was nearly insupportable, cleanliness being impossible. I stepped to the hatchway; it was secured by iron bars and cross bars, and pressed against them were the heads of the slaves below.

This account is not surprising insofar as it reflects the suffering that abolitionists had campaigned so hard against. What is more shocking is that, according to Harrison Rankin, the situation only worsened after their arrival. In the heavy rain, Harrison Rankin watched as the task of counting the liberated Africans was undertaken. He notes that a 'black boatswain seized them one by one, dragging them before us for a moment ... and they were instantly swung again by the arm into their loathsome cell, where another negro sat, with a whip or stick, and forced them to resume the bent and painful attitude necessary for the stowage of such a large number.' Conveyed to shore in overcrowded canoes, one died before Harrison Rankin's eyes.[1]

Whether the majority of liberated Africans in the earliest days in Freetown understood what had happened to them, especially given this kind of treatment, is a moot point. Watching captured slave ships arrive in 1815–16, a US captain named Samuel Swan explained that as slaves had already passed through so many hands on their journey to the coast and then, after arrival in Sierra Leone, were confined in a large barracks and only told in English that they were no longer slaves, they most likely had no idea what had occurred. Some were thought to believe that they were in the Americas and about to be sold. Such terror could continue for months in the minds of liberated Africans.[2] A number apparently believed that missionaries were nursing them back to health just so that they would be worth more when they were eventually sold.[3] As Mary Church wrote in the 1830s when a slave vessel arrived at Freetown, they 'have no means of being aware of what is wished to be done for them'. Some chose suicide over what they believed was just a new form of terror.[4]

This was clearly not what the abolitionist leaders had envisioned, but what they had intended or expected is unclear. When the Abolition Act took force in 1808 and naval ships were deployed to catch those breaking the ban, it had not been fully thought through as to what would happen to the Africans they recaptured from the illicit trade. Certainly they were to be 'free', but nobody really thought too much about what that meant to those who would receive this 'gift'. Few Europeans understood, or perhaps cared, that Africans arriving in shackles did not seek their freedom in terms of individuality of action and autonomous decision-making. They had not shouted huzzah for Liberty or Death, guillotined aristocratic necks in the name of *liberté*, nor proclaimed the air of their country so pure that all simply must be free born. They had been snatched from extended family and community, deprived of the set roles and relationships that governed all aspects of life. They had been kidnapped from all that gave their life meaning and identity.

Even by European or American standards, however, the idea of liberty flaunted by the abolitionists was no utopia. It did not include more than a passing glance at anything akin to equality. The idea of the African as 'a man and a brother', as engraved into history by Josiah Wedgewood, was little more than a pretty fiction. Even after 'liberation', the African was on his knees. As Michel-Rolph Trouillot has argued, late-eighteenth- and early-nineteenth-century Europeans did not even have the language to express equality between races. It was beyond their horizons.[5] In the long run, the abolition of the slave trade was a mere moment in the evolution of racism.[6] Most Britons, including abolitionists, imagined that liberated Africans could be put to work in some way that contributed to imperial progress. Once British authorities had anointed slaves with pompous blessings and declared them free – 'mummery' was Samuel Swan's description of it – they could be kept in various degrees of non-freedom as long as they were just the right side of outright slavery.[7] Sometimes the line was very fine indeed. As Marcus Wood has argued, 'emancipation [was] a mean-spirited and highly efficient plan for the continued exploitation of the African body as both commodity and resource'.[8]

This chapter will examine how the hotchpotch of ideologies, practicalities and realities played out in Sierra Leone in the first days of the anti-slavery squadron. It will show that there was no single policy but rather an array of possible outcomes, often dependant on the whims of who was in charge. The governors of Sierra Leone during the early anti-slavery era had different ideas about how to deal with the liberated Africans who were under their purported care and command. Thomas Ludlum, serving his third period of governorship in 1808, favoured apprenticeships, but Thomas Perronet Thompson who followed him felt that solution too close to slavery. Edward Columbine, a naval man, reinstated apprenticeships but sent others to newly created villages in the area surrounding Freetown. Charles Maxwell continued sending the newly arriving 'recaptives' to the villages but also recruited many into the armed services. Charles MacCarthy, who governed for ten years from 1814, had the most comprehensive policies. He sent many of the liberated Africans to the colony's villages and used the Church Missionary Society to further his vision of creating a Christian, 'civilised' peasantry.[9]

In 1813, authorities in Sierra Leone conducted a census. It provides considerable insight into how these policies played out in the first six years of the liberated Africans' story. It is an incomplete list, as the fate of the 4,224 Africans who had arrived in the colony prior to 1813 is recorded only if their circumstances changed in that year. But for those arriving in 1813, the list is comprehensive, beginning with a man named 'Quaco' at 1 and ending with 4,669, a man named 'Manga'. As it records the immediate fate of these men, women and children, the census is an invaluable resource for identifying what happened to liberated Africans in the first six years of the campaign against the slave trade. It allows us to recover some of the individual stories that existed behind the governors' policies and to recall that each and every African captive sold across the Atlantic Ocean was an individual with his or her own narrative.

Serving a new master

In the earliest days of liberated Africans' arrival in Freetown the focus was on apprenticeships, which uncomfortably crossed the line into chattel bondage in some cases. The first slaves brought into the colony after the ban were ten boys kidnapped from Robana by a Rhode Island slave trader. They were 'indentured as servants to three of the [Sierra Leone] Company's employees who paid $100 each for them'.[10] Then in March 1808, when two US slave ships arriving in Sierra Leone were captured by the naval patrol, the slaves found aboard were 'sold' as apprentices to Freetown's citizens for $20. Governor Ludlum, having no instructions on what to do with them, simply followed the earlier example. This was a very strange type of freedom since they remained wearing iron shackles. Unsurprisingly, the buyers thought they were purchasing chattel slaves whom they would own in perpetuity.[11]

Whatever the ambiguities over the meaning of freedom, this was too scandalous for many abolitionists. Thomas Perronet Thompson, who became governor in July 1808 a few months after this sale, was horrified. He declared void all apprenticeships signed before his arrival, believing, as he wrote to his fiancée, that the scheme 'introduced actual slavery'. William Wilberforce and his fellow anti-slavery 'saints' had 'at last become slave traders with a vengeance' because of their support for apprenticeships, raged Thompson.[12] Even during Thompson's governorship there were advertisements in the *African Herald* that hint at similar problems, however. In fact, Thompson had little choice but to go on apprenticing those who arrived during his governorship. In November 1809, Moses Grief advertised a $60 reward for the return of three 'New Negro Fellows' who had gone off with abolitionist literature in their pockets.[13] The following week's paper advertised for the return of Cupid (who, tellingly, called himself Osman not Cupid while a fugitive). The man had been rescued from a slave ship a few months earlier and he had run off, it was said, 'in consequence of the light whipping given to his wench'.[14] It is not hard to see parallels between these advertisements and those for runaway slaves that were common in the slave societies of the Americas.

Thompson was recalled to Britain over his undiplomatic words about Wilberforce, and there were no more of the open sales of liberated Africans as had occurred in 1808. Even so, in place of outright sale came negligence. When Edward Columbine replaced Thompson as governor there were allegations that liberated Africans went hungry and had to go around the town 'begging & stealing for subsistence'. Columbine apparently remained unapologetic, declaring on one occasion, '[t]is enough that we give them liberty'.[15] Preoccupied with finances, Columbine's words reveal his less than idealist motivations. In July 1810, hearing that twelve slaves had been liberated and were to be delivered to Freetown, he declared that such a small number was hardly worth the effort. Leaving aside any abolitionist sentiment, Columbine had to try to capture slave ships because, as he made clear, he needed the prize money urgently, being unable to survive on his salary alone.[16]

Charles Maxwell took over the governorship in 1811. There was little change as he was 'bidden to continue Columbine's regime of economy'.[17] Samuel Swan, who visited Freetown just as Maxwell was passing on the baton of governorship to Charles MacCarthy, wrote:

> as no particular fund had been appropriated for the maintenance of the captive negroes brought into the colony, the governor and superintend-ants [sic] of prizes condemned there seem to have been more eager to secure their proportions of the profits from the sale of the ships than to ameliorate the condition of their unhappy sufferers.[18]

Even apprenticeships, which would later be resurrected as a frugal method of 'civilising' the liberated Africans, were off the agenda for the time being, or almost so: a few children were still indentured.[19] It was not until MacCarthy's era that apprenticeships were abolished altogether.[20]

It was this very limited freedom, complete with floggings for the unruly, that led to the relatively high number of runaway apprentices. Around 1810, just two years after slave-trade abolition, around eighty liberated Africans had already fled the colony.[21] The government argued that they were trying to return to their homelands, but given the very high risk of re-enslavement this seems to be a large number. The census of 1813 shows that early arrivals kept on fleeing. Perhaps the starkest record about them is how very young they were; several of those who ran from their masters during 1813 were only 8 or 9 years of age.[22]

Around the time that the 1813 census was taken, the focus of gubernatorial policy shifted from apprenticeships to military service. Governor Charles Maxwell's solution was to choose the strongest and most able of teenage or adult males for enlistment in the army. It was not an entirely original idea; 129 slaves were taken ashore from a captured US brig in April 1810 and put 'into the lower story of the barrack on Falconbridge Point' until the corporal at Bunce could enlist the men.[23] After November 1811, when a 'Black Company' had been added to the Royal African Corps, the Collector of Customs was required to turn over those considered fit for military service.[24] Maxwell, however, pursued the policy with new verve. When the census of 1813 began, five men on its first page were marked as having been enlisted into the Royal African Corps. On the second and third pages every single man and boy, down to an 11-year-old named Mohammed, was listed as having been 'sent to the African recruiting department'. Hardly surprisingly given this level of enlistment, by 1814 Maxwell had more than four companies of his envisaged African army.[25]

The Royal African Corps was not the only route into the military for liberated Africans in the early years of abolition. In some ways those taken into the Royal African Corps were fortunate since they remained in Africa. The West India Regiment also recruited men in Freetown and took many others of those arriving in 1813. These men would cross the Atlantic Ocean not as slaves but as soldiers destined to fight for Britain's imperial causes.[26] In 1813, the recruiting depots for both the West India Regiment and the Royal African Corps were at Bunce Island; the census sometimes marked their fate as 'gone to Bance Island' rather than 'recruiting depot'. There was considerable irony in this taking of liberated Africans to the most infamous slaving depot of the region. The same buildings that had held slaves were thought particularly suitable for holding the new recruits because to escape from them was almost impossible.[27] Before arriving at Bunce they were given new names, their old identities stripped away as profoundly as if a new master had called them Caesar or Pompey. In later years Captain J. F. Napier Hewitt met liberated African soldiers called everything from Michael Angelo to Napoleon Bonaparte, Inigo Jones to Charles Dickens, the weird and wonderful Lucius O'Trigger to Pertinax Max Sycophant.[28] Frederick Harrison Rankin, who watched liberated Africans march away into the army in the 1830s, saw them given names like 'Mark Anthony and Scipio Africanus'. They were bundled down to the cathedral to be summarily baptised, their indigenous beliefs or Islamic heritage considered irrelevant.[29]

We can trace this process through 22 men, part of a group of 233 captives who arrived together from the Windward Coast and were drafted into the Royal African Corps after their appearance at Freetown. Only five days after they set foot in Sierra Leone these men appeared on the Royal African Corps' muster. The approximations of their African names written down by the British clerk were abandoned. Men who had given their name as Kangaree, Fallee, Baloo or Nacoi had, by the alchemies of the time, become David Neptune, Isaac Newton, John Newton, John Nero and Tom Parrott. Rather than letting his imagination roam free, the clerk on this occasion obviously decided not to mess up his alphabetisation and so gave all twenty-two men surnames beginning with the letters N, O or P. Who was who is lost. It is possible that Kangaree, number 4,339, became William Nash and so on in order so that Wojoe, at 4,400, the last destined for the Royal African Corps, became Bob Patten.[30] There is no way of being certain, however.

This could be seen as an inevitable step, since the loss of freedoms for any soldier, of any ethnic background, was part of military service in this era. But other experiences confirm the inequalities that belie this argument. At the time of their recruitment, liberated African men received a bounty of 8 guineas, barely more than half the 15 guineas given to white men.[31] The gulf was supposedly filled with 'Barley Corn Beads assorted', amber and coral, tobacco, iron bars and snuffboxes.[32] In other words, the new recruits were made to accept the sort of gewgaws that dealers had tried to trade for slaves for hundreds of years. Moreover, the military recruitment of liberated Africans was not so much a step forward as a forced march, since many of those who arrived at the recruitment depot were not aware of the 'choice' they were making. Colonel Alfred Burdon Ellis, who spent years in West Africa with the West India Regiment, wrote of the liberated Africans: 'they could not possibly have any idea of the engagement into which they were entering'.[33] Frederick Harrison Rankin believed the truth was darker still. He saw 'the most muscular [liberated Africans] ... drafted at once into the King's service ... marched in a string, *nolentes volentes* ... under strong escort'.[34] A Freetownian told him that the recruits were 'forced to march and labour against their will when the white men pleased' and so were widely considered to be slaves.[35] The bigger picture is also indicative. For British men the West India Regiment and especially the Royal African Corps were convict corps, a punishment for those who had committed some crime or deserted from another regiment. The white man's punishment was to be the black man's liberation.

If the most common fate of adult and teenage males around the 1813 period was military service, the equivalent for younger boys was sometimes the navy. Captain Edward Scobell of the anti-slavery patrol's HMS *Thais* advocated taking liberated African boys aboard his fleet. He took a 9-year-old boy named Bamba (liberated African number 1,599) onto the *Thais*, and then wrote to the Admiralty Office later in 1813 explaining why he had taken twelve more boys. '[M]any, of the younger subjects especially, might be useful on board HM ships', he wrote, acknowledging that the army had first call on the older men. With 'excellent materials afforded in the African nature' they could save English sailors from death in tropical climates. Afterwards, he believed, they would go home and tell their fellow liberated Africans how wonderfully munificent were the British.[36] The twelve boys taken onto the *Thais* were aged between 11 and 8 years old and all seem to have been destined for the general lowest shipboard ranks, among the equivalent European boys, with the exception of an 8-year-old, named simply Prince, who was to serve as Lieutenant Watkins's personal servant. As with soldiers the boys were given new names: Famoi, Nacoi, Jongo and all the others became Black Andrew, Boy Jack, New Tom, Ben Williams, William Coff, George, William (Bill) Williams, Jack Bew, Tom Freeman, Ben Liverpool and Samuel Davis.[37]

Other passing naval ships also sometimes took liberated African boys aboard. HMS *Albacore*, anchored in Freetown harbour in mid-1813, took aboard six 8-year-old boys, two 11-year-olds and the youngest of all, a 6-year-old named Pay. They were listed on the *Albacore*'s muster separately as 'black boys from the colony of Sierra Leone'. Their names originally rendered as Wona, Ghema, Corree, Coona, Yorrow and Pay, they became Tom Handyman, John Cardigan, Roderick Random, John Junk, Jerry Pounce, James Marline, Timothy Chipps and William Warwick.[38] We can trace what happened to some of these liberated Africans through the Royal Navy's musters. Few of them served for long. Tom Handyman and John Cardigan were both discharged within weeks. Jerry Pounce also left before the *Albacore* sailed from Freetown. But others became part of the Royal Navy's cannon fodder. Both William Warwick, aged 10, and Timothy Chipps who was even younger, were sent from the *Albacore* to HMS *Prince* in late December 1813. Another boy found himself alone in England. For James Marlin, not yet 10 years old, freedom was to be left on the docks in Portsmouth on 21 December 1813. What happened to the poor, lost boy after that is not known.[39] He must have been freezing.

There was also a seaborne fate for one liberated African listed on the 1813 census, one of the last brought in during that year. His destiny shows how extremely precarious freedom could be. When he stood in the King's Yard after his arrival in Freetown the British recorded the boy's name as 'Za alias Jack Phoenix'.[40] 'Za' was probably Sahr, the name Kono and Kissi women give to their first-born son, and 'Phoenix' was from the slave ship he was found aboard. The *Phoenix* had not been captured by the naval patrol but by Captain John Roach of the *Kitty* who had a letter of marque in the War of 1812. After going to Freetown to be officially registered among the liberated Africans, Za/Jack stayed with Roach aboard the *Kitty*, becoming part of her crew. This liberated African was to serve aboard a ship that was involved in capturing slave traders.

The tenuousness of freedom for Za/Jack can be seen in what happened next. In January 1814 the *Kitty* found itself under attack. It happened as they were apprehending a slave ship off Gallinas and five 'Spaniards' came alongside asking if they could enlist aboard. They were told that the *Kitty* had a full crew but Roach allowed them to board as he needed hands to sail the captured slaver to Freetown. It was a terrible error of judgement. That evening, as Roach and his First and Second Mates sat down to dinner in the cabin, the five men pounced and declared that they were holding them as prisoners of war. Roach yelled 'no' but as he stood from his chair he was stabbed 'through the heart'. First Mate Richard Blundell, himself bleeding from stab wounds, was chased to the fore-rigging where he threw himself overboard. Dragged back on deck, he saw Roach lying prostrate on the floor in death throes. Second Mate Michael Williamson, cut with a handspike, jumped from the port window. Outside the cabin, the *Kitty*'s sailors heard only a loud noise and saw the Kru jump overboard. They rushed into the fray but were overpowered. Williamson, thrashing about in the sea, saw one of the Kru men have his legs bitten off by a shark. Another sailor gave Williamson an oar that he managed to cling to until he could get into a boat and reboard the *Kitty*.[41]

By then the attackers had control of the whole brig and were busy plundering. The following morning the surviving members of the *Kitty*'s crew were put into a small boat with some bread and water and allowed to make the best of the way to shore. But the Africans from the ship were kept, detained 'in a state of Slavery'. They included 'nineteen Kroomen coming to Sierra Leone', a woman from the colony called Venus Murray who worked as the *Kitty*'s cook, the infant son of a trader from Cape Coast Castle who was a passenger, and Jack Phoenix.[42] The men in the boat eventually got to shore and arrived in Freetown a week or two later to tell their tale. Aboard the Spanish schooner, Venus Murray saw Captain Roach's body thrown overboard and his belongings stolen, along with the *Kitty*'s ivory, gold, cloth, 'bottles of Lavender', bedding, dollars and doubloons, 'six pigs ... one Bull, one Sheep ... six Goats, thirty ducks, three coops Fowls ... a number of Parrots ... a Crown bird' and a 'walking stick which changed into a spy glass'.[43]

In Freetown, Governor Maxwell believed that Roach's murder was no spontaneous strike but was carried out at the behest of some slave traders based in Cuba who had been angered at Roach's repeated assaults on their ships. A Gallinas slave dealer named Crawford was also complicit; so familiar with the attackers was he that they 'hugged him round the body' and said 'Crawford *sta bona*' [*sic*].[44] Maxwell and the British authorities believed that the man behind the attack was 'Anthony Scott' [really Antonio Escoto] of Havana, 'who has been in the habit of carrying on, under cover of the Spanish flag, an illegal trade in slaves with the subjects of Great Britain and America'. This trade was carried on at 'Mesurado'.[45] Also implicated was a Cuban captain named Bodega.[46] Venus Murray somehow escaped to tell her tale.[47] Too young to testify even if he did somehow miraculously escape, Za remains in the historical shadows, his fate unknowable. British authorities at Freetown certainly believed that he had been sold at Havana, a far worse fate even than those who had been forced into military or naval service at Sierra Leone.

Freedom in the villages

Not all male liberated Africans in the earliest years of arrival were drafted in the armed or merchant services. The policy of settling them in villages scattered in the countryside around Freetown was most popular during the governorship of Charles MacCarthy but also occurred under Maxwell's regime. This was, arguably, a more tangible freedom but it was still within the confines thought appropriate by Britons at the time rather than any indigenous model. In the villages the liberated Africans would be encouraged to behave like British labourers with 'proper' wooden houses, 'decent' clothing and regular attendance at church.

A few of the villages were actually established in the years before Maxwell. Regent, high in the hills above Freetown, was one of the oldest villages, originally founded on 10 April 1809 when Governor Thompson laid the first stone of the village he called Hogbrook.[48] Leicester was also established that same year and there Maroon Charles Shaw oversaw the liberated Africans in the early years, ruling 'summarily, the unruly, men and women, were publicly flogged'.[49] But it was in Maxwell and MacCarthy's eras that these settlements really took off. In 1813 an influx of men and women settled in Hogbrook, by then re-christened Regent, while Leicester greatly expanded when MacCarthy gave 1,000 acres to the Church Missionary Society for former slaves to culti-vate with the aim of their becoming self-sufficient.[50] MacCarthy also renamed Cabenda, calling it Wilberforce after the great abolitionist leader. Other villages were also formed: Gloucester, Charlotte, Kent and Bathurst, the latter afterwards absorbing the settlement of Leopold.

There were both negative and positive reasons to isolate the newly arrived liberated Africans in villages outside of Freetown. In some ways it was because there was resentment towards them among the original settlers, as the current president of the Krio Descendants Yunion has recounted in telling her own family history:

> My mother's mother's family we can trace to Gloucester village because it was the policy of Governor MacCarthy to settle the Liberated Africans, when they arrived in batches, in the villages. The Nova Scotians and the Maroons they were already in Freetown and so he sent the liberated slaves to the villages so that it wouldn't cause conflict with those who already had settled in Freetown.[51]

It would be decades before this trouble ended. In the 1830s, Frederick Harrison Rankin observed, 'the haughty black Settlers sneer at the new importation of savage Captives'.[52] Derisorily referred to as 'Willy-foss [Wilberforce's] niggers', there were reports of 'guns ... fired all night', thefts, the burning of property, destroying planted crops, and the savage beating of a liberated African who married a settler.[53] One old lady, apparently agitated that the liberated Africans had their own hospital, said, 'it is only my wonder dat we settlers do not rise up in one body and *kill* and *slay*'.[54]

There were more optimistic forces behind the settlement of the villages, too. MacCarthy and other governors felt that it was the best method of putting the liberated Africans under the influence of Christianity and 'civilisation'. The things MacCarthy ordered to 'reflect his vision' illustrate the kind of freedom they were supposed to enjoy in the villages:

> Bells, clocks and weathercocks were ordered from England for church towers, forges for village blacksmiths, scales and weights for village markets. Quill-pens and copy-books, prayer books and arithmetic books were ordered for the schools, with tin cases for the children to carry them in, lamps to read them by. Hats were ordered for the men, bonnets for the women, shoes for all; gowns and petticoats, trousers and braces— buttons too, with needles, thread and thimbles, soap and smoothing- irons, even clothes-brushes, nothing was forgotten.[55]

Often the Church Missionary Society's ministers had more or less total control over the people under their care. Reverend Düring, for instance, had charge of around 100 of the ex-slaves at Gloucester. Most famous of all was Reverend William Augustine Bernard Johnson who presided at Regent. Still today the people of Regent know Johnson as 'the apostle'.[56] Only in his mid-20s when he arrived at Sierra Leone in 1816, he had trained as a sugar refiner, not a missionary.[57] It was the most challenging of postings in a region thought to be 'pre-eminently reigned over by the Evil One', and Hogbrook itself a place where there 'mingled wickedness, woe, and want'.[58] Throwing in the old chestnut about Noah's son causing blackness, he noted that the people were 'the degraded race of Ham'.[59]

Despite the warnings, when Johnson arrived at Regent he was aghast. The people at Hogbrook were 'the off-scourings of Africa', he lamented, living in 'a complete wilderness'. His nerve wavered. 'I think I shall be of no use among so wild a race as that at Hogbrook', he wrote, wondering what on earth he had got himself into. But he soon rallied. He might have been among 'some of the wildest cannibals in Africa', but he hoped he could soon stop all manner of devilry and replace blood lust with English cuisine.[60] It only needed the hand of God. On a more practical level he set about feeding Regent's people and inoculating them against smallpox.[61] Against all the odds he was remarkably successful, aided by his apparently superhuman power. It

[65]

was said he could strike doubters lame through the sheer power of his invective, leaving them unable to walk away.[62] With such a force of nature in the pulpit even the most intractable became 'tame and civil', it was claimed, and Hogbrook was converted 'to a smiling village'.[63] When Reverend Garnon visited only two years after Johnson's arrival to see what he was up to he found the place delightful: 'in all directions are seen the houses of the Liberated Negroes'. After a marathon four services in one day Garnon found himself 'well satisfied with the conduct of these dear Negroes'.[64] In fact four services was one short of the usual total: Johnson normally held two prayer meetings and three rounds of divine service each Sunday.

Soon Regent became a model village. The local newspaper raved that 'the young men settled there have furnished an example which will long be admired, and not easily surpassed'. The settlers had constructed 'two excellent stone bridges' and laid roads remarkably 'solid and level' as well as building a hospital. The journalist saw 'the hand of Heaven' in such works done by people only just rescued from the holds of slave ships.[65] Three years later, some of the liberated Africans of Regent were considered so 'civilised' that they were called for jury service in Freetown.[66] By the mid-1820s, no fewer than one in three people living in Regent could read and write.[67]

In the years before he left Regent, Johnson was aided in his mission by two particular liberated African men, William Tamba and William Davis. Appointed 'messengers of salvation in native districts', these two men showed how forcefully some liberated Africans took up the word preached to them by the CMS missionaries.[68] They both toured around the region, going far past the border of the colony and into lands where slave trading was still endemic, trying to preach the word. Tamba at one point went to St Mary's, later Banjul, in Gambia, where he taught at a school for what was a newly created outpost where some liberated Africans were sent. Later, when Reverend Düring had to leave due to illness (and then died when the ship carrying him away was lost at sea), Tamba was placed in charge at the village of Gloucester, presiding over, he wrote, a 'church filled with hypocrites'.[69] This was an astonishing progression for a man who had arrived in the colony only in 1813.

Not all liberated Africans adopted Christianity. When Garnon visited Regent one man explained the difficulties that he met with while trying to preach the gospel:

They called him 'White Man's Child;' and told him that white man make him fool. He went one day to see some of them, and tell them 'God's palaver [sic].' Ten or twelve were present. One man, worse than the rest, said, 'Me no want God. Me no want Jesus Christ. Where he live? Me no look him. Me want cassada to eat. Me no like white man's fashion: suppose me sabby [Krio for to know/understand] white man's fashion, me be fool.' The other answered, 'Suppose you no sabby Jesus Christ, and suppose you die, you go to hell.' 'Hell!' said he, 'what place that? I no look that place in my country.' 'Why Hell be one place where big fire live for ever and ever.' 'Ah!' said he, 'I like that. Suppose you give me plenty of cassada [*sic*] to roast, that be good too much. Me sabby go there!' The poor fellow knew not how to reply to such a reprobate, while he continued, 'What good thing Jesus Christ do for you? You sabby him – you be fool.'[70]

In other ways, however, it seemed to many at the time that the liberated Africans were often more receptive to the missionaries' message than the earlier settlers, particularly the Maroons. Reverend Garnon even claimed that '[t]he Liberated Negroes, it is confidently hoped, will, for the future, stimulate them [the settlers] by their example'.[71] Mary Church, observing the liberated Africans a few decades later, similarly noted that, 'charms and incantations are superseded by an outward observance at least of the forms of Christianity' and from there 'follow industry and order; and in a few years, the savage is found either a useful artizan [*sic*] in the town, or a labourer in the villages'.[72] This was the ultimate aim of the mountain villages of Sierra Leone as perceived by the early governors: a Christianised peasantry that could prove 'useful' to the colony as a whole.

The villages were also home to many of the schools in the early colony, a central part of the plan for liberated African children. It was often girls who were put into school in the earliest days, the boys having more alternatives, although both sexes were sent into the schoolroom. They were taught reading and writing, with the girls also learning skills such as needlework and dressmaking to make them useful about town.[73] One liberated African explained that boys and girls learned the English alphabet in their first year and to say the Lord's Prayer, and by a few years later were tackling words 'of 4 syllables' and 'ciphering simple multiplication'.[74] The object was not, as one English observer put it, 'the mere education of letters, but in all the moral duties of civilized society'.[75]

Liberated African women

Although women were sent to live in the mountain villages almost as regularly as men, in some ways the fate of liberated African women was divergent. In the era of apprenticeships, Governor Columbine wrote that though there was a great demand for 'allotted negro' girls, adult women were harder to settle.[76] He did, however, manage to apprentice out the women of the *Doris* and another slave ship arriving in April 1810, all being indentured to local settlers.[77] The most urgent task that liberated African women faced was to find themselves a husband who could support them. Under a later governor, newly arrived women had only three months to find themselves a husband before being summarily cut from the government's food allowance.[78] This was not only an economical measure but part of the greater plan of Christianising the new arrivals and shaping them into an Anglo-style workforce. Marriage was seen as a safeguard against immorality, and missionaries aimed to swap '[t]he lax intercourse of the sexes' with 'the obligations of marriage', as Mary Church described it.[79]

There was an aspect of this that seemed rather degrading to some at the time, never mind to modern eyes. The women were shipped around for display in the various villages as if they were marketable goods seeking a willing purchaser.[80] Harrison Rankin wrote, 'the women are submitted for choice to such negroes as express desire for conjugal happiness'. They had to agree to marry any man who wanted them and so were, 'carried off to joy by liege lords, who assume their unasked consent'. 'The ladies' will is not consulted,' lamented Harrison Rankin, believing that most liberated African men took a wife solely as a 'servant and labourer, tiller of the ground, grinder of corn, water-bearer'.[81] It is hard to imagine how the authorities squared some of these marriages with their European Christian principles. Nine-year-old Many, for example, married off to a soldier at the recruiting depot, was definitely not protected by the norms of European society.[82]

It is possible that there was a happier aspect to this, however, at least in some instances. Harrison Rankin believed that most of the liberated Africans could not speak to their new spouse chosen in this way because they understood different languages.[83] This was undoubtedly the case in many of these hasty marriages, but the census also reveals the number of women who did manage to find a 'countryman' to live with. A number of women on the census of 1813, such as 27-year-old Blango and 16-year-old Banga, were living with men who were their countrymen. Others too found 'country people' to live with, either in marriage-style relationships or just as companions, proving that the bonds of language, culture and ethnic origin were not always broken in the early days of the colony. Some liberated African women may well have found men to marry in a similar manner to that in which they had lived prior to their enslavement and these arrangements allowed them to recreate some semblance of normality in the colony.

Conclusion

The census carried out in 1813 reveals some tantalising anomalies in the fate of liberated Africans arriving at Freetown. What, for example, of Evay de Roche, number 4,241, who is listed as having 'Returned to Brazil, March 1st 1813'? Possibly he was a free black seaman caught aboard a slave ship who opted to return to Brazil rather than remain in Freetown. Joshua Krooman, number 4,440, was very probably a free Kru sailor caught up in events rather than a captive destined for the slave markets of the Americas.[84] On the whole, however, the fates of the liberated Africans fell into a few categories. The abolition era began with apprenticeships for most of those arriving at Freetown. Later, for men deemed fit and healthy, a common outcome was to be sent to the recruiting department to enlist as a soldier. Likewise, some boys had gone into the Royal Navy. Others were living in the colony, often in the villages where CMS missionaries tried to shape them into a rural peasantry. Liberated African women, seen as a moralising influence, were also an important part of these expectations. They were often to be found living about the colony, married off to either settlers or formerly enslaved men in the hope of helping them to form small agricultural units. Liberated African girls might work as servants or be in school.

The bigger picture suggests that freedom for many liberated Africans arriving at Sierra Leone in the first years after the abolition of the transatlantic slave trade was an uncertain, and often tenuous, proposition. Ill thought out and unpredictable, liberation was badly financed and sometimes resulted more from the necessity of economy than from any higher, humanitarian cause. What became of these individuals was as much about the day and month they stepped ashore than any grand design to help them to build new lives. Their lives as liberated Africans in Sierra Leone did not reflect freedom as it was understood for Europeans, but a novel form of direction and coercion. Entry to Freetown was not just an end of their enslavement but an introduction to a totally new sort of life. It might include military or merchant service; it would almost certainly involve Christianity. Henceforth, they would be expected to live on the European fringes, culturally and religiously if not geographically. Yet left to their own devices, some found 'country people' to live with, showing that being stolen from their homeland could not totally break the ties of language, let alone culture. They adopted (and transformed) the new, but they never forgot the old, no matter the limits of their liberty.

Notes

1   F. Harrison Rankin, *The White Man's Grave*, 2 vols (London: Richard Bentley, 1836), ii, pp. 119–22.
2   George E. Brooks Jr., 'A View of Sierra Leone ca. 1815', *Sierra Leone Studies* 13 (1960), 24–31.
3   A. P. Kup, *Sierra Leone: A Concise History* (Newton Abbot: David and Charles, 1975), p. 151.
4   Mary Church, *Sierra Leone: or, The Liberated Africans, in a Series of Letters from a Young Lady to her Sister in 1833 and 34* (London: Longman and Co., 1835), p. 29.
5   Michel-Rolph Trouillot, *Silencing the Past: Power and the Production of History* (Boston, MA: Beacon Press, 1995), pp. 82–3, 88–9.
6   Seymour Drescher, 'The Ending of the Slave Trade and the Evolution of European Scientific Racism', *Social Science History* 14 (1990), 415–50; Philip D. Curtin, *The Image of Africa: British Ideas and Action, 1780–1850* (Madison, WI: University of Wisconsin Press, 1964).
7   Brooks, 'A View of Sierra Leone ca. 1815', p. 30.
8   Marcus Wood, *The Horrible Gift of Freedom* (Athens, GA: University of Georgia Press, 2010), p. 14.
9   Kup, *Sierra Leone*, pp. 151–2.
10 Christopher Fyfe, *A History of Sierra Leone* (Oxford: Oxford University Press, 1962), pp. 105–6.
11 *The African Herald*, 25 November 1809; 2 December 1809; Fyfe, *History of Sierra Leone*, p. 106.
12 Michael J. Turner, 'The Limits of Abolition: Government, Saints and the "African Question", c. 1780–1820', *English Historical Review* 112, (1997), 319–57; John Peterson, *Province of Freedom: A History of Sierra Leone* (London: Faber and Faber, 1969), pp. 51–4.
13 *The African Herald*, 11 November 1809.
14 *The African Herald*, 18 November 1809.
15 Samuel Swan, 'Journal of a Voyage Along the West African Coast, 1815–16', in Norman R. Bennett and George E. Brooks, Jr. (eds), *New England Merchants in Africa: A History Through Documents, 1802–1865* (Boston, MA: Boston University Press, 1965), pp. 72–3.
16 Entry for July 12 1810 and March 1810, E. H. Columbine Papers, Sierra Leone Collection, Richard Daley Library, University of Illinois at Chicago.
17 Fyfe, *History of Sierra Leone*, p. 116.
18 Swan, 'Journal', p. 72.
19 The National Archives, Kew (hereafter TNA), CO 267/38: Sierra Leone Correspondence, 1814.
20 Francis A. J. Utting, *The Story of Sierra Leone* (London: Longmans and Co., 1931), p. 119.
21 Fyfe, *History of Sierra Leone*, p. 115.
22 CO 267/38.
23 Entry for April 1810, Columbine Papers.
24 Arthur Porter, *Creoledom: A Study of the Development of Freetown Society* (Oxford: Oxford University Press, 1963), p. 37; J. J. Crooks, *A History of Sierra Leone* (London: Cass, 1972), p. 87.
25 Peterson, *Province of Freedom*, p. 58.
26 Brian Dyde, *The Empty Sleeve: The Story of the West India Regiments of the British Army* (London: Readers Book Club, 1997), pp. 30–1.
27 Dyde, *The Empty Sleeve*, p. 31.
28 Captain J. F. Napier Hewett, *European Settlements on the West Coast of Africa* (London: Chapman and Hall, 1862), p. 128.
29 A. B. Ellis, *History of the First West India Regiment* (London: Chapel and Hall, 1885).
30 CO 267/38; TNA,WO 12/10344: Muster Book, African Corps, 1813; and TNA, WO 12/10345: Muster Book, African Corp, 1814.

31 S. C. Ukpabi, 'West Indian Troops and the Defence of British West Africa in the Nineteenth Century', *African Studies Review* 17 (1974), 133–50.
32 Dyde, *The Empty Sleeve*, p. 32.
33 Ellis, *History of the First West India Regiment.*
34 Harrison Rankin, White *Man's Grave*, ii, p.107.
35 Harrison Rankin, *White Man's Grave*, ii, p. 112.
36 TNA, ADM 1/2537, Captains' Letters, 1813; TNA, ADM 37/4430: Muster Book of HMS *Thais*, 1 January 1812–30 June 1813.
37 TNA, ADM 37/4430; TNA, CO 267/38.
38 TNA, ADM 37/4462: Muster Book of HM Sloop *Albacore*, 1 August 1812–28 February 1814.
39 TNA, ADM 37/4462.
40 TNA, CO 267/38.
41 TNA, CO 267/38, testimony of Michael Williamson and John Gustave.
42 TNA, CO 267/38, testimony of Richard Blundell, Michael Williamson and Venus Murray.
43 TNA, CO 267/38, testimony of Richard Blundell, Michael Williamson and Venus Murray.
44 TNA, CO 267/38, testimony of Richard Blundell.
45 TNA, CO 267/38, Maxwell to Bathurst, 1 May 1814.
46 *Twelfth Report of the Directors of the African Institute, read at the General Meeting 9th Day of April 1818* (London: Hatchard, 1818), p. 162; Voyage identification no. 14675.'Voyages: The Transatlantic Slave Trade Voyages Database', Emory University, www.slavevoyages.org. Accessed 9 June 2014.
47 TNA, CO 267/38, testimony of Venus Murray.
48 *Sierra Leone Gazette*, 15 April 1809.
49 Fyfe, *History of Sierra Leone*, p. 115.
50 G. R. Collier and Charles MacCarthy, *West African Sketches: Compiled from the Reports of Sir G. R. Collier, Sir Charles MacCarthy and Other Official Sources* (London: Seeley and Son, 1824), p. 187; Kup, *Sierra Leone*, p. 153.
51 Author's interview with Mrs Cassandra Garber of the Krio Descendant's Yunion, Freetown, 2009.
52 Harrison Rankin, *White Man's Grave*, ii., p. 105.
53 Leo Spitzer, *The Creoles of Sierra Leone: Responses to Colonialism 1870–1945* (Madison, WI: University of Wisconsin Press, 1974), p. 11; W. A. B. Johnson, *A Memoir of W.A.B. Johnson, a Missionary at Sierra Leone, 1816–23, compiled by R.B. Seeley* (London: Thames Ditton, 1852), p. 122.
54 Elizabeth H. Melville, *A Residence at Sierra Leone* (London: John Murray, 1849), pp. 240–2. Original emphasis.
55 Fyfe, *History of Sierra Leone*, p. 131.
56 Author's interview with Prince Morgan-Williams, Regent, 2010.
57 A. B. C. Sibthorpe, *The History of Sierra Leone* [1881] (London: Frank Cass, 1970), p. 29; Stephen H. Tyng, *A Memoir of the Rev. W.A.B. Johnson, Missionary to the Church Missionary Society in Regent's Town, Sierra Leone* (Memphis, TN: General Books, 2010), p. 3.
58 Tyng, *Memoir*, pp. 207–8.
59 Tyng, *Memoir*, p. 207.
60 Johnson, *Memoir*, pp. 26, 32–4, 36; Arthur Tappan Pierson, *Seven Years in Sierra Leone: The Story of the Work of W.A.B. Johnson* (London: J. Nesbit and Co., 1897), pp. 15–6, 37, 39, 41; Peterson, *Province of Freedom*, p.107.
61 Johnson, *Memoir*, pp. 36–7, 56.
62 Fyfe, *History of Sierra Leone*, p. 129.
63 Sibthorpe, *History of Sierra Leone*, pp. 33–4.
64 'Memoir of the Late Rev. William Garnon' at 'Project Canterbury', the Church of England, http://anglicanhistory.org/africa/sl/garnon1819.html. Accessed 5 June 2014.
65 *Royal Gazette and Sierra Leone Advertiser*, 19 December 1818; Johnson, *A Memoir*, p. 126.

66 Sibthorpe, *History of Sierra Leone*, pp. 32–3.
67 Joe A. D. Alie, *A New History of Sierra Leone* (London: Macmillan, 1990), p. 69.
68 Pierson, *Seven Years*, pp. 152–3; *Missionary Register* 7 (1819), 491–2.
69 Johnson, *Memoir* , p. 363; Samuel Abraham Walker, *The Church of England Mission in Sierra Leone* (London, 1847), pp. 175–6.
70 Garnon, 'Memoir', p. 289.
71 Garnon, 'Memoir', p. 289.
72 Church, *Sierra Leone*, p. 48.
73 William Tamba to the Church Missionary Society (CMS), 25 May 1824, Reel 94, CA 0203, CMS archive, Section IV: African Missions, Adam Matthews Publications.
74 Tamba to the CMS, report of Wellington, midsummer 1826.
75 James Holman, *Travels in Madeira, Sierra Leone, Teneriffe, St. Jago, Cape Coast Castle Fernando Po, Princes Island, etc.* (London: George Routledge, 2nd edn, 1840), p. 105.
76 Columbine Papers. Entry for 22 April 1810 and 25 May 1810.
77 Columbine Papers. Entry for 23 April 1810.
78 Sibthorpe, *History of Sierra Leone*, p. 38.
79 Church, *Sierra Leone*, p. 48.
80 Crooks, *History of Sierra Leone*, pp. 131–2.
81 Harrison Rankin, *White Man's Grave*, ii, pp. 107–8, 125.
82 TNA, CO 267/38.
83 Harrison Rankin, *White Man's Grave*, ii, p. 108.
84 TNA, CO 267/38.

CHAPTER FOUR

A 'most miserable business':[1] naval officers' experiences of slave-trade suppression

Mary Wills

Personal testimonies of daily life on the West Africa Squadron in journals, letters and remark books provide insights into the attitudes, beliefs and individual experiences of naval officers charged with upholding abolition. In particular, such sources uncover the extent of their emotional commitment to the anti-slavery cause. Assessment of commitment to this role is not without difficulties. Employment on the squadron offered a paid wage at a time when naval jobs were increasingly scarce; discussion of personal motivations for service must take place in awareness that few volunteered for any particular naval station.[2] Nevertheless, suppression of the Atlantic slave trade was extraordinary employment. Its intensity transcended normal workloads, and without doubt had significant impact on the lives of those involved.

What affected commitment? Some officers were driven by, or certainly exposed to, a new notion of duty fuelled by abolitionism and an expression of British morality emanating from the political elite. For others, any enthusiasm for suppression was tempered by the difficult living and working conditions they faced, including tropical climate, disease, the threat of attack, and the trauma of witnessing the human consequences of the slave trade. Many experienced, in the words of Commodore Charles Hotham in 1847, 'a general disgust at the character of the service'.[3] This chapter examines, firstly, the conditions and experiences of service in the context of naval officers' understanding of their work on the West African coast. Secondly, it explores the motivations that served to balance their emotional and physical distress: the financial incentives of prize money and belief in the virtues of the anti-slavery cause.

Conditions of service

Service on the West African coast presented abundant risks, arising from tropical heat and heavy rain, threats of disease and violence, all of which gave rise to the view of West Africa as a 'horrid hole'.[4] Employment there was notoriously unpopular. In his published narrative of service on the anti-slave-trade patrols, naval surgeon Peter Leonard summed up the concerns and fears of many. He wrote that as he sailed to Sierra Leone in 1830 he regretted leaving 'cheerful society' at home, having 'exchanged [it] for intercommunity with savages, dull looks, and gloomier thoughts, and the perpetual risk, at every step, of death from a poisoned atmosphere'.[5]

Work on the squadron was 'frequently of a most harassing and dangerous character'.[6] The threat of the climate to the health of naval personnel is covered in John Rankin's chapter in this volume. Also perilous were encounters with slaver crews angered by the Royal Navy's interference. One infamous case which caused public outcry in Britain

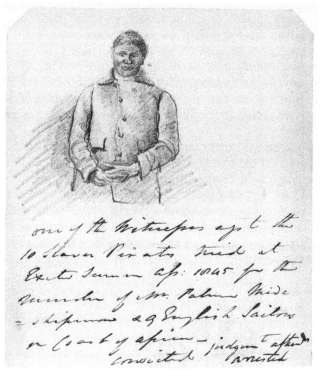

Figure 4.1 Sketch from the *Felicidade* trial. (© National Maritime Museum, Greenwich, London, ZBA2553)

was the trial in July 1845 of ten Brazilian and Spanish crew-members from the slavers *Felicidade* and *Echo* for the murders of midshipman Thomas Palmer and nine seamen of HMS *Wasp*. At the time of their murders the British sailors were transporting the *Felicidade* to Sierra Leone for condemnation.[7] Figures 4.1 and 4.2 show sketches by an unidentified artist depicting, as the annotations explain, one of the witnesses in the case, and Janus Majaval, the 'Slaver pirate who ran the knife into Mr Palmer midshipman'. There were also dangers from encounters with Africans on shore, where naval personnel disembarked to secure treaties with local rulers. Midshipman Cheesman Henry Binstead related an encounter in the River Bonny in his journal of 1823. He found the 'natives' to be 'desperate thiefs', who 'attempted to kidnap our men' and 'wood [*sic*] no doubt have murdered them were they not seen'. Relations worsened to conflict, 'in which fray Lieut. Stokes received a spear thro the neck'.[8]

The excitement of identifying and chasing slave ships, or 'prizes', was for some a positive part of the service. Fleet Engineer John M'Kie,

Figure 4.2 Sketch from the *Felicidade* trial: Janus Majaval.
(© National Maritime Museum, Greenwich, London, ZBA2554)

who served on HMS *Rattler* in 1850, wrote in his memoirs that the 'capture of a full slaver had a very exhilarating effect[,] it raised the spirits of all hands to the highest pitch of excitement'.[9] Midshipman Astley Cooper Key's published letters are imbued with the glory and adventure of the chase. He reported a near-miss with a slaver on the West Indies Station in 1840. 'It would have been a glorious cutting-out expedition', he wrote to his mother. 'I was sharpening my sword in the most butcher-like manner all the chase.'[10]

Analysis of these narratives must take into account their provenance and intended readership; letters written home in particular often placed emphasis on the author's bravery. Boredom and disillusionment were more common experiences than Key's excitement. Royal Navy vessels often spent months patrolling the West African coast with little prospect of capturing a slaver. Surgeon Alexander Bryson described service in the Bight of Benin as 'irksome and monotonous'. He wrote of the practice in the earlier years of suppression of empty slave vessels waiting off shore until an opportunity was found to take their human cargo on board. In these situations cruisers could 'spend two, three, or four months in succession, standing "off and on the land" under easy sail'.[11] The situation changed with the introduction of equipment clauses into anti-slave-trade treaties from the 1830s, which made possible the seizure of empty vessels with renovations indicating the intention of carrying slaves. A change in methods in the 1840s, when patrolling the coast was increasingly replaced by the blockade of ports and embarkation points, enhanced the squadron's success but led to fewer chases and captures, contributing to the sense of monotony.[12] Patrol was wearing for Lieutenant Thomas Davies, on board HMS *Cygnet* and HM Brig *Spy* between 1850 and 1852. His journal entries over a four-month period feature little more than commentary on the weather, most frequently 'continual rain all day and night'.[13] 'I am beginning to feel more like a cat than a midshipman,' reported Midshipman Augustus Arkwright of the *Pantaloon* in a letter home in 1842, 'for I so seldom am inclined to do anything but sleep and feed.'[14] Midshipman Arthur Onslow wrote in his journal off Lagos in 1852 that his days consisted of '[m]iserable dull work. There is nothing whatever to do this service is insupportable.'[15]

Morale was undermined by the complex international dimension to suppression: the labyrinthine network of anti-slave-trade treaties between Britain and other powers, and ambiguities over the Royal Navy's rights of search, capture and condemnation, contributed to frustrations.[16] Fundamentally, slave dealers showed no sign of acceding to the British abolitionist dictate, and there was a common perception that the labours of the West Africa Squadron were in vain in the face of demand for slaves from Cuba and Brazil in particular.[17] Naval personnel alluded to the contradictory effects of suppression, whereby slave traders were paid more for their cargos in recognition of the risks involved in evading capture. Commander Hugh Dunlop reported on a conversation with a slave captain in 1848:

> He repeatedly said to me that the *very worst thing* for him & those employed in the slave vessels would be for England to withdraw the men of war from the Coast, as that would at once reduce their remuneration, and that he as Captain of a Slaver instead of receiving 10,000 for a successful trip, when no risk was attached to it, would only receive about 300 or 400 dollars![18]

Speculation in Britain that the squadron was ineffective and ill-managed added to despondency. Questions were raised over the quality and efficiency of the vessels employed; small ships in the early years were nicknamed 'floating coffins'.[19] In a pamphlet published in 1848, Commander Henry James Matson called the squadron 'a mere paper blockade' and wrote of how many ships were 'the very worst description of vessels we have in the service'.[20] The escalating costs of maintenance, treaty payments to foreign governments and running the Admiralty courts compounded misgivings, as did several publications critical of the squadron.[21] Disapproval peaked in 1845, when MP William Hutt led a parliamentary campaign for the total withdrawal of the squadron, claiming that the horrors of the Middle Passage had been exacerbated by the naval presence.[22]

Such criticism was not confined to politicians. A published letter from a naval officer in West Africa in July 1845 remarked on the perceived futility of suppression, and stressed the argument that naval methods increased the suffering of the enslaved:

> We look upon the affair as complete humbug ... The absurdity of blockading a coast 2,000 miles in extent must be obvious to the meanest capacity ... The loss of life and demoralizing effect to our Service are very great, the climate and service being of that nature to prevent the proper exercise of discipline, and ships are anything but men of war ... the naked fact of our exertions in favor of the African slave having increased his miseries to an awful extent, with an immense sacrifice of life, is uncontradicted by the best-informed advocates of slave measures.[23]

In private correspondence of 1848, Commodore Charles Hotham captured much of the frustration felt by naval officers. He claimed: 'this blockade service has been twisted & turned by almost every Politician and naval officer each naturally thinks that if his views were adopted success would be attainable ... You can no more stop the slave trade by y[ou]r present system than you can turn the course of the Danube.'[24]

Financial rewards

The conditions of service on anti-slavery patrols clearly sapped enthusiasm for the cause; in recognition of the risks, dangers and plummeting morale, officers and men required financial incentives to serve. Since the early eighteenth century, it was customary to issue a proclamation at the beginning of each war, allowing the value of captured enemy ships to be divided up among the officers and crews of the ships that took part in its capture.[25] Under the Prize Regulations of the Act of 1807, prize money was similarly paid to those engaged in the suppression of the slave trade. 'Headmoney' was paid for every slave captured and liberated, to be distributed between officers and crew on a fixed scale according to rank. The introduction of equipment clauses into treaties also made possible the seizure of empty vessels and subsequent division of prize money.[26]

The opportunity to make money was clearly a motivating factor. Commodore Hotham wrote in 1847 that the 'love of prize money makes this a popular station with seamen' meaning that 'the brigs are all well-manned'.[27] Captain George Hastings wrote to Captain Eden in 1850 that 'the prize money of course, is the boon'.[28] The notion of 'good' or 'poor' prizes, in reference to the amount of net profit made from each capture, frequently features in narratives. In 1822, Master William Hall described the 'Prize Brig Esperanza with 149 slaves' as a 'good prize'.[29] Similarly, naval surgeon Dr McIlroy wrote in a letter of 1841 that a slaver with 450 Africans on board captured by HMS *Fantome* was a 'valuable prize'.[30] In these examples, prize vessels were regarded primarily as objects of financial worth. Naval men also wrote about the best parts of the coast to make captures and prize money. McIlroy noted that a section of the coast south of the equator had been redistributed to the South American Station, and so, 'we lose our cruizing ground. We have all been extremely sorry at this news, as we had the best part of the coast.'[31] Career advancement was also a priority. Areas of patrol were traded and regarded as instrumental in promotions, as McIlroy implied about the area between Badagry and the River Benin: '[i]t is a part of the coast, whether or not good for making Captains is yet to be seen'.[32]

For some, like naval surgeon Robert Flockhart, financial gain was one of the main motivations to serve: 'If it was not for the excitement in chasing vessels ... and making prize money this would be a dull monotonous station.'[33] Others lamented the lack of material success, highlighting that service on these patrols was regarded as paid employment like any other and as worthless without material reward. Commander Alexander Murray wrote to his brother in 1847 from HMS *Favorite* that 'there is no prize money to be made[;] at least I have never seen a slaver'.[34] The following year, he described his involvement in the service as 'a rich man's ruin'.[35]

In March 1845, Francis Meynell was Acting Lieutenant of HM Sloop *Albatross* when the vessel captured the slave ship *Albanoz* near St Paul de Loanda. Meynell was part of a prize crew tasked with transporting the prize to Sierra Leone, a voyage that lasted six weeks. 'We lost on the voyage 150 slaves three or four dying every day', he wrote in a letter to his father. '500 were landed but near 30 have died since[,] it's a very horrible business this slave trade.'[36] Meynell's watercolours depicting the slaver and its slave-hold are among the few visual eyewitness representations of suppression and of enslaved Africans, capturing the suffering, fatigue and bodily trauma experienced (Figures 4.3 and 4.4).[37] Compared to the more brutal imagery of the slave trade publicly distributed by the abolitionist movement, Meynell paints the slave-hold as quiet, still and melancholic; but while there is humanity in the painting, it also feels emotionally withdrawn.[38] Read alongside later letters from HMS *Cygnet* informing his family of his prize money, it becomes apparent that Meynell measured his success in the liberation of enslaved Africans in monetary terms:

Figure 4.3 Francis Meynell, 'Slave deck of the *Albanoz*' (1845).
Album of Lt Meynell's watercolours. (© National Maritime Museum, Greenwich, London, MEY/2 D9317)

Figure 4.4 Francis Meynell, 'Rescued Africans on deck of HM Sloop *Albatross'* (1845). Album of Lt Meynell's watercolours. (© National Maritime Museum, Greenwich, London, MEY/2 D9316)

we took a good prize which in 2 years time I suppose will be payable, with 560 slaves ... in the last 3 months I share in 4 prizes which will give me upwards of £150[;] good work for a few months[,] it beats China even but it is active work for an officer at any rate and he deserves all he gets and a little more ... £50 or 60£ more in my pocket thank God.[39]

Such observations can be interpreted in a number of ways. Meynell wrote with what appeared to be limited sympathy for the enslaved; he was concerned more with financial gain. Or, perhaps the nature of his work and what he had witnessed had caused Meynell such distress that the financial recompense was the only positive news he could report back home.

Belief in the anti-slavery cause

Meynell's letters exemplify the variety of emotions experienced by officers on anti-slave-trade patrols, but imply that prize money was one of the few advantages of the service. For others, notions of abolitionism, humanitarianism and morality played a more significant role in defining their commitment to the cause. The *Instructions for the Guidance of Her Majesty's Naval Officers Employed in the Suppression of the Slave Trade* of 1844, issued to all officers serving on the patrols, began with the statement: 'The Slave Trade has been denounced by all the civilized world as repugnant to every principle of justice and humanity.'[40] But how far did naval personnel agree? Anti-slavery campaigns before and after 1807 have been characterised as the embodiment of a uniquely British devotion to freedom and moral progress.[41] The navy's suppression activities provided the British with a focus for this crusade, in a belief that they could lessen the sense of national guilt and reassert the national character as a liberty-loving nation.[42] The anti-slavery cause had at its heart religious belief translated into the language of political protest by abolitionist leaders. It was also at various times a popular movement, with the involvement of many levels of society in generating pressure for abolition and emancipation.[43] To what extent did abolitionist impulses inspire naval officers?

Evangelical belief provided conviction and inspiration for the anti-slavery movement.[44] There was a concurrent surge in evangelical sentiment in the navy by the beginning of the nineteenth century, a minority movement that promoted religious observance, morality and humanitarianism for the reformation of naval society.[45] Prominent evangelicals in the navy included Sir Charles Middleton, appointed as First Lord of the Admiralty in 1805, who moved in a social circle that included William Wilberforce and other leading abolitionists.[46]

By mid-century Sunday service was compulsory throughout the navy and religious observance had become a significant part of naval life.[47]

Captain Claude Henry Mason Buckle served on West African patrols between 1841 and 1845 in command of HMS *Growler*. His journals reveal his daily private reading as invariably composed of evangelical texts such as 'Scott's Bible and Commentary'. Thomas Scott, a founder of the Church Missionary Society, condemned virtually all forms of contemporary slavery. Buckle was a great admirer: 'How truly scriptural, spiritual and practical is Scott, how opposed to the mere nominal Christian.'[48] Among Buckle's personal papers is an engraving of the abolitionist Granville Sharp and a handwritten copy of the inscription on Sharp's memorial tablet in Westminster Abbey, in which he is described as 'among the foremost of the honorable band associated to deliver Africa from the rapacity of Europe'.[49] However, Buckle scorned the religiosity and devotion of his ship's company. As he noted in a Sunday journal entry: 'Performed divine service on deck & read one of Cooper's sermons to ship's co. – I fear to very little purpose, – they are very practical and scriptural and truly evangelist – not what our ignorant and polluted & thoughtless men like to hear, nor I believe the officers either.'[50] In the case of Buckle and his crew, examples of religious belief amongst sailors of the West Africa Squadron appear to be of an individual rather than a collective nature.

Yet if religion held an insecure place in naval life, its presence provided fertile ground for the development of anti-slavery ideas amongst naval crews.[51] Some were clearly influenced by Christian conviction prevalent in anti-slavery thought and literature, and many expressed moral condemnation of the slave trade. Captain Edward Columbine was governor of the newly established crown colony of Sierra Leone from 1809 until his death in 1811.[52] Columbine saw action in the West Indies as a junior officer, and again in 1803–04 when he undertook hydrographical work off Trinidad. Perhaps as a result of these experiences, he had deep sympathies with the abolitionist movement.[53] He also had strong ties with Wilberforce and his abolitionist allies, not least in his role as a Commissioner of the African Institution, founded in 1807 in order to promote the suppression of the slave trade and the 'civilisation' of Africa through Christianity.[54] Columbine certainly subscribed to the views of leading abolitionists that complicity in the slave trade degraded the moral reputation of the nation. Columbine condemned the 'atrocious traffic', which represented 'an indelible stain' on Britain's moral integrity. He wrote: 'No man who is alive to the Honour of his Country, but must feel the Disgrace, not the *Dignity*, of permitting its Flag to wave for so many years over a line of Slave-holes.' Columbine also referred to the shame brought upon the navy from its role in protecting the slave trade: 'Oh! That the same flag should fly triumphant over the head of our immortal Nelson; and be prostituted to protect the Slave-dealer in his den.'[55] As chapter 3 in the present volume highlights, however, Columbine's evangelical concern for national character did not translate to humanitarian concern for the wellbeing of liberated Africans.

In recognition of the significance of African agency in the supply of slaves, naval personnel were employed in negotiations with African rulers to end slave trading and replace it with 'legitimate' trade. In 1815, John Tailour commanded HMS *Comus* on the West African coast as part of one of the earliest squadrons sent there on anti-slave-trade duty. His description of an encounter with locals 'up Calabar River' is suffused with abolitionist rhetoric, but also illustrates the difficulties naval personnel faced as Britain's representatives in encouraging abolition while only ten years earlier having being seen to support the slave trade:

> My language was new to them. I spoke of humanity. I described the miserable wretched existence these poor slaves whom they sell off their coast have to go through ... they had never met with any man who thought ill of the slave trade. Their fathers in short their grandfathers – and they knew not how many generations before them they said had been led by King George to consider the trade as then only good.[56]

Tailour clearly believed in the moral imperative of suppression, although as a protagonist in the early days of the squadron he had less cause for disillusionment. His language was punctuated with racial stereotypes, but revealed sympathy and paternalism for the enslaved:

> Some would have us believe that these black slaves are an insensible unfeeling race. I wish you had seen the effect produced on the first party which were brought on board here, to these vessels. When after knocking their irons off & giving each a waist cloth, I took up a pair of the shackles, showed it them all round & with indignation of countenance threw them into the sea. It had the power of an electric shock. Joy in all its forms ... they showed all which can be discovered in the Human Kind of these feelings.[57]

Sir George Ralph Collier was the first Commodore of the West Africa Squadron between 1818 and 1821. He was a committed abolitionist, as his reports to the Admiralty make clear; he declared that British naval officers under his command were working with 'commendable zeal in the cause of humanity'.[58] Collier wrote passionately that the slave trade 'is more horrible than those who have not had the misfortune to witness it can believe, indeed no description I could give would convey a true picture of its baseness & atrocity'.[59] He expressed humanitarian concern for the enslaved: 'It is to me a matter of extreme wonder that any of these miserable people live the voyage through; many of them indeed perish on the passage, and those who remain to meet the shore, present a picture of wretchedness language cannot express.'[60] His reports were widely read and consulted, and this passage in particular was quoted in numerous newspapers of the period.[61] In other correspondence, Collier wrote of 'the sickening and desponding appearance of most of the wretched victims' of the slaver *Anna Maria* taken by HMS *Tartar* in 1821, 'confined more loathsomely and more closely than hogs brought to a morning market for sale', the experience of which 'was so appalling and distressing to our feelings'.[62] Collier was notable in linking humanitarianism to his understanding of duty on the West African coast. He wrote that his actions were performed with 'no view to personal merit, for I did what humanity, and therefore my duty, only required'.[63] Collier was elected an honorary Life Member of the African Institution in 1820 for his work on the squadron.[64]

Joseph Denman was one of the most publicly committed abolitionists on the patrols. In 1833, he served as lieutenant on HMS *Curlew* off the coast of South America when it captured the Portuguese slaver *Maria de Gloria*, with 423 Africans on board. As Brazilian courts had no jurisdiction over Portuguese ships, Denman conveyed the slaver to Sierra Leone in a failed attempt to secure its condemnation. 'I was 46 days on that voyage', he wrote, 'and altogether 4 months on board of her, where I witnessed the most dreadful sufferings that human beings could endure'.[65] Subsequently Denman did much to improve tactics and organisation of the squadron, frequently clashing with other officers over the most efficient methods of suppression.[66] In 1850 Denman wrote that the anti-slavery movement was working in the 'great and holy principles of right' and that the slave trade was 'a custom manifestly unjust, unlawful, and in violation of the law of nature'.[67] He also gave evidence at select committees commissioned to examine the slave trade; in his defence of the squadron Denman was supported by his father Lord Chief Justice Denman, himself an outspoken abolitionist.[68]

Alongside the undercurrents of religious belief and abolitionist sentiments, the commitment of naval men was undoubtedly influenced by their first-hand experiences of the brutality of the slave trade. This was especially the case for those placed in charge of prize vessels, often with full cargos of enslaved Africans on board, taken to be presented for prosecution at the Admiralty courts, typically at Sierra Leone. These accounts reveal emotions of humanity and paternalism but also racial assumptions and anxieties.[69] The emotional anguish in Commodore John Hayes's flag officer reports to the Admiralty from HMS *Dryad* off the West African coast in 1830–31 is striking. He described conditions for enslaved Africans on a recently detained slave vessel:

> the *scalding perspiration* was running from one to the other, covered also with their own filth, and where it is no uncommon occurrence for women to be bringing forth children, and men dying by their side, with full in their view, living and dead bodies chained together, and the living, in addition to all their other torments, labouring under the most famishing thirst.[70]

Hayes denounced the 'nefarious traffic' and the 'horrible crimes, worse than murder, perpetrated on those wretched creatures'. His compassion for the enslaved led him to plead with the Admiralty to 'reflect on what must be the sufferings of upwards of five hundred of these miserable people chained together, and crammed in between the decks of a vessel only half the tonnage of a Ten Gun Brig. Gracious God! Is this unparalleled cruelty to last for ever?'[71] Hayes, like Collier, wrote with emotive and rhetorical language in his correspondence with the Admiralty regarding what he had witnessed of the slave trade, expressive of his distress and sympathy.

Naval officers spent many days on prize vessels and were ordered to manage and keep charge of the ship like any other. As a result, for some naval officers feelings of compassion and duty collided, and notions of humanity were overwhelmed by the demands of service. In 1849, Midshipman Henry Rogers of HMS *Pluto* was ordered to convey the *Casco*, a Brazilian slaver with 440 Africans on board, from Ambriz to St Helena. In his journal, Rogers displayed sympathy for the plight of the enslaved and recognition of their emotional distress. The demands of managing a large number complicated his feelings towards them, however. For example, the daily routine on board the prize vessel inevitably led him to treat and write about those under his supervision in collective terms: 'At 6am our daily task commenced, the first operation was to get the slaves on deck, wash them and make them clap their hands ... At 7 we gave the slaves their water and swept the slave deck.'[72] Rogers suffered insomnia brought on by distress at the thought of an uprising and 'how easily a man might have got up taken my sword, drawn and soon have killed me and given the other slaves a chance of rising'.[73] Perhaps as a result of these fears, Rogers described how, 'a big slave having nearly throttled a small one', he was 'obliged to proceed to punishment':

> I administered a small dose to him, consisting of 2 dozen, inflicted with a rope-end ... pretty severely. This must not be mistaken for cruelty, as it is a well known fact that in large communities with little intelligence, any outbreak against the laws that preserve the weak from the attacks of

the strong must be punished immediately and severely. The poor slaves appear very docile, good creatures generally, and many of them have tolerably intelligent features.[74]

Parts of Rogers's account echo the subjugation of slaves by slave ship seamen; here and in other testimonies there are certainly similarities between conditions on prize vessels and slave ships.[75] Rogers also revealed paternalistic and racial assumptions reflective of his time. Ingrained belief in their racial difference and inferiority undoubtedly affected how naval personnel viewed African peoples.[76] This is also made clear in the attitudes of naval officers towards efforts aimed at the betterment of Africa.

Anti-slavery and the 'improvement' of Africa

For many naval men, their allegiance to the anti-slavery cause was fuelled by pride in Britain as an abolitionist beacon for the rest of the world. This sentiment took form in belief in Britain's moral superiority to nations who continued to trade in slaves, and also in the notion of 'imperial stewardship': Britain taking care of those peoples who, it was believed, could not care for themselves.[77] Britain dominated the maritime world in the nineteenth century, and regarded its role as the main enforcer of the abolitionist agenda as a key part of that supremacy.[78] A fundamental feature of British abolitionist policy was to insist that other countries follow and accord to its moral lead. As a result, those involved in suppression condemned other nations that still traded in slaves. The surgeon Peter Leonard described in exemplary terms the 'supineness, indifference, or bad faith' of those who were not committed to abolition.[79]

Furthermore, the anti-slavery mission, centred on a very British conception of freedom and progress, dominated British relations with Africa in the nineteenth century.[80] Abolitionists and missionaries viewed the slave trade as having destroyed African society, and felt that Britain had an essential role to play in bringing about the civilisation of the continent. There was a belief that Africans could be shown to be capable of the development of agriculture and commerce, and responsive to 'useful' arts and Christian values.[81] Naval personnel joined these debates about remedies for the slave trade. An unidentified officer from HMS *Thalia* wrote in 1834 that education from missionaries was the best means for 'improvement' of the liberated Africans at Sierra Leone; it could 'prevent a return to barbarism'.[82] Such observations were freighted with notions of British humanity, but invariably linked to a belief that Africans were incapable of progress without British assistance. Commander Walter Estcourt believed that

British influence would 'encourage the legal trade and raise the moral character of the people'. As he wrote in his journal in 1845, legitimate commerce would 'extend morals', embed 'habits of industry' and ensure there was 'a way opened for the introduction of Christianity'.[83]

Commander Arthur Parry Eardley Wilmot articulated a commitment to Britain's sense of moral responsibility to African society. In 1852 he wrote to the Commander in Chief of the forces at Abbeokuta to promote the elevating example of the Christian faith, which would encourage the African people to 'do good & endeavour to benefit their fellow creatures'. Wilmot's letter expressed confidence and pride in the British anti-slavery mission. This was especially in comparison with the Portuguese who '*do not care* for you ... They have no interest in the permanent prosperity of your country. If all of you were to die tomorrow, they would laugh & sing as usual.' Britain, on the contrary, 'longs to release her [Africa] from those chains of bondage and misery in which she has been bound for so many years past'.[84] Naval officers like Wilmot were actively engaged with the role of this imperial rhetoric in mid-nineteenth-century relations between Britain and African polities.

Ambiguities and pro-slavery sentiment

However, that some naval officers involved in suppression did not support anti-slavery efforts was made clear as early as 1810. In that year, Edward Columbine noted his offence at having heard a report of a naval officer, Lieutenant Bourne, involved in selling slaves. Employed in charge of a detained slave brig, Bourne was directed to Sierra Leone, but instead ventured to Princes Island where the brig was condemned. Columbine wrote: 'He sold her & the slaves to a Portuguese merchant; taking in payment bills on Rio Janeiro, 1300 dollars & a small schooner.'[85] Similarly, in a letter of 1838, naval surgeon Robert Flockhart reported that a former Royal Navy officer was profiting from the slave trade by posing as an American captain of a slave ship. He 'turns out to be a man of the name Graham who served for two years on this coast in the Lynx[,] one of our cruisers'.[86] While the number of similar occurrences cannot be known, such cases are significant in revealing a disregard for abolitionism by some in the navy, whereby financial gain was clearly more important than acting against the slave trade.

Officers were aware of the nuances of 'freedom' and the realities of suppression beyond ideology and rhetoric. This was particularly the case in relation to liberated Africans at Sierra Leone, many of whom were dispatched to the West Indies as apprentices and labourers, or recruited into military service.[87] Midshipman Henry Rogers wrote his journal from St Helena after landing the prize vessel *Casco* in 1849. Of the Africans on board he wrote, 'one in particular wanted to stay with me but poor fellow he is not free and must go where he is sent. For their freedom is but nominal, they are now being prepared for *emigration* to our Colonies, as there are now three vessels waiting for slaves.'[88] Rogers did not believe that the process of liberation by British naval vessels made the enslaved 'free'. Nor did he alter his terminology in respect to the liberated Africans, still referring to them as 'slaves', only this time in the context of British colonies.

As already seen, racial attitudes played their part in affecting the commitment of naval men to the cause and led some to argue in favour of the institution of slavery. In his journal of 1866, naval surgeon Fleetwood Buckle recounted a discussion with the clergyman on board HMS *Bristol* off the West African coast: 'Had a long talk with Pemberton about the negro and his position – he quite agrees with me that he was intended for a slave & must be *made* to work.'[89] Commander Alexander Murray wrote letters on a similar subject from HMS *Favorite* in 1847:

> The more I see of the whole system the more I am convinced that the attempt to stop the emigration of Africans is an error ... if ever any progress is made in our day in the civilization of Africa it will be by using slavery as an assistant therein instead blindly shutting the eyes and waging war against the social institutions of a continent which are coeval with the races in which they exist. Were I, Mr Colonial Government, I would become a slave owner myself.[90]

Writing two years later, Murray aired views in private correspondence that would have likely had to be disguised in public debates: 'my opinions are for nothing much less than a return to the old slave system as far as Africa is concerned'.[91] Clearly, even considering the impact of abolitionism on British society, there was an endurance of eighteenth-century pro-slavery rhetoric amongst some in the navy.

Others held more ambiguous views. George Augustus Elliot, Commander of HMS *Columbine* in 1840, was seemingly indifferent to the plight of the enslaved, a state of mind induced by concerns for his own hardships. In a letter to Lord Melgund (private secretary to the First Lord of the Admiralty) he declined to offer much reflection on his experiences 'unless by the by you are contemplating a speech on antislavery'. He continued:

> One idea I will give as a sample of the rest which rather amused me at first. The Portuguese keep the slaves as they buy them in barracoons or sheds until they are embarked. They are chained together to prevent escape and therefore cannot work consequently they are twice a day

compelled to holla for an hour without stopping by way of exercise, you can fancy the sort of row perhaps a thousand of them together and the Portuguese applying the lash if they leave off or don't holla loud enough. You can hear the poor wretches for miles off.[92]

A sympathetic tone can be traced here, but at the same time Elliot's amusement is revealing. While he accepted that his experiences would fuel anti-slavery arguments, he also appeared detached from the distress of the captured Africans. In the same letter, he wrote of his disgust at the nature of service on 'this abominable coast', and suggested it strong enough to outweigh any commitment to the cause: 'one or two of my chases have been rather interesting and some of the boat work has also afforded excitement but all other points connected with this service is disgusting enough, unless one happens to be impressed with an extraordinary degree of philanthropy'.[93] For Elliot, unlike many of his colleagues, a personal commitment to anti-slavery service required an almost incomprehensible level of compassion and belief in the cause.

Conclusion

Conditions of service on the anti-slave-trade patrols were at best uncomfortable and tedious and at worst pestilent, dangerous and traumatic. With plummeting morale, many questioned their commitment to the service and were concerned solely with financial incentive. Others went further and concurred with Elliot that disgust at life and work on the West African coast overrode all else, including the rewards of prize money or promotion. Captain George Hastings wrote conclusively in a letter of 1850, 'I would not accept of [sic] another command to come out here, and to remain one moment longer by my own free consent if I were safe of making ten thousand pounds. It is the most disagreeable service I was ever employed on, and a year is quite sufficient in one's life.'[94]

The commitment of some to extinguishing the slave traffic was clearly driven by abolitionist sentiment, but the lofty rhetoric of abolitionism lost impact when confronted with the reality of life on the ships at the frontline of suppression. It must not be assumed that all naval men were, or aspired to be, humanitarians motivated by the moral imperative to end slaving and 'improve' Africa. The official obligations of naval personnel must be remembered: the element of choice in their employment was rare, and support for the humanitarian cause was not necessarily required or expected.[95] Yet the service was out of the ordinary and rarely allowed for fixed views: officers and men were exposed to the brutality of the slave trade which undoubtedly had an impact on how they viewed their employment. As the naval surgeon Richard Carr McClement wrote in his journal after visiting the prize *Clara Windsor* at Sierra Leone in 1861: 'It would be utterly impossible to describe the sight which presented itself to us when we first went on board;– and; it would be equally difficult for any one who had not seen it, to comprehend the amount of misery, the suffering and, the horrors, that were contained within the wooden walls of that little craft.'[96] In reality, commitment to the cause may not always have been driven by anti-slavery sentiment. But to judge these men for being more concerned with other rewards is to ignore the human element to this story. Their experiences reveal pride in the British cause, emotions of sympathy and humanity, but also anxieties and racial tensions regarding the ambiguities of freedom, and their own struggles for survival on the West African coast.

Notes

1 National Maritime Museum (hereafter NMM), MEY/5, Letter from Lieutenant Francis Meynell to his father, 17 August 1845.
2 For despondency in the post-Napoleonic Wars navy, see Michael Lewis, *The Navy in Transition, 1814–1864: A Social History* (London: Hodder and Stoughton, 1965); Margarette Lincoln, *Representing the Royal Navy: British Sea Power, 1750–1815* (Aldershot: Ashgate, 2002), chapter 8.
3 Qtd in Christopher Lloyd, *The Navy and the Slave Trade: The Suppression of the African Slave Trade in the Nineteenth Century* (London: Longmans, 1949), p. 119. Hotham was reporting to a Parliamentary Committee.
4 R. M. Jackson, *Journal of a Voyage to Bonny River on the West Coast of Africa in the Ship Kingston from Liverpool*, ed. Roland Jackson (Letchworth: Garden City Press, 1934), Journal entry for 6 June 1826, p. 133. Jackson was referring to his residence in the River Bonny.
5 Peter Leonard, *Records of a Voyage to the Western Coast of Africa, in His Majesty's Ship Dryad, and of the Service on that Station for the Suppression of the Slave Trade, in the Years 1830, 1831 and 1832* (Edinburgh: William Tait, 1833), p. 13.
6 Alexander Bryson, *Report on the Climate and Principal Diseases of the African Station* (London: William Clowes and Sons, 1847), pp. 1–2. Bryson wrote this report at the request of the Admiralty.
7 *The Times*, 11 July 1845, 14 July 1845; Lloyd, *Navy and the Slave Trade*, p. 86.
8 National Museum of the Royal Navy, Portsmouth (hereafter NMRN), 2005.76/2, Diaries of Cheesman Henry Binstead, 9 June 1823.
9 National Library of Scotland (hereafter NLS), MS 24633, Memoirs of John M'Kie, fos 67–8.
10 Sir Astley Cooper Key, *Memoirs of the Admiral the Right Honorable Sir Astley Cooper Key*, ed. P. H. Colomb (London, 1898), p. 54.
11 Bryson, *Report on the Climate*, p. 19.
12 Lloyd, *Navy and the Slave Trade*, pp. 94–6.
13 NMM, JOD/42, Journal of Thomas Davies.
14 Derbyshire Record Office, D5991/10/72-73, Augustus Peter Arkwright to his mother from Sierra Leone, 19 June 1842.
15 Mitchell Library, State Library of New South Wales, MSS 2050, Journal of Arthur Onslow, 5 January 1852.
16 David Eltis, *Economic Growth and the Ending of the Transatlantic Slave Trade* (Oxford: Oxford University Press, 1987), pp. 85–90.

17   For the increase in the price of slaves bought in Brazil and Cuba from the transatlantic slave trade, see Eltis, *Economic Growth*, Appendix C; David Eltis and David Richardson, *Atlas of the Transatlantic Slave Trade* (London: Yale University Press, 2010), map 182, p. 278.
18   Special Collections and Archives Department, Nimitz Library, United States Naval Academy, MS 59, Remark Book of Commander Hugh Dunlop, 17 April 1848. Original emphasis by underlining.
19   Lloyd, *Navy and the Slave Trade*, p. 124.
20   Commander Henry James Matson, *Remarks on the Slave Trade and African Squadron*, 3rd edn (London: James Ridgeway, 1848), p. 64.
21   Eltis, *Economic Growth*, pp. 7, 27. For example, Thomas Fowell Buxton, *The African Slave Trade and Its Remedy* (London: John Murray, 1840).
22   Leslie Bethell, *The Abolition of the Brazilian Slave Trade: Britain, Brazil and the Slave Trade Question 1807–1869* (Cambridge: Cambridge University Press, 1970), pp. 260–1. The motion was narrowly defeated.
23   *Hampshire Advertiser & Salisbury Guardian*, 11 October 1845.
24   Hull History Centre: Hull University Archives (hereafter HHC), DDHO 10/11, Charles Hotham to Captain Hamilton, 1 November 1848.
25   Brian Lavery, *Nelson's Navy: The Ships, Men and Organisation, 1793–1815* (London: Conway Maritime Press, 1989), p. 116.
26   Lloyd, *Navy and the Slave Trade*, pp. 79–84. Later, the Naval Pay and Prize Act of 1854 ordered that all prize bounty should be paid into a centralised prize account.
27   HHC, DDHO 10/8, Charles Hotham to the Earl of Auckland, 3 April 1847.
28   NMM, TRN/10, Copy letter from George Fowler Hastings to Captain Charles Eden, 11 February 1850.
29   The Cadbury Research Library: Special Collections, University of Birmingham (hereafter CRL), MS 27, Journal of William Hall, 1 May 1822.
30   NMM, LBK/41, Dr McIlroy to his brother, 3 October 1841.
31   NMM, LBK/41, Dr McIlroy to his brother, 3 August 1841.
32   NMM, LBK/41, Dr McIlroy to his brother, 25 November 1841.
33   National Archives of Scotland (hereafter NAS), GD 76/458, Copy letter from Robert Flockhart to Dr Craig Ratho, 12 December 1838.
34   NAS, GD 219/304/36, Alexander Murray to John Dalrymple Murray, 22 September 1847.
35   NAS, GD 219/304/38, Alexander Murray to John Dalrymple Murray, 5 May 1848.
36   NMM, MEY/5, Francis Meynell to his father, 2 May 1845.
37   See Marcus Wood, *Blind Memory: Visual Representations of Slavery in England and America, 1780–1865* (New York: Routledge, 2000), chapter 2, particularly pp. 23–5, for discussion of Meynell's painting of the slave-hold.
38   For an overview of the visual culture of the abolition movement in the eighteenth century, see John Oldfield, *Popular Politics and British Anti-Slavery: The Mobilisation of Public Opinion against the Slave Trade 1787–1807* (Manchester: Manchester University Press, 1995), chapter 6.
39   NMM, MEY/5, Francis Meynell to his father, 12 January 1846.
40   *Instructions for the Guidance of Her Majesty's Naval Officers Employed in the Suppression of the Slave Trade* (London: T. R. Harrison, 1844), p. 1.
41   Christopher Leslie Brown, *Moral Capital: Foundations of British Abolitionism* (Chapel Hill: University of North Carolina Press, 2006), pp. 28–9.
42   Linda Colley, *Britons: Forging the Nation, 1707–1837* (London: Yale University Press, 1992), pp. 321–2, 359–60; James Walvin, *England, Slaves and Freedom, 1776–1838* (Basingstoke: Macmillan, 1986), pp. 173–5.
43   Seymour Drescher, 'Public Opinion and the Destruction of British Colonial Slavery', in James Walvin (ed.), *Slavery and British Society 1776-1846* (London: Macmillan, 1982), pp. 22–48; James Walvin, 'The Public Campaign in England against Slavery, 1787-1834', in David Eltis and James Walvin (eds), *The Abolition of the Atlantic Slave Trade: Origins and Effects in Europe, Africa and the Americas* (Madison, WI: University of Wisconsin Press, 1981), pp. 63–79.

44 Roger Anstey, *The Atlantic Slave Trade and British Abolition, 1760–1810* (London: Macmillan Press, 1975), chapter 8.
45 Richard Blake, *Evangelicals in the Royal Navy 1775–1815: Blue Lights and Psalm-Singers* (Woodbridge: Boydell Press, 2008).
46 Brown, *Moral Capital*, pp. 341–4.
47 Blake, *Evangelicals*, p. 287.
48 West Sussex Record Office (hereafter WSRO), Buckle Papers 470, Journal of Claude Buckle, 7 October 1844; Roger Anstey, *Atlantic Slave Trade*, pp. 188–9.
49 WSRO, Buckle Papers 524.
50 WSRO, Buckle Papers 470, Journal of Claude Buckle, 7 October 1844. Buckle is likely referring to Edward Cooper's *Practical and Familiar Sermons*, evangelical passages first published in 1809.
51 This is not to suggest that religious belief automatically equated to anti-slavery sentiment. Many evangelicals hated slavery but accepted racial inequality and held a lack of faith in Africans' ability to 'civilise' themselves. For example, see Catherine Hall, 'An Empire of God or of Man? The Macaulays, Father and Son', in Hilary M. Carey (ed.), *Empires of Religion* (Basingstoke: Palgrave Macmillan, 2008), pp. 64–83.
52 Christopher Terrell, 'Columbine, Edward Henry (1763–1811)', *Oxford Dictionary of National Biography*, Oxford University Press, 2004, www.oxforddnb.com/view/article/64853. Accessed 9 March 2009. A permanent anti-slavery squadron did not operate until after 1815, but a small naval force under Columbine's command captured and condemned several slave ships.
53 Terrell, 'Columbine'.
54 Wayne Ackerson, *The African Institution (1807–1827) and the Antislavery Movement in Great Britain* (New York: The Edwin Mellen Press, 2005).
55 University of Illinois at Chicago Library (hereafter UIC), Sierra Leone Collection: Series III, Folder 9, Journal of Edward Columbine, 12 January 1810, fos 50–2. Original emphasis. That Nelson himself had little time for abolitionist arguments is illustrative of the ideological conflicts surrounding suppression during this early period. For Nelson's views, see Hugh Thomas, *The Slave Trade: The History of the Atlantic Slave Trade 1440–1870* (London: Picador, 1997), pp. 545–6.
56 NLS, Pasley Papers MS 9879, Copy letter from John Tailour to General Sir Charles William Pasley, 3 May 1815, fos 333–5.
57 NLS, Pasley Papers MS 9879, Copy letter from John Tailour to General Sir Charles William Pasley, 3 May 1815, fos 333–5.
58 NMRN, MSS 45, 'Second Annual Report on the coast of Africa by Commodore Sir George Collier, 1820', fo. 13.
59 NMRN, MSS 45, 'Second Annual Report', fo. 13.
60 NMRN, MSS 45, 'Second Annual Report', fos 241–2.
61 For example, *The Morning Chronicle* (2 October 1821) and *Glasgow Herald* (19 October 1821).
62 George Collier to the Registrar of the Court of Mixed Commission, 26 March 1821, *British and Foreign State Papers, 1821–1822* (London: J. Harrison and Son, 1829), pp. 272–3.
63 George Collier to the Lords of the Admiralty, 27 December 1821, *British and Foreign State Papers, 1821–1822* (London: J. Harrison and Son, 1829), pp. 215–6.
64 John Marshall, *Royal Naval Biography* (London, 1825), vol. 4, pp. 539–40.
65 Qtd in Lloyd, *Navy and the Slave Trade*, pp. 92–3. The court at Sierra Leone concluded that as the slaver was seized south of the line (and therefore permitted to trade under Portuguese law), it was to be returned to Rio and its owner.
66 As commander of the northern division of the squadron in 1840, Denman entered into a treaty with the local rulers at Gallinas by which all slave factories there were destroyed, slave dealers expelled and slaves liberated. This action caused much debate in naval circles and Denman was unsuccessfully sued for the loss suffered by the slave owner.
67 Joseph Denman, *The African Squadron and Mr Hutt's Committee*, 2nd edn (London: John Mortimer, 1850), pp. 4, 64.

68 See *A Letter from Lord Denman to Lord Brougham on the Final Extinction of the Slave Trade*, 2nd edn (London: J. Hatchard and Son, 1848).

69 See Robert Burroughs, 'Eyes on the Prize: Journeys in Slave Ships Taken as Prizes by the Royal Navy', *Slavery & Abolition* 31 (2010), pp. 99–115, for a reading of chaplain Pascoe Grenfell Hill's published account of a harrowing prize-ship journey on the East African coast.

70 The National Archives, Kew (hereafter TNA), ADM 1/1, John Hayes to Captain George Elliot (Secretary of the Admiralty), 20 January 1831, fos 259–61. Original emphasis by underlining.

71 TNA, ADM 1/1, Hayes to Elliot, 20 January 1831.

72 Private, Journal of Henry Rogers, 29 November 1849.

73 Private, Journal of Henry Rogers, 29 November 1849. Such fears were not unrealistic. Up to one in ten slave vessels experienced insurrection. David Richardson, 'Shipboard Revolts, African Authority and the Atlantic Slave Trade', *The William and Mary Quarterly* 58 (2001), 69–92.

74 Private, Journal of Henry Rogers, 29 November 1849.

75 See Marcus Rediker, *The Slave Ship: A Human History* (London: John Murray, 2007); Emma Christopher, *Slave Ship Sailors and Their Captive Cargoes, 1730–1807* (Cambridge: Cambridge University Press, 2006), particularly chapter 5; Burroughs, 'Eyes on the Prize', p. 102. However, such disciplinary action should also be understood in the context of the harsh punishments handed out to sailors. See N. A. M Rodger, *The Wooden World: An Anatomy of the Georgian Navy* (London: Fontana Press, 1986), chapter 6.

76 Philip D. Curtin, *The Image of Africa: British Ideas and Action 1780-1850* (Madison, WI: University of Wisconsin Press, 1964), especially pp. 479–80; P. J. Marshall and Glyndwr Williams, *The Great Map of Mankind: British Perceptions of the World in the Age of Enlightenment* (London: J. M. Dent & Sons, 1982), p. 3. However, personal testimonies make clear that while some were quick to term all Africans 'savages', others took time to distinguish between tribes and attribute positive characteristics to them. This was particularly the case with West African seamen, notably the Kru, employed by the anti-slave-trade squadron to assist with navigation and transporting men between ship and shore.

77 Brown, *Moral Capital*, p. 213; Andrew Porter, 'Trusteeship, Anti-Slavery, and Humanitarianism', in Andrew Porter (ed.), *The Oxford History of the British Empire: Volume III: The Nineteenth Century* (Oxford: Oxford University Press, 1999), pp. 198–221.

78 See Paul Kennedy, *The Rise and Fall of British Naval Mastery* (London: Allen Lane, 1976), chapter 6, for the idea of 'Pax Britannica'. The scale of the British commitment to suppression dwarfed that of other nations, as illustrated by Eltis and Richardson, *Atlas*, p. 282, map 185.

79 Leonard, *Records of a Voyage*, p. 19.

80 Eltis, *Economic Growth*, p. 102; A. G. Hopkins, 'The "New International Economic Order" in the Nineteenth Century: Britain's First Development Plan for Africa', in Robin Law (ed.), *From Slave Trade to 'Legitimate' Commerce: The Commercial Transition in Nineteenth-Century West Africa* (Cambridge: Cambridge University Press, 1995), pp. 240–64.

81 T. C. McCaskie, 'Cultural Encounters: Britain and Africa in the Nineteenth Century', in Andrew Porter (ed.), *The Oxford History of the British Empire: Volume III: The Nineteenth Century* (Oxford: Oxford University Press, 1999), pp. 665–89. See Howard Temperley, *White Dreams, Black Africa: The Antislavery Expedition to the River Niger 1841–1842* (New Haven and London: Yale University Press, 1991) for an account of Thomas Fowell Buxton's Niger Expedition for the purposes of 'improving' Africans.

82 UK Hydrographic Office Archive, MP 90, 'Remark Book of His Majesty's Ship Thalia between the 6th of June and the 31st December 1834 on her passage from England to the Cape of Good Hope', fos 59–97.

83 Gloucestershire Archives, Sotherton-Estcourt Papers D1571/F543, Journal of Walter Estcourt, 5 January 1845.

84 CRL, Church Missionary Society Archives, CA2/08/04, Arthur Parry Eardley Wilmot to Obba Shoron, 3 April 1852. Original emphasis. Wilmot became Commodore of the squadron in 1863.

85 UIC, Sierra Leone Collection: Series III, Folder 10, Journal of Edward Columbine, 10 December 1810.

86 NAS, GD 76/458, Copy letter from Robert Flockhart to his family, 12 November 1838.

87 Johnson U. J. Asiegbu, *Slavery and the Politics of Liberation, 1787-1861: A Study of Liberated African Emigration and British Anti-slavery Policy* (Harlow: Longmans, 1969); Rosanne Adderley, *"New Negroes from Africa": Slave Trade Abolition and Free African Settlement in the Nineteenth-Century Caribbean* (Bloomington & Indianapolis, IN: Indiana University Press, 2006); Eltis and Richardson, *Atlas*, p. 289, map 189.

88 Private, Journal of Henry Rogers, 19 December 1849. Original emphasis by underlining.

89 Wellcome Library, MS 1396, Diaries of Fleetwood Buckle, 6 August 1866. Original emphasis by underlining. Much has been written about the hardening of racial attitudes from the mid-nineteenth century and the rise of 'scientific racism'. It is fair to assume that naval personnel like Buckle were affected by such changes in public sentiment.

90 NAS, GD 219/304/36, Alexander Murray to John Dalrymple Murray, 22 September 1847.

91 NAS, GD 219/304/39, Alexander Murray to John Dalrymple Murray, 8 May 1849.

92 NLS, Minto Papers MS 12054, George Elliot to Lord Melgund, 6 January 1840, fos 176–8. Elliot was nephew of the Second Earl of Minto, First Lord of the Admiralty between 1835 and 1841, and son of Admiral Sir George Elliot.

93 NLS, MS 12054, Elliot to Melgund, 6 January 1840.

94 NMM, TRN/10, Copy letter from George Fowler Hastings to Captain Charles Eden, 11 February 1850.

95 See Jane Samson, 'Hero, Fool or Martyr? The Many Deaths of Commodore Goodenough', *Journal for Maritime Research* 10 (2008), 1–22, for an examination of the conflicts between idealism and professionalism in the career of Commodore Goodenough in the Pacific Islands in the later nineteenth century.

96 Scottish Catholic Archives, GB 0240 FA/67/3, Diary of Richard Carr McClement, 7 January 1861, p. 118, www.scottishcatholicarchives.org.uk/Learning/DiaryofRichardCarrMcClement/DiaryExtracts/Empire/tabid/186/Default.aspx. Accessed 20 June 2011.

CHAPTER FIVE

British and African health in the anti-slave-trade squadron

John Rankin

Nineteenth-century medical journals provide important insights into the lives and deaths of African and European sailors. Parliamentary reports and published first-hand accounts from naval surgeons, especially Alexander Bryson and Morris Pritchett, make clear that service in the West Africa Station proved to be extremely dangerous for 'unacclimatised' European bodies. These sources illuminate European sailors' fears of the region's fevers.[1] Scholarly interest in the West Africa Station has been confined to the politics and processes of slave-trade suppression and, if these studies do mention health, they echo the opinions of the likes of Bryson and Pritchett without development or context.[2] African experiences are largely ignored even though medical sources offer a rare glimpse at the roles of African mariners and the Royal Navy's attitudes to race. Through the use of naval records this chapter will draw attention to the importance of African mariners in maintaining anti-slavery efforts in West Africa, and will examine how European sailors treated and categorised the African body in the age of abolition. Comparison of the health of African and European sailors serving on the West Africa Station will provide insight into the degree to which naval medicine was racialised in the early nineteenth century. This information will expose how Britons perceived, understood and, in a practical sense, dealt with the African body.

The primary data employed in this analysis is derived from medical journals of eight Royal Navy ships whose dates of service ranged from 1831 to 1861. These comprise all such records for the West Africa Station between 1800 and 1861 extant in the National Archives. The total number of morbidity cases (episodes of ill health) in this data set is 1,961. These medical journals are buttressed by quarterly and annual reports from a military hospital in Sierra Leone that, on occasion, treated Royal Navy personnel. Journals from ships' surgeons and military surgeons who came into contact with Royal Navy personnel are valuable, but their extant reports tended to emphasise the sensational, spilling little ink over everyday health complaints. Since African mortality proved so low and Africans for the most part avoided the fevers that often afflicted Europeans, Africans do not feature prominently in these medical summaries. Nonetheless, the limited descriptions of African patients and their interaction with European surgeons do provide the opportunity to examine and compare the treatment methods received by both European and African sailors.

Four categories were employed to describe and to differentiate the African work force on the West Africa Station. These four categories were: 'Kroomen' (or Kru), liberated Africans (both boys and men), Africans, and Blacks. The first and most numerous of hired Africans were Kru who came from what is today eastern Liberia and actively sought employment upon European vessels as experienced seamen. 'Liberated African' was a term employed by the British to describe any African who had been rescued from a slaver and 'repatriated' to Africa. 'African' was a term used by the Admiralty to describe any African serving in the station who was neither Kru nor a liberated African.[3] 'Blacks' referred to sailors of African descent, who had been born, or at the time of recruitment, were living, outside of Africa. Blacks were only employed on one ship under my study, HMS *Wilberforce*.

To these four categories I have added that of European. Europeans are distinguished from Africans in the medical journals, for European sailors had their rank or occupational status recorded while African sailors usually were only identified by ethnic group (i.e. Kru or liberated African). 'European' is here used as a general description for Europeans and those of European descent. For the purposes of this investigation it was not necessary to inquire into the origins of the European personnel but, as a general observation, the substantial majority were born in England, Wales, Scotland and Ireland.

Europeans comprised 79% of all ship board personnel on the eight ships: Africans and Blacks made up the remaining 21%. There were 1,001 Europeans; 265 Kru, liberated African, and 'African'; and eleven 'Blacks'. The 220 hired Kru comprised 80% of all non-Europeans. 'African' was the next most common designation with 31 hired, comprising 10.9% of the non-European group. There were fourteen liberated Africans in the records of the ships surveyed (5.1% of non-Europeans). Only two of these sailors were adults; the other twelve were recorded as being liberated African boys. Eleven Blacks served upon HMS *Wilberforce*; they comprised 4% of all non-European personnel on board the ships surveyed. For the distribution of non-European personnel hired for service on the eight ships under investigation, see Figure 5.1.[4]

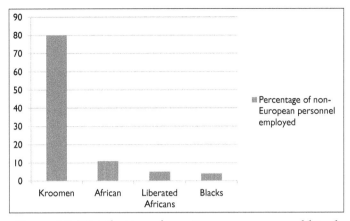

Figure 5.1 Distribution of non-European personnel hired
for service, 1831–61.

The Royal Navy was particular in the Africans it employed and, as the numbers demonstrate, preferred Kru to all others. According to nineteenth-century commentators, Kru lived along the West African coast between Cape Mount and Cape Palmas.[5] Kru were well aware that the British believed them to be expert seafarers and eagerly propagated the myth that they alone among the African peoples were 'naturally' suited for seafaring.[6] The Kru who served upon a Royal Navy vessel placed themselves under the authority of a single Headman.[7] The Headman had authority over all his Kru acting as a mediator between them and the British officers. In return, the Headman took a portion of each Kru's salary.[8] The British accepted this effective chain of command as superior to the haphazard recruitment and instruction of a variety of unattached individuals not under the supervision and authority of a single African leader.[9]

African personnel were hired to refresh ships' complements weakened by death and disease and to engage in work considered too dangerous to the health of Europeans. Kru were viewed as an auxiliary labour force and often had no stated status, quality or rank on board ship except that of being a 'Krooman'. They were often responsible for engaging in the most labour-intensive and low-status jobs, including going ashore to acquire fresh water and cutting fire wood.[10] While the Admiralty also used those classified as 'Africans' as a general labour force, 'Africans' were much more likely to serve as members of the ships' crew. One of the most common jobs for hired 'Africans' was that of ship's steward. The steward was responsible for the preparation of and cleaning up after meals. After the advent of the steam-powered ship, 'Africans' often served as stokers, responsible for stoking coal fires. This position was labour intensive, low status, extremely uncomfortable and sometimes dangerous. However, some 'Africans' did have opportunities for advancement. Jake Campbell, who served on HMSS *Trident* in 1859, was promoted to the rank of engineer after the ship's engineering staff was taken ill, suggesting some Africans were familiar with the workings of European steam ships.[11] On the whole, when Europeans became too ill to fill their duties, it was those classed as 'Africans' such as Campbell who took over their roles, not Kru. This suggests that the British perceived the responsibilities and capabilities of Kru and 'Africans' differently. It may also indicate that Kru were seen more collectively, as members of a team serving under a Headman, whereas 'Africans' entered the ship's books as individuals and, thus, may have been selected for skills which were seen as better placed for advancement.

Naval surgeons had three official means of dealing with incapacitated personnel. They could discharge the patient to a hospital for further care, they could declare the patient invalided and arrange transport home, or they could complete treatment on board. Surgeons on the West Africa Station rarely ordered a patient to hospital for further care.[12] The reason for this is hard to determine, but it was probably a product of surgeons' belief in their own abilities and also the result of simple logistics. Ships were often far away from a hospital and, consequently, no matter whether the surgeon thought the patient warranted hospital care, this form of treatment was not always immediately available. Only one hospital, on Ascension Island far to the south of Sierra Leone, was of much value to the navy. Ascension Island, located 1,600 km off the coast of Africa, was the major supply depot and sanatorium for the sailors of the West Africa Station. In addition, the Royal Navy occasionally used the colonial Kissy Hospital located in Freetown and army hospitals located in the Gambia and Sierra Leone. Although these hospitals were willing to accept and treat patients for the Royal Navy, they were not set up for this sort of care. The logistical difficulty of discharging a patient to hospital for further treatment meant that it was common to have someone on the sick list for over two months before being discharged to a hospital. For example, Thomas Strong and John Wright remained on the sick list for 119 days after sustaining gunshot wounds until HMS *Arrogant* finally docked near a hospital on 20 June 1861.[13]

The practice of invaliding home was even rarer. Only 1% of all European patients were invalided and not a single hired African. Few hospital records exist and it is impossible to know how often these institutions ordered home naval patients who had previously been placed in their care. However, the infrequent use of hospitalisation meant that the numbers could not have been substantial. Naval surgeons on the West Africa Station primarily handled the medical needs of their crews on board.

Mortality

The Royal Navy's reliance upon African labour was partly a consequence of the disease environment. In the first half of the nineteenth century, the West Africa Station proved more deadly than any of the navy's other foreign stations.[14] Those who survived long enough to formulate an opinion of the climate most likely agreed with Dr Bryson, who called service in the West Africa Station, 'the most disagreeable, arduous and unhealthy service that falls to the lot of British officers and seaman'.[15] Bryson was well equipped to make an assessment; he served for nine years as a surgeon in West Africa and published the standard analysis of the 'healthiness' of the Station. *Report on the Climate and Principal Disease of the African Station* examined the mortality rates of sailors serving in the navy over a twenty-year period beginning in 1825. Bryson demonstrated that the West Africa Station deserved its reputation as the deadliest station. The mortality rate from disease was 54.4 per thousand, or three times that of the West Indian Station, which possessed an average mortality rate of 18.1 per thousand.[16] Bryson calculated the mortality per thousand from all causes (both diseases and accidents) in the West Africa Station to be 64.9.[17] The reason that the West African environment proved so hostile to European bodies was the high incidence of endemic and epidemic fevers, for which most of the naval work force had little or no resistance. The existence of

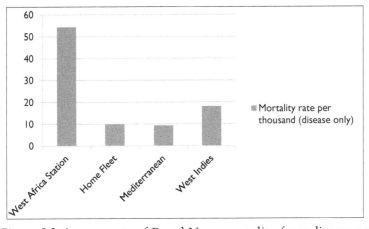

Figure 5.2 Average rate of Royal Navy mortality from disease on select stations, 1825–45.[18]

endemic malaria and epidemic yellow fever, in particular, combined to make the West Africa Station the most deadly posting in the whole of the Royal Navy. For the mortality rate for naval personnel in select stations, 1825–45, see Figure 5.2.

Bryson's statistics covered the period 1825–45. The eight ships serving during the period 1831–61 for which records are available suffered an overall mortality rate of 43.9 per thousand for the whole ships' complements, and 56 per thousand for Europeans.[19] This was lower than the mortality rate of 64.9 per thousand calculated by Bryson.[20] This drop is perhaps explicable because in the 1840s naval surgeons abandoned bleeding as their primary method of treatment and began to adopt instead quinine both to prevent and treat fever.[21] These changes appear to have had a positive effect. The application of quinine significantly reduced the deadliness of malaria,[22] while surgeons no longer needlessly weakened their patients by bleeding, giving them a better chance of recovery. Considering that this was the deadliest naval station, an average yearly loss of less than five out of each hundred lives for the eight ships surveyed appears to be rather low compared to the experiences of European soldiers in West Africa. For the period 1819–36, the mortality rate amongst European troops in Sierra Leone was 483 per thousand.[23] Although a comparison for the same years and exact locales is not possible, the European mortality on board HMS *Atholl* (1831–32), HMS *Aetna* (1837–38) and HMS *Scout* (1837–38) provide a valuable comparison. Despite the fact that the HMS *Aetna* had experienced an outbreak of yellow fever, the three ships had a combined average mortality of 65.3 per thousand,[24] approximately seven times lower than the mortality rate experienced by soldiers (and almost identical for the twenty-year average up to

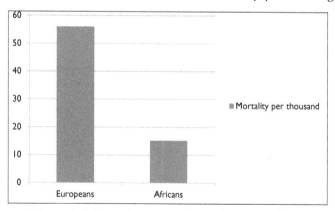

Figure 5.3 Mortality rate of naval personnel per thousand for the eight ships surveyed, 1831–61.[25]

1845 produced by Bryson). There was a significant difference between sailing the West African coast and serving out one's duty on West African soil. For the mortality rate of naval personnel for the eight ships under investigation, see Figure 5.3.

Mortality amongst Africans serving on the naval patrols of West Africa was very low. On the eight ships under examination, Africans accounted for 21% of the labour force but only 6.6% of the deaths. The causes of the four Africans' deaths were recorded as an abscess, pericarditis, heart clot and apoplexy.[26] This low mortality explains the preference for hired Africans. Europeans comprised 79% of all personnel, and accounted for 93.4% of the total mortality. African labour was therefore vital in sustaining the West Africa Station, although the labours of Africans in suppressing the slave trade have been virtually ignored to date. Figure 5.4 compares African and European naval and military mortality.

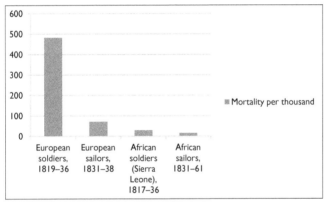

Figure 5.4 African and European naval and military mortality.[27]

The mortality rate for Africans serving in the British navy can be compared with the mortality rates for African soldiers serving in West Africa. For the years 1817–36, African soldiers serving in Sierra Leone died at a rate of 30 per thousand,[28] compared to African sailors who between 1831 and 1861 died at a rate of 15.2 per thousand. For a direct comparison using the three ships that served in the 1830s, HMS *Atholl* (1831–32), HMS *Aetna* (1837–38) and HMS *Scout* (1837–38), not a single African amongst the seventy-eight who served on these vessels died. Whether African or European, it was less deadly to be a sailor in the West Africa Station than to serve as a soldier in West Africa. The reason can be explained in part by two sets of diseases: smallpox, which gravely affected Africans; and the 'fevers' which attacked European soldiers and sailors. One reason European sailors did not suffer the same high mortality rate as European soldiers was that sailors spent much of their time either at sea or moored miles off the coast.[29] At this distance, crews would have been located outside the reaches of mosquitoes and thus, for much of the time, sailors were significantly safer than European soldiers in West Africa. This distance gave sailors a much better chance of surviving the West African 'climate'. Smallpox proved a constant threat to West Africans. Despite the efforts of British colonial, medical and military officers, smallpox caused the highest level of mortality amongst African soldiers serving in Sierra Leone.[30] Despite its deadliness on land, not a single case of smallpox was found in the records of the eight ships surveyed. This outcome may well have been the result of compulsory naval vaccination. That smallpox proved so deadly on land compared to at sea helps explain why African soldiers suffered twice the mortality rate as African sailors serving in West Africa.

Philip Curtin proposes that British West Africa experienced a mortality revolution during the 1870s when European soldiers survived service in the region much more often thanks to the introduction of quinine.[31] The Royal Navy had also experienced a mortality revolution, but much earlier – around mid-century – and the decline in mortality was much more rapid. Indeed, for the years 1854–58 the total mortality for European sailors serving in the West Africa Station had dropped dramatically to 15.5 per thousand.[32] This was a significant decline, for according to the figures compiled by Bryson the mortality rate for the years 1840–45 for all personnel was 45.1 per thousand.[33] Only in the early twentieth century did the British army reduce its mortality rate for service in West Africa to a level experienced by the navy in the 1850s.[34] By keeping a distance from the coast, limiting shore time,[35] hiring Africans to engage in labour considered too dangerous for European bodies, including 'wooding and watering',[36] and by adopting quinine, the navy successfully experienced a mortality rate that the army could only match after both the application of the germ theory and the verification of the mosquito as the vector in the transmission of malaria and yellow fever.[37] The differing patterns of mortality for soldiers as compared to sailors provide another perspective on the hazards of West Africa for European labour.

The mortality rates aboard the eight ships examined affirm that the Royal Navy in West Africa experienced a 'mortality revolution' around mid-century (see Figure 5.5). If the eight ships surveyed are divided into two groups, one comprising the four ships up to and including the Niger Expedition of 1841–42 and the other group the four ships of 1846–61, the evidence is striking. For the first set, the mortality rate was 80.2 per thousand, whereas for the second it was 41.5 per thousand.

This drop confirms Curtin's assertion that by the mid-1840s, largely due to the use of quinine, the navy experienced a dramatic reduction in the mortality of (European) seaman on the West Africa Station. [38]

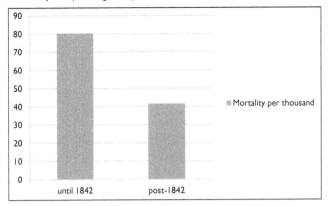

Figure 5.5 European mortality per thousand on board the eight ships examined in the West Africa Station before and after 1842.[39]

'Fever' proved to be by far the most likely disease category to claim a European sailor's life. Fever accounted for forty-seven out of the fifty-one fatalities attributed to disease (92.4%).[40] Other causes of European mortality included three cases of gunshot wounds,[41] two occurrences of fractured skulls,[42] and one drowning.[43] Fever proved deadly in only one out of every ten cases. Without tropical fevers, the death rate for European sailors would have dropped from 56 to 10 per thousand (see Figure 5.6).

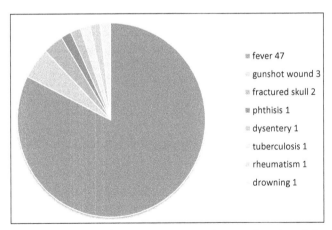

Figure 5.6 Attributions for European naval mortality for eight ships, 1831–61.[44]

An examination of the mortality experiences of both European and African sailors allows for two important conclusions. First, regardless of nativity, service was significantly less deadly aboard a ship than in the army. For Africans it was about twice as deadly to serve as a soldier in West Africa than as a sailor. For Europeans it was almost seven times more deadly.[45] Second, European sailors and soldiers suffered a much higher mortality rate – nearly seven times higher for sailors and sixteen times higher for soldiers – than their hired African counterparts. It made sense, therefore, that British officials endeavoured to replace European soldiers and sailors with Africans. In 1829, British authorities, baffled and frustrated by the high mortality rates amongst soldiers serving in West Africa, replaced most of the remaining European troops (high-ranking officers excepted) with 'coloured' soldiers from the West India Regiments.[46] British officials recognised the dangers associated with service in West Africa and altered their military plans either to protect the lives of European soldiers or to optimise military effectiveness. Some officials worried about the loyalty of these soldiers,[47] but the British acknowledged that 'coloured' troops had immunities to the environment not afforded to European soldiers. Race was an important part of British military plans in West Africa. At sea, for numerous logistical reasons, British officials could not simply replace all European naval personnel. Instead the Royal Navy tried to minimise mortality within a skilled workforce by hiring Africans, especially Kru, to do the labour considered the most injurious to European life. In general, this was effective: more Europeans likely survived as a result.

Morbidity

There was a noticeable difference in the morbidity rates of European and African personnel serving in the West Africa Station. Morbidity, whether from illness or debility, is defined for the purposes of this investigation as being placed on the ship's sick list. The difficulties of employing these lists to examine health include that personnel may have been ill or unwell long before being placed on the list, their injury or illness may not have been severe enough to gain notice from the ship's surgeon or judged ill or injured severely enough to be placed on the sick list. It may also be the case that African and European personnel concealed injury or illness from the ship's surgeon. It is also true that the determination of incapacitation possessed cultural features, and that it varied according to the schedule of a vessel's responsibilities and its moments of crisis. Despite these limitations, morbidity rates as calculated from the sick lists remain the best statistical measure of health for the nineteenth-century Royal Navy.

An examination of morbidity demonstrates how frequently naval personnel were unable to attend their duty. It also provides the opportunity to examine which of the Admiralty's classification of personnel were most likely to be placed on the sick list, and which groups were most likely to avoid it. On average, three out of four European sailors who worked on the eight ships surveyed entered medical care on the sick list. Even the surgeon of HMS *Scout*, which experienced the lowest level of morbidity for ships surveyed, placed half of all sailors on the sick list.[48] Africans on board British vessels experienced lower morbidity rates, with approximately four out of ten hired Africans being placed on the sick list. The range of morbidity for hired Africans extended from a low of 29.1% to a high of 57.1%, depending upon the vessel. The morbidity rate of European personnel ranged from 50.7 to 86.1%. Europeans comprised 79% of all sailors on the eight ships examined; however, they accounted for 89.5% of all recorded morbidity. Hired Africans constitute 21% of personnel, but accounted for only 10.5% of the total morbidity (see Figure 5.7).

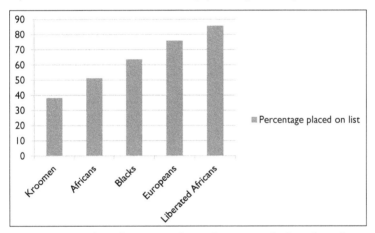

Figure 5.7 Classifications of naval personnel placed on the daily sick lists, 1831–61.[49]

Liberated Africans, whether boys or men, were the most likely of all sailors, European or African, to become ill. Of the fourteen individuals identified as liberated Africans, twelve entered the sick list and one of them died. The likely reason is extensive pre-service ill-health as a result of the slave trade. Once slavers were condemned by the Mixed Commission for the Suppression of the Transatlantic Slave Trade at Sierra Leone, the court that adjudicated whether a vessel was involved in the slave trade, liberated Africans immediately became the responsibility of the colonial government.[50] Liberated Africans would then be subjected to a quick medical examination determining who was in need of medical care and who could be put to work. This precaution should have ensured that liberated Africans were ready for employment. As Emma Christopher's chapter in this volume explores in more depth, however, in an attempt to minimise costs colonial governors and officials put the freed victims of the slave trade to work as soon as possible.[51] Liberated Africans were in demand with the army and other employers. The army's hiring policy was so aggressive that they enlisted liberated Africans still in poor health. Army surgeons complained of this practice and the poor condition in which the liberated Africans arrived for service.[52]

The navy displayed similarly questionable judgement.[53] The case of six liberated African boys recruited for work on HMS *Aetna* in 1837 is illustrative. Having all entered service together on 1 December four had been placed on the sick list with pre-service cases of yaws within three days. Yaws is an infection of the skin, bones and joints caused by the spirochete bacterium. It is spread from direct skin to skin contact. It leads to the development of lesions at the point of contact and if not treated can spread all over the body. Although rarely fatal, yaws causes chronic disability and disfigurement. Within the week, a fifth boy joined them, having come down with fever.[54] That most of the six liberated African boys had fallen sick within a week of joining HMS *Aetna* illustrates the suffering inflicted by the slave trade on those who survived. Given the relative low morbidity of all other African groups onboard British ships, and the fact that those liberated Africans who fell ill did so within days of beginning their service, it is reasonable to assume the navy had a similar experience to the army in recruiting from this group. It should be noted that twelve of the fourteen liberated Africans under study were children. Their young age may have made them prone to illness or more likely to be placed under care.

Seven of eleven Blacks born or domiciled in the West Indies, Canada, the USA and England brought to Africa to serve on board HMS *Wilberforce* in the Niger Expedition were placed on the sick list. This proportion (63.6%) is high, in fact the highest except for Europeans and liberated Africans on all the ships examined. On the same voyage, six of eleven (54.5%) of Kru fell ill, as did fourteen of twenty-four (58.3%) of other 'Africans'. Forty of the HMS *Wilberforce's* forty-seven European sailors were placed on the sick list resulting in morbidity per thousand of 85.1%. The ship's hiring pattern was unique, in part because the 'Blacks' aboard had been born in Europe or the Americas. The other seven vessels did not rely so heavily on Africans of all backgrounds.

Blacks born outside Africa fell ill often and, if they recovered, often suffered further episodes of sickness. The experiences of William

Jackson illustrate this point. Born in Jamaica, the 22-year-old appeared on the sick list five times in the span of only six months having suffered catarrh twice, fever twice and colic once for a total incapacitation of forty-four days.[55] It was this frequent recurrence of disease amongst Blacks born or domiciled across the Atlantic that prompted Morris Pritchett, one of the surgeons on the Niger Expedition, to conclude that since 'many of the blacks and mulattos we had onboard having become accustom[ed] to colder climates of the North, they were probably at least as liable to be attacked with disease as Europeans'.[56] He points out: '[i]t was among the men of colour in fact, that the first cases of the disease [fever] occurred'.[57] Blacks, according to Pritchett, were not only a liability as unhealthy employees but a hazard placing all sailors at risk of infection. Although other hired Africans were also placed on the sick list multiple times over the expedition's duration of two years and eight months, not one of the eleven Kru was placed on the sick list more than once. The British apparently learned a lesson from HMS *Wilberforce* and the Niger Expedition. After 1841 it appears that the Admiralty returned to hiring predominantly Kru; never again, on the four ships surveyed after 1842, were 'Africans' preferred over Kru, nor were Blacks born or domiciled outside Africa hired for service within these four ships.

Africans' lower mortality and morbidity rates made them essential to British naval activities on the coasts of West Africa. This is all the more impressive given that Africans were expected to do work considered too dangerous for Europeans.[58] While European sailors generally avoided shore duty, and thus the dangers of 'marsh miasma', Africans were sent to the shore to gather wood and water.[59] Over three-quarters of Europeans employed on the ships of the West Africa Station contracted an illness sufficiently severe to place them on the sick lists; for Africans, of all classifications, the figure was 42.3%. When Africans became ill they required similar recovery times as European personnel. On average, sailors placed on the sick list remained there for twelve days. Once Europeans or Africans became ill, they just were as likely to become ill again. On average, all sailors placed on the sick list once were likely to be placed on the list once more before the end of their term of service. Once Africans became ill, their experiences, in terms of the number of days sick and the likelihood of becoming ill again paralleled that of European sailors. Where Africans differed, and why they were so valuable, was their ability to avoid incapacitation in the first place.

For the eight ships under consideration, fever was responsible for nearly a quarter of all European morbidity (24.1%) and a third of the total number of days spent by Europeans on the sick list.[60] Fever required one of the longest recovery periods, taking on average 16.6 days for a patient to be released from the sick list. Africans did not escape fever; it accounted for 11.8% of their total morbidity. On average Africans who contracted fever spent 10.4 days on the sick list. Despite these numbers, some surgeons maintained that Africans were immune to fever.[61] Fever was a health problem for employed Africans, but it never proved deadly. Nor when contracted did the affliction lead to a hospital stay. The shorter stay on the sick list may have reflected an expectation by the ship's officers that Africans could quickly get back to active duty. It would be misleading to attribute the higher morbidity rates amongst Europeans exclusively to fever. Even if fever is temporarily removed from the analysis, the pattern of morbidity does not change. Certainly the *mortality rate* of Europeans drops dramatically from 56 per thousand to 10 per thousand, while the total average days spent on the sick list for all diseases drops from 12.1 days to 10.6. However, the frequency of European morbidity would not be affected. Ignoring fever, Europeans (who comprised 79% of all personnel) would still have accounted for 87% of total morbidity and 88% of the total days spent on the sick list. A possible reason that the removal of fever does not have such a large statistical impact is that while fever most markedly divided European and African mortality, in almost all categories of disease it was Europeans and not Africans who were most likely to be placed on the sick list. The exceptionality of fever needs to be noted and its influence on the European statistics shown; however, regardless of how deadly some fevers were, Europeans were more likely overall to become ill – or at least to enter the sick list – than their African counterparts. For the impact of fever upon the average number of days on the daily sick list for European personnel, see Figure 5.8.

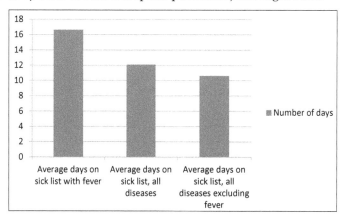

Figure 5.8 Average number of days on sick list for European personnel.[62]

The analysis of morbidity presents an opportunity to examine, in addition to fever, a few ailments at a closer level in order to acquire further insight into the health experiences of African and European sailors. The sick lists show that, with the exception of fever, diseases that occurred infrequently required some of the longest recovery times. Bubo, a swelling of lymph nodes in either the groin or armpits used to identify plague or plague-like symptoms,[63] is an example of this. The six Europeans who contracted the disease had an average stay on the sick list of 16.7 days, while the two afflicted Kru spent an average of 18.5 days on the sick list. One African boy (Admiralty classification) diagnosed with Bubo spent five weeks under treatment.[64] Parasitical infections provide another example as they were rarely diagnosed, averaging only a single case per ship. Those who contracted them, regardless of race, spent on average upwards of four weeks in care. The most striking example of an uncommon disease causing a long convalescence is phthisis or, as it later became known, tuberculosis. Of the eleven cases contracted by Europeans, the average stay on the sick list was 47.4 days. One patient was discharged to hospital for further care,[65] and three others invalided home.[66] There was a single diagnosed case of phthisis among Africans: a Kru sailor spent 22 days on the sick list.[67]

Venereal disease, an acknowledged problem for the army and navy in the nineteenth century, had relatively little impact on the eight ships surveyed. It sent twenty-seven Europeans and six Africans to the sick bay. While the incidence of venereal disease was, for the navy, low, those who were incapacitated by a venereal disease spent weeks recovering. The recovery time for the twenty-seven Europeans who contracted some form of venereal disease was, on average, 21.2 days. Four of these Europeans were then sent to a shore hospital for further treatment while another was invalided. For Africans incapacitated by venereal disease, the average recovery time was also around three weeks. Venereal disease appeared intermittently, and usually on ships after they had docked at certain locations. HMS *Arrogant* suffered a limited outbreak of syphilis after the ship had visited St Helena in January 1861.[68] Ship's surgeon Hart Ginlette blamed St Helena's populace for spreading syphilis. Ginlette stated that although most Europeans had contracted a mild form, others suffered from 'secondary symptoms'.[69] Ginlette reported that the two Kru who contracted syphilis did not experience any secondary complications.[70] Once incapacitated by syphilis, European sailors often required a long convalescence as the disease evolved into other stages. It is noteworthy that in an era of heightened concern venereal disease remained a small and manageable problem for the eight ships surveyed.

Perhaps due to the strenuous demands of their employment, Africans were somewhat more likely than Europeans to wind up on the sick list because of trauma. Trauma encompassed most physical injuries such as a sprains, fractures, wounds and contusions. Trauma placed twenty-one Kru, six 'Africans' and one liberated African boy on the sick lists. In total, 15.3% of all medical cases involving Africans were the result of injuries. The source of injuries to Africans ranged from a gunshot wound to burns acquired while stoking.[71] Severity varied from treatable contusions that required rest and recovery to skull fractures that resulted in immediate death. Europeans of course were not exempt from the 'rigours of the sea', with 12.5% of all cases involving Europeans attributed to a physical trauma. In total, 210 Europeans were placed on the sick list due to physical trauma, with thirteen cases referred to a hospital, while a further six ended in death. Three of these deaths resulted from gunshot wounds, two from a fractured skull and one from drowning.[72] None of these fatalities appeared on the sick lists for more than a day. Their deaths likely followed soon after being placed in the surgeon's care. Not a single African died or was placed in hospital after sustaining a physical trauma. Given that Africans and Europeans suffered from similar physical injuries (although severity cannot be ascertained) it is noteworthy that not a single African died or was sent to the hospital because of physical injury. The explanation for this may lie in the general perception that Africans were blessed with a durable constitution and thus would recover quickly from physical trauma.[73]

Two of the most common ailments on board the eight ships surveyed were catarrh and abdominal complaints. Catarrh, a catch-all diagnosis that refers to a host of possible ailments that produce a discharge from any mucous membrane, was responsible for 7.7% of European cases, and 11.8% of recorded cases involving Africans. Catarrh never proved deadly, although in one case a European patient was sent to a hospital. Europeans diagnosed with catarrh spent on average 7.6 days on the sick list compared to 9.6 days for their African counterparts. The somewhat greater reliance on catarrh as an explanation for African disease may suggest that surgeons had difficulty in diagnosing African complaints and, instead of achieving precise diagnosis, relied on a term that covered a variety of ailments with similar symptoms.

Abdominal complaints, dysentery, diarrhoea and general stomach pain routinely afflicted European sailors. Given the quality of the naval diet and the propensity of European sailors to drink large quantities of palm wine, to which their stomachs were unaccustomed, it is no surprise that they often suffered from bowel complaints.[74] Indeed, 12.3% of all European complaints consisted of diagnosed bowel problems. Although the incidence of stomach complaints was high, the severity of these complaints was, for the most part, low. Europeans on average spent 5.7 days on the sick list. Bowel complaints accounted for 5.6% of all African ailments while stays on the sick list averaged 9.3 days. The reason why fewer Africans were diagnosed with bowel complaints is unknown though it may have to do with their familiarity with the cuisine and sparse diet.[75] It is difficult to know why Europeans suffering from bowel complaints recovered their health faster than their African counterparts. It appears that neither age nor class played a factor, as the distribution was equal among all ages and ranks of sailors. The most obvious area of difference was that when diagnosed with dysentery Europeans recovered nearly six days faster than African personnel. Again, the reason for this is unknown but may be due to the fact that the threshold for placing Europeans on the sick list was lower than that for Africans. Thus Europeans with milder cases of dysentery (which may have really been a bad case of diarrhoea) were placed onto the sick list while an African in a similar condition was not brought to official notice or considered incapacitated.

African personnel were much less likely to be placed on the sick list than their European counterparts. Africans were familiar with the climate, less likely to be incapacitated by malaria or yellow fever, and believed to be more durable. In all likelihood the better ability of African labourers to endure or avoid illness, whether real or perceived, helped sustain the British presence on the West African coast.

Although limited, medical journals furnish the opportunity to evaluate treatment methods. An important question is whether European surgeons treated African and European sailors suffering from the same ailments in identical ways. If not, what was the basis for differentiated treatment? Because both African and European personnel placed on a sick list received medical treatment from the same personnel, it is possible to offer tentative answers. The entries for fever are often the most detailed accounts found in the medical journals and their frequency provides enough examples to venture conclusions. European physicians and surgeons were nearly unanimous in their belief that Europeans were more likely to contract fever and that, while an attack of fever for a European could be life threatening, fever had only a mild effect on Africans. Despite this common belief, Morris Pritchett of HMS *Wilberforce* treated Africans and Europeans with yellow fever identically. He believed the best treatment for the malady, regardless of race, was to apply a soothing lotion to cool the skin, to open the bowels and to blister the temples.[76] Replacement surgeon James Farnaley of HMSS *Trident* also treated European and African patients diagnosed identically so far as the records allow us to tell. His treatment consisted of quinine, wine and a nutritious diet employed alongside a purgative of calomel and jalap.[77] Pritchett's and Farnaley's chosen treatments buttress Curtin's assertion that, although bleeding as a cure for fever may have been on the decline by mid-century, other forms of heroic or aggressive medicine, especially purging, continued to be practised in conjunction with the relatively new use of quinine.[78]

Even if these surgeons applied similar methods to treat African and European fever patients, naval surgeons delayed sending African personnel diagnosed with fever to the hospital. The probable explanation for this lack of urgency is that naval surgeons generally agreed that amongst Kru, 'as well as all of the race', fever could only take a very mild form and, thus, there was no need for urgency.[79] This assertion appeared to be well founded. Numerous Europeans died from fever on the eight ships surveyed, but fever did not kill a single African. When HMSS *Trident* was in quarantine off Ascension in June 1859, Farnaley exercised a policy of immediately discharging into hospital for further care any European who showed 'signs of fever'.[80] This same policy was not extended to Kru sailors who contracted fever. They stayed on board and many were only sent to the hospital after spending upwards of two weeks on the sick list.[81] The only likely reason that Farnaley ordered the sick Kru to the hospital was that the whole crew needed to leave the ship as it was about to return to England. It is possible that Farnaley delayed in sending Kru who contracted fever to the hospital because he believed that Africans suffered only the mildest forms of fever. Farnaley, or the hospital authorities, may also have been concerned about hospital space or segregation and desired to reserve the limited space for Europeans. African personnel may also have resisted the idea of being sent to a hospital. It is likely that injured or sick Kru would not have relished the idea of being separated from their companions and sent to Ascension Island Hospital, for example.

Another reason why Farnaley may have delayed in sending Africans to the hospital was that as it was the responsibility of Kru to care for sick Europeans during the course of a fever epidemic he may have been unwilling to part with this help. In the case of HMSS *Trident*, once all sailors were removed to shore, it was Kru, and not European, personnel who were given the responsibility of caring for the sick in a makeshift hospital erected there.[82] Farnaley was not happy with their performance and stated: 'More intelligent nurses would certainly be desirable.'[83] He explained that the use of Kru was a necessity as 'the Europeans had a very great objection to going near the sick'.[84] Although in this period European Royal Navy sailors commonly served as emergency nurses, Farnaley accepted their fear of contagion as a reason for not carrying out this duty. The idea that Africans were resistant to fever was near universal and did much to direct the tasks assigned to Africans who served on board British vessels.

Farnaley's criticism of Kru nursing abilities was not universal. R. Henderson Brown, surgeon to HMS *Scout* in 1838, praised the Admiralty for allowing him to hire a Kru to serve as his medical assistant and was so satisfied with his assistant's ministrations that he called for the practice to be extended to every naval vessel serving in the West Africa Station. [85] This ship, with 113 Europeans and 29 Africans on board at that time, in fact experienced the lowest morbidity rate of the eight vessels (48.2% compared to the average for the eight of 68.3%). For the *Scout*, the principal causes of illness were stomach complaints, particularly diarrhoea and colic. Fever was not a concern. While the exact reasons for the lower morbidity on the *Scout* are unknown, surgeon R. Henderson Brown believed that his Kru nurse deserved some of the credit for the good health of the crew.

On occasion, borne either of necessity or convenience, African and European sailors would be discharged to a military – not a naval – hospital for further care. In the military hospital, European and African seaman were at times given quite different treatments for similar complaints. The treatments administered to John Ogden, a European marine from HMS *Growler* in 1845, and an unnamed Kru from HMS *Penelope* in 1845, suggest that this could be the case. Staff surgeon W. Johnston of the First West India Regiment gave John Ogden, identified as having remittent fever, a 'sample of calomel' followed three hours later by a solution of sulphate of magnesia in peppermint water, while his body was sponged with lime juice and water.[86] Instead of the soothing treatment of lime juice and water, the Kru, though also diagnosed by Johnston with remittent fever, was 'bled immediately on admission to the extent of twenty ounces' and, according to Johnston, due to the severity of this treatment, 'fainted'.[87] After three hours, a sample of calomel and jalop purge was administered. A blister was also applied to the Kru man's 'affected' side and a mercurial injection was administered to his groin.[88] Thus, two naval personnel, diagnosed and treated for presumably the same disease, by the same surgeon, at the same time and location, received substantially different treatments.

This apparently racialised approach to the treatment of African and European patients was not unique. Arthur Hayden, a liberated African and a new recruit to the Second West India Regiment, and Richard Months, a European of HMS *Waterworld*, were admitted to Dr Johnston's care in 1845, both suffering from fever. Hayden was bled whereas Months, instead of receiving the lancet, was 'lathered with lime juice and water to produce perspiration'.[89] What led Dr Johnston to treat these four patients, admitted within months of each other, in such significantly different ways? Since one of the European patients died and both Africans were able to resume their duties, it seems unlikely that the Africans received more extreme forms of treatment because their cases were considered the more life threatening. This differentiated treatment may have been the result of the perception of Africans as possessing stronger constitutions than Europeans, thus enabling harsher, more aggressive, treatments. This was not out of line with contemporary European medical beliefs, as those who appeared to be the most healthy were afforded 'stronger' doses and treatments than those who were classified as weak.[90]

The different treatments administered to European and African patients extended to other ailments. When European sailor William Wills injured his big toe after accidentally shooting himself in the foot in 1861, assistant surgeon Keenan of HMS *Ranger* washed the wound and wrapped the injured toe. According to Keenan this mode of treatment 'was peculiar [worthy of notice] only in its simplicity'.[91] Impressed by the ease of treatment, Keenan credited his patient's temperate habits and otherwise excellent health.[92] A Kru by the name of Jack Smart was also sent to Keenan to have his toe examined, for he was reported to be in the habit of applying a very tight ligature to his right little toe and had worn the toe raw. The frustrated surgeon stated that the patient had applied the ligature 'without being able to assign [to me] any reason for doing so'.[93] Instead of instructing Smart to stop applying the ligature and dressing the injured toe as he had done with Wills, Keenan believed the best remedy was amputation. After amputation the healing process was 'rather slow owing to the cartilaginous state of the ends of the flaps', which resulted in another surgery to promote 'further healing'.[94] It is noteworthy that after having so much success with wrapping a severely damaged toe, this surgeon ordered immediate amputation of Smart's digit. Keenan may have feared gangrene, but if so he did not state this in his medical journal.

There were some racialised differences in the treatment of Europeans and Africans, but not all variations were due to racial ideas of physiology or constitution. A language barrier sometimes made it difficult for surgeons to treat Africans. Hart Ginlette, surgeon to the Commodore's ship HMS *Arrogant*, complained in 1861 of that barrier.[95] Effective medicine requires an exchange of information and without this diagnosis can be difficult. In one instance diagnosis was so difficult that Ginlette listed three diseases as the possible source of one Kru's discomfort: pericarditis, pleuritis and bronchitis. Instead of treating a specific ailment, Ginlette acted more generally, 'due to the difficulty of communication with the patient the treatment was adopted to the most prominent symptoms'.[96] Given the lack of an accurate diagnosis, Ginlette relied upon blisters, brandy and the use of turpentine enemas, but none of these treatments arrested the progress of the disease.[97] The inability of Ginlette to reach a diagnosis may have contributed to the death of this Kru after ten days of treatment. Ginlette found treating this individual to be frustrating and dismissed Africans as unintelligent, their approach to medicine backward.

Ginlette's attitude is evident in the following case when he attempted to cure a Kru of guinea worm. One John Nimrod was found to be suffering from a small swelling above the left ankle. When opened with a lancet, the surgeon saw no pus but instead the head of a small white worm which he said caused much excitement for the Kru who joyfully exclaimed: 'I got him last year at Accra'. The surgeon then took a piece of cocoa nut fibre, wrapped it around the worm and began to draw the worm out slowly.[98] Removing a worm is a delicate process that could take many days; it is important not to break the worm as it would only continue to grow inside. Although the surgeon had instructed Nimrod not to 'meddle with the worm', the patient ignored this advice and applied 'a whole host of Kroo remedies' including onions and palm oil to the wound.[99] Eventually when almost eighteen inches of the worm had been withdrawn, the patient, while employing his own remedies, accidentally broke the worm, forcing the surgeon to start the tedious process afresh. This second attempt was successful and after a total of thirty days the patient was deemed completely recovered.[100] This episode reveals that Kru at times resisted or at least attempted to complement European treatment on board ship. Kru may have had more faith in traditional healing methods than the Westernised medicine prescribed by European surgeons. The nature of the documentation makes it difficult to measure the scope of resistance to, or modification of, European medicine, but, if resistance did occur, it may have manifested itself in not reporting or trying to hide ailments from naval surgeons. Avoidance could be one reason for the lower morbidity rates recorded for hired Africans. Of course, the Royal Navy also possessed a history of its European personnel attempting to avoid painful, unpleasant, or embarrassing medical treatments. For this workforce, medical care was both a right and a requirement. Medical officers attempted to encompass Africans within the ship's medical system, although the surviving records are not sufficiently rich to touch upon the topics of sanitary hygiene, sick diets and the like. Similarly, both self-help and group cooperative help rarely appear in the documentation for either Africans or Europeans. Resistance to treatment was not uniquely African, but avoidance may have been more achievable.

Not all European surgeons had difficulty in treating Kru, nor were they always opposed to the application of traditional African forms of healing. In 1849, when a Kru accidentally got jammed between the capstan's 'bars and bits', the surgeon to HMS *Albatross* ordered that the frightened man needed rest and should be left undisturbed. Instead of obeying the surgeon's orders, a fellow Kru was observed 'jumping on the man's hurt back' and 'kneading him with his feet as if he were on the steps of a treadmill'.[101] The next day the injured Kru declared himself better and ready to return to his duties. When the surgeon was told that the Kru directly disobeyed his orders in employing 'kroo remedies', he was astounded that such treatment worked and was pleased that, despite not adhering to his mode of treatment, his patient had recovered.[102] In the Royal Navy, failure to follow prescribed courses of treatment often led to punishment of European sailors. This episode suggests that a degree of latitude not granted to European personnel may have been granted to injured or sick Africans. Dr Lawson, a military surgeon, was so impressed with the efficacy of traditional healing methods that in cases of remittent fever, rather than utilising cold water to cool the patient, as many European surgeons and physicians prescribed, he relied upon the native cures of warm baths to produce perspiration.[103] Dr Johnston also favoured this mode of treatment and even applied it to European fever patients but (oddly) continued to bleed his African patients.[104] Whether Johnston was aware of this contradiction is unknown.

Conclusion

At times, Europeans and Africans received similar treatment, but important differences existed. Hired Africans were almost never discharged to a hospital for further care and when suffering from fever their cases were rarely considered urgent. The limited evidence suggests that Africans may have preferred their own treatments and at times resisted European medicine. Some surgeons did not racialise their treatment and treated Africans and Europeans suffering from the same ailment in identical ways, but other surgeons, such as Dr Johnston, gave Africans harsher and more extreme forms of treatment. The lack of a coherent doctrine of racialised medicine left naval surgeons to decide for themselves the validity of a racialised approach to health and healing. This seems to support wider studies of Victorian racism which determined that racialism was powerful but rather varied.[105] The application of racial thinking was never constant, but heavily influenced by situation, place and time.

African labour helped sustain British slave-trade suppression in the West Africa Station. Africans had a significantly lower mortality rate and were far less likely to be incapacitated by disease. One of the reasons for this difference was the response to fevers, which had relatively little effect on African personnel while causing one-third of the European morbidity and upwards of 90% of European deaths. While, on average, three out of four Europeans appeared on the sick list, Africans were more likely to remain healthy and able to attend to their duties. Once sick, however, Africans and Europeans appear to have had similar health experiences in terms of the number of days spent on the sick list and had a comparable risk of being placed on the sick list again. Where African employees differed, and why they were so valuable, was their ability to avoid sickness in the first place.

Africans' ability to remain active and at their posts made them valuable employees and crucial to sustaining British presence along the West African coast. For the eight ships under my analysis it is possible to calculate the number of Europeans that would have been needed and the subsequent mortality rate if the British had been unable or unwilling to hire Africans as employees. Assuming that Europeans hired to serve in place of Africans would have sustained the same morbidity rates as other Europeans, the navy would have required an additional 650 European sailors to replace the 276 Africans it hired. The cost of hiring these additional employees would have been heavy, especially if every ship in the West Africa Squadron was manned only by Europeans. Without Africans, not only would the financial cost have been much higher, so too would have been the loss of European lives. Assuming these additional Europeans hired for service on the eight ships under study suffered the same mortality rates as other Europeans, an additional thirty-six European sailors would have lost their lives. Clearly, the navy benefited from its reliance on local African labour which proved crucial in British efforts to stop the illegal transportation of slaves. The story of suppression is not solely made up of European efforts, but rather Africans and Europeans working on the same ships, risking their lives in what was often dangerous and difficult work.

Notes

1 For example, *Parliamentary Papers* (henceforth *PP*), 'Select Committee on West Coast of Africa, Report', 1842 (551-II), appendix, pp. 423–30; Alexander Bryson, *Report on the Climate and Principal Diseases of the African Station* (London: William Clowes, 1847); Morris Pritchett, *Some Account of the African Remittent Fever Which Occurred on Board Her Majesty's Steam-Ship Wilberforce in the River Niger and Whilst Engaged on the Western Coast of Africa: Comprising an Inquiry into the Causes of Disease in Tropical Climates* (London: John Churchill, 1843).
2 For example, William Law Mathieson, *Great Britain and the Slave Trade, 1839–1865*

(London: Longmans, 1929), p. 91; W. E. F. Ward, *The Royal Navy and the Slavers: The Suppression of the Atlantic Slave Trade* (London: Allen & Unwin, 1969), p. 99.

3 To avoid confusion, I have placed the Admiralty term 'African' in quotation marks throughout this chapter to distinguish it, as a specific nineteenth-century categorisation, from my present-day usage of the term.

4 The National Archives, Kew (hereafter TNA), ADM 101/81/2: Medical Journal of HMS *Aetna*, 4 October 1837 to 13 November 1838; TNA, ADM 101/130: Medical Journal of HMS *Arrogant*, 30 August 1860 to 31 August 1861, TNA, ADM 101/88/3: Medical Journal of HMS *Atholl*, 2 September 1831 to 21 February 1832, TNA, ADM 101/132: C. Keenan, Medical Journal of HMS *Ranger*, 1 January 1861 to 31 December 1861; TNA, ADM 101/116/4: Medical Journal of HMS *Rapid*, 2 January 1846 to 2 January 1847; TNA, ADM 101/120/1: Medical Journal of the HMS *Scout*, 25 November 1837 to 12 June 1838; TNA, ADM 101/129: Medical Journal of HMSS *Trident*, 28 June 1858 to 17 July 1859; TNA, ADM 101/127/3: Medical Journal of HMS *Wilberforce*, 14 November 1840 to 14 September 1842. All figures in this chapter (5.1 to 5.8) have been derived from these data sources.

5 G. R. Collier and Charles MacCarthy, *West African Sketches: Compiled from the Reports of Sir G. R. Collier, Sir Charles MacCarthy and Other Official Sources* (London: Seeley and Son, 1824), p. 85.

6 Diana Frost, 'Diasporan West African Communities: The Kru in Freetown and Liverpool', *Review of African Political Economy* 29 (2002), 285–300, at pp. 288–9.

7 George E. Brooks, Jr, *The Kru Mariner in the Nineteenth Century* (Bloomington, IN: Indiana University Press, 1971), p. 9.

8 Brooks, *The Kru Mariner*, pp. 9–10.

9 *PP*, 'West Coast of Africa', 1842 (551) (551-II), p. 239.

10 Brooks, *The Kru Mariner*, p. 14; TNA, ADM 101/132: C. Keenan, Medical Journal of HMS *Ranger*.

11 TNA, ADM 38/5209: Ship's Musters of the HMSS *Trident*, July 1858 to March 1859.

12 Apart from the sailors quarantined from the HMSS *Trident* at Ascension Hospital in June 1859, only 3% of all sick Europeans and 1.4% of hired Africans were discharged to a hospital for further care.

13 TNA, ADM 101/130, Medical Journal of HMS *Arrogant*.

14 Bryson, *Diseases of the African Station*, p. 177.

15 Bryson, *Diseases of the African Station*, p. 166.

16 Bryson, *Diseases of the African Station*, p. 177.

17 Bryson, *Diseases of the African Station*, p. 177.

18 Bryson, *Diseases of the African Station*, p. 177.

19 Calculated from the sources identified in Figure 5.1. Mortality per thousand is calculated by taking the number of deceased members of a ship's crew, dividing this number by the total number of men, and then multiplying by a thousand. Average mortality is calculated in the same way except those deceased are divided by the total mean force for a given period.

20 Bryson, *Diseases of the African Station*, p. 177.

21 Philip D. Curtin, 'White Man's Grave: Image and Reality, 1780–1850', *Journal of British Studies* 1 (1961), 94–110, at pp. 106–110.

22 Philip D. Curtin, 'The End of the "White Man's Grave"? Nineteenth-Century Mortality in West Africa', *Journal of Interdisciplinary History* 21 (1990), 63–88, at p. 74.

23 Philip D. Curtin, *Death by Migration* (Cambridge: Cambridge University Press, 1989), pp. 7–8, table 1.1.

24 Calculated from TNA, ADM 101/88/3: Medical Journal of HMS *Atholl*; TNA, ADM 101/81/2: Medical Journal of HMS *Aetna*; TNA, ADM 101/120/1: Medical Journal of the HMS *Scout*.

25 See note 4.

26 Pericarditis is inflammation of the membrane that surrounds the heart. This membrane, known as the pericardium, is responsible for protecting the heart and inflammation of this thin layer of tissue can cause major complications including

heart attack. Apoplexy was used to describe uncontrolled bleeding of the internal organs including the brain. It was often also used as a synonym for a stroke.

27 Philip D. Curtin, 'African Health at Home and Abroad', *Social Science History* 10 (1986), 369–98; Curtin, 'The End of the "White Man's Grave"', p. 65. Also calculated from sources listed in Figure 5.1.
28 Curtin, 'African Health at Home and Abroad', pp. 371–2.
29 Curtin, 'The End of the "White Man's Grave"', p. 74.
30 Curtin, 'African Health at Home and Abroad', p. 373.
31 Curtin, 'The End of the "White Man's Grave"', p. 74.
32 *PP* 1857–58, vol. LXI and 1861, vol. LXIV extracted from Lloyd, *The Navy and the Slave Trade*, p. 289.
33 Bryson, *Diseases of the African Station*, p. 177.
34 Curtin, 'The End of the "White Man's Grave"', p. 72.
35 Curtin, 'The End of the "White Man's Grave"', p. 74.
36 C. Keenan, TNA, ADM 101/132: Medical Journal of HMS *Ranger*.
37 Validated in the late nineteenth century, the germ theory, known alternatively as the pathogenic theory of medicine, proposes that microorganisms are the cause of many diseases. For a straightforward analysis of the germ theory and the process of its discovery, see John Waller, *The Discovery of the Germ* (London: Icon Books, 2002). For the perception and application of germ theory in the nineteenth century, W. F. Bynum, *Science and the Practice of Medicine in the Nineteenth Century* (Cambridge: Cambridge University Press, 1994). For the discovery of the vector in the transmission of yellow fever, Francois Delaporte, *The History of Yellow Fever: An Essay on the Birth of Tropical Medicine* (Cambridge, MA: MIT Press, 1991). For malaria, Gordon Harrison, *Mosquitoes, Malaria, and Man: A Story of the Hostilities since 1880* (New York: Dutton, 1978).
38 Curtin, 'The End of the "White Man's Grave"', p. 74.
39 See note 4.
40 Physical trauma is defined as any fracture, contusion, wound or broken bone that required medical assistance.
41 TNA, ADM 101/130: Medical Journal of HMS *Arrogant*.
42 TNA, ADM 101/127/3: Medical Journal of HMS *Arrogant*; Medical Journal of the HMS *Wilberforce*.
43 TNA, ADM 101/127/3: Medical Journal of HMS *Wilberforce*.
44 See note 4.
45 Curtin, *Death by Migration*, pp. 7–8; Bryson, *Diseases of the African Station*, p. 177.
46 Curtin, 'The End of the "White Man's Grave"', p. 70.
47 Christopher Fyfe, *A History of Sierra Leone* (London: Oxford University Press, 1962), p. 118.
48 TNA, ADM 101/120/1: Medical Journal of the HMS *Scout*.
49 See note 4.
50 For the role of the mixed commissions, see Leslie Bethell, 'The Mixed Commissions for the Suppression of the Transatlantic Slave Trade in the Nineteenth Century', *The Journal of African History* 7 (1966), 79–93.
51 Charles Turner, Governor of Sierra Leone, expressed the need to employ liberated Africans, for according to him they had too long 'been supported in idleness by the government'. In this letter to Earl Bathurst he congratulates himself on reducing the number of liberated Africans being supported by the government by one half. TNA, CO 267/71 fo.24: Charles Turner to Henry Bathurst, Earl Bathurst, Sierra Leone, 25 January 1826.
52 Although no evidence of this practice exists for the navy, army surgeons complained that they were being sent ill Africans who had recently been liberated from the hold of a slaver. For examples of these complaints, see the quarterly and yearly reports for the years 1844–50 contained in TNA, WO 334/168. According to Dixon Denham the military was so anxious to recruit liberated Africans that immediately upon being 'liberated' the military would give them a quick health inspection and try to get them to sign up for military duty without the 'poor creatures' understanding

what they were agreeing to. When Denham became governor in May 1828 he put an end to this policy. TNA, CO 267/94: Dixon Denham to William Huskisson, Sierra Leone, 14 May 1828.

53 TNA, ADM 101/87/6: Thomas Brownrigg, Ascension Island Hospital, Medical Journal, 1 October 1837 to 19 January 1839.

54 TNA, ADM 101/81/2: Medical Journal of HMS *Aetna*.

55 TNA, ADM 101/127/3: Medical Journal of the HMS *Wilberforce*.

56 Pritchett, *Some Account of African Fever*, p.2.

57 Pritchett, *Some Account of African Fever*, p. 2.

58 TNA, ADM 101/129: James Farnaley, Medical Journal of HMSS *Trident*.

59 TNA, ADM 101/129: James Farnaley, Medical Journal of HMSS *Trident*.

60 All calculations involving the number of days spent on the sick exclude the data from HMSS *Trident* during its time in quarantine from 28 June to 25 July. The reason for this is that European fever patients were likely only to spend a day on the sick list before being transferred to the hospital and their inclusion would severely skew results for calculations involving the total days spent on the sick list.

61 Robert Clarke, *Sierra Leone. A Description of the Manners and Customs of the Liberated Africans: With Observations upon the Natural History of the Colony and a Notice of the Native Tribes* (London: James Ridgway, 1846), p. 86; James Lind, *An Essay on Diseases Incidental to Europeans in Hot Climates: With the Method of Preventing their Fatal Consequences* (London: T. Becket and P. A. de Hondt, 1768), pp. 224–5.

62 See note 4.

63 Although most often reserved for plague, Bubo was used to describe a variety of other ailments including gonorrhoea, tuberculosis and syphilis.

64 TNA, ADM 101/120/1: Medical Journal of HMS *Scout*.

65 TNA, ADM 101/129: Medical Journal of HMSS *Trident*.

66 Two of these cases occurred upon the HMS *Arrogant* in 1861 and the final case happened on HMS *Atholl* 1831.

67 TNA, ADM 101/127/3: Medical Journal of the HMS *Wilberforce*.

68 TNA, ADM 101/130: Medical Journal of HMS *Arrogant*.

69 TNA, ADM 101/130: Hart Ginlette, Medical Journal of HMS *Arrogant*.

70 TNA, ADM 101/130: Hart Ginlette, Medical Journal of HMS *Arrogant*.

71 TNA, ADM 101/130: Medical Journal of HMS *Arrogant*; N.A., ADM 101/132: Medical Journal of HMS *Ranger*.

72 TNA, ADM 101/130: Medical Journal of HMS *Arrogant*; TNA, ADM 101/127/3: Medical Journal of the HMS *Wilberforce*; TNA, ADM 101/127/3: Medical Journal of the HMS *Wilberforce*.

73 Pritchett, *Some Account of African Remittent Fever*, 2.

74 In the late eighteenth and early nineteenth century prominent naval surgeons turned their attention to both the dangers and therapeutic properties of different forms of alcohol. See for example, Sir Gilbert Blane, 'Observations on the Diseases of Seaman', in *The Health of Seamen: Selections from the Works of Dr. James Lind, Sir Gilbert Blane and Dr. Thomas Trotter*, ed. Christopher Lloyd (London: Navy Records Society, 1965), pp. 136–74; Thomas Trotter, *An Essay, Medical, Philosophical, and Chemical, on Drunkenness, and Its Effect on the Human Body*, 2nd edn (London: Longman, 1804).

75 Kenneth Kiple, *The Caribbean Slave: A Biological History* (Cambridge: Cambridge University Press, 1984), pp. 23–8.

76 TNA, ADM 101/127/3: Medical Journal of the HMS *Wilberforce*.

77 TNA, ADM 101/129: Medical Journal of HMSS *Trident*.

78 Curtin, 'The End of the "White Man's Grave"', p. 108.

79 TNA, ADM 101/129: James Farnaley, Medical Journal of HMSS *Trident*.

80 TNA, ADM 101/129: James Farnaley, Medical Journal of HMSS *Trident*.

81 TNA, ADM 101/129: Medical Journal of HMSS *Trident*.

82 TNA, ADM 101/129: James Farnaley, Medical Journal of HMSS *Trident*.

83 TNA, ADM 101/129: James Farnaley, Medical Journal of HMSS *Trident*.

84 TNA, ADM 101/129: James Farnaley, Medical Journal of HMSS *Trident*.
85 TNA, ADM 101/120/1: R. Henderson Brown, Medical Journal of HMS *Scout*.
86 TNA, WO 334/168: W. Johnston, Quarterly Summary Report on Disease, West Coast of Africa, 1 July to 30 September 1844, p. 44.
87 TNA, WO 334/168: W. Johnston, Quarterly Summary, 1 July to 30 September 1844, p.54.
88 TNA, WO 334/168: W. Johnston, Quarterly Summary, 1 July to 30 September 1844, pp. 54–55.
89 TNA, WO 334/168: W. Johnston, Quarterly Summary, 1 July to 30 September 1844, pp. 58–61.
90 Wendy Churchill, 'Female Complaints: The Medical Diagnosis and Treatment of British Women, 1590–1740' (PhD dissertation, McMaster University, 2005), p. 148.
91 TNA, ADM 101/132: C. Keenan, Medical Journal of HMS *Ranger*.
92 TNA, ADM 101/132: C. Keenan, Medical Journal of HMS *Ranger*.
93 TNA, ADM 101/132: C. Keenan, Medical Journal of HMS *Ranger*.
94 TNA, ADM 101/132: C. Keenan, Medical Journal of HMS *Ranger*.
95 TNA, ADM 101/130: Hart Ginlette, Medical Journal of HMS *Arrogant*.
96 TNA, ADM 101/130: Hart Ginlette, Medical Journal of HMS *Arrogant*.
97 TNA, ADM 101/130: Hart Ginlette, Medical Journal of HMS *Arrogant*.
98 TNA, ADM 101/130: Hart Ginlette, Medical Journal of HMS *Arrogant*.
99 TNA, ADM 101/130: Hart Ginlette, Medical Journal of HMS *Arrogant*.
100 TNA, ADM 101/130: Hart Ginlette, Medical Journal of HMS *Arrogant*.
101 TNA, ADM 101/82/1: Medical Journal of HMS *Albatross*, 31 December 1848 to 1 January 1850.
102 TNA, ADM 101/82/1: Medical Journal of HMS *Albatross*.
103 TNA, WO 334 /168: Dr Lawson, Annual Report on the Diseases which have Prevailed among the Troops at Sierra Leone, 1 April 1847 to 31 March 1848, 203.
104 TNA, WO 334/168: W. Johnston, Quarterly Summary, 1 July to 30 September 1844, pp. 58–61.
105 Peter Fryer, *Black People in the British Empire: An Introduction* (London: Pluto Press, 1988), pp. 66–8.

PART III

Representations

CHAPTER SIX

Slave-trade suppression and the culture of anti-slavery in nineteenth-century Britain

Robert Burroughs

Introduction

With the culmination of the West Indian emancipation movement in 1838, politicians and anti-slavery leaders turned their attention increasingly to slave-trade suppression.[1] Public interest in, if not support for, the cause was roused, as from the late 1830s until the early 1850s – especially in the 1840s when its efficacy became the subject of political debate – the Africa Squadron was the topic of countless newspaper and periodical articles and tens of pamphlets.[2] It further attracted description and commentary, often of an expansive and colourful character, in travelogues and memoirs and a handful of fictional texts. The authors working in these different literary forms varied greatly in terms of their social background, political views, the extent of their technical knowledge and their rationale for writing about the matter. Nor was the focus of their discussion uniform: while some first-hand officers of wide-ranging experience described its many elements, the majority of writings on naval suppression were slanted toward one geographical region of activity, or particular aspects of the work and its outcomes, according to authors' expertise or readers' interest or both. A number of accounts by missionaries resident in Sierra Leone centre upon the Liberated Africans Department at Freetown, for example, whereas officers involved in signing anti-slave-trade treaties with local traders and potentates catered for the public interest in narratives of travel in West Africa. Reports by naval surgeons are unsurprisingly dominated by descriptions of the climatic conditions in the so-called 'White Man's Grave' of West Africa, and the impact of these upon crews.[3]

Of all these subjects and locales, it was the seaborne actions that figured most prominently in creating a picture of naval suppression in in the mind's eye of the reading public. Even though many testified that offshore patrolling of the West African coast was mostly tedious and unrewarding work, authors of published eyewitness accounts joined writers of fictional narratives in focusing upon episodes of danger and excitement at sea likely to arouse their readers' curiosity and sympathy: chases of and battles with slave ships; shipboard interactions with slave traders and their captives; perilous cruises to shore in dilapidated prize vessels; outbreaks of disease and the death of British sailors. It might seem natural that reports of this work at the coal-face of Britain's anti-slave-trade policy should take centre-stage in its cultural dissemination. Regency Britain witnessed a rise in esteem for the gentleman-officer of the navy – above all, Nelson, who was enshrined, following his death, as the embodiment of imperial duty and sacrifice[4] – which would seem to have guaranteed admiration for patrollers of the slave trade. But when it is considered that eminent lords of the Admiralty and naval officers, not least Nelson, had until 1807 protected the British slave trade in line with the navy's remit to defend national mercantile interests, it becomes apparent that the construction of positive imagery of naval suppression was part of a process of re-identification of Britain as a nation opposed to the slave trade and, later, slavery in the Americas. The ease of the changeover from the leading profiteers of the human traffic to its pre-eminent opponents cannot be assumed.

In this chapter I examine this transition in national self-perception, and demonstrate that as well as inspiring much patriotic and religious fanfare, naval suppression also was a thorny and divisive topic. In both fictional and non-fictional written representations of the recapture of enslaved Africans at sea, critics of the campaign highlighted what they saw as the failings of Britain's abolitionist policies, and cast doubt upon the moralistic and spiritual arguments which are encoded in writings by the supporters of naval suppression. The Royal Navy's mission to eliminate the Atlantic slave trade helped to keep alive a culture of anti-slavery in nineteenth-century Britain, but its place in the hearts and minds of the people that created that culture was never secure. The rise of racial sciences is one notable cause and symptom of the decline in support for the campaign towards the middle of the century. The following two sections of this chapter analyse in turn a range of celebratory and critical representations of the Africa Squadron, connecting these to contemporary debates on nation and empire, class, gender and race. To begin, I examine celebratory images of the patrols within the religious and moralistic frameworks of writing about slavery and travel at sea.

Writing redemption

To understand how representations of naval suppression suggested the moral and spiritual redemption of the nation, it is profitable to read them in the broader discursive context of the sea voyage. As with their Romantic-era forebears, Victorian writers took great interest in tales of maritime peril and mishap. Narratives of hazardous travel at sea provided more than simple entertainment in the suffering of others; they also projected, and sometimes challenged, social and political identities. For people still persuaded by religious explanations of chance and accident, the perilous sea voyage stood metaphorically for the providential vulnerability of all human life, in which faith in God was essential. Disasters were taken as evidence of supernatural punishment, whereas epic tales of survival suggested divine intervention on behalf of the endangered seafarer. Narratives of seaborne danger assumed social and political significance because the religion, or religious fervour, nationality, gender, social rank and racial identities of mariners were reckoned with to account for their endurance or destruction. Frequently tales of shipwreck operated to consolidate the existing order by attributing the hand of God to the survival of those in positions of authority on ships. At other times, their typically small cast of socially diverse individuals battling against the elements enabled writers of shipwreck narratives to explore areas of tension and ambiguity in social relations.[5]

Representations of the Middle Passage frequently employ such metaphoric interpretations of disaster and survival at sea, and the spiritual autobiographies of John Newton (1725–1807) epitomise them. Newton was a slave-ship sailor and then captain who in later life became an evangelical crusader and public critic of the slave trade. In his youth he suffered impressment by the Royal Navy, and was himself enslaved while seeking refuge from what he vaguely termed his own 'passions and follies' on West Africa's Windward coast. But the religious awakening that led him eventually to condemn the slave trade began, according to Newton's own testimonies, when, in 1748, his ship was caught in a violent storm on the home leg of a slaving voyage. He attributed his survival to 'the good providence of God [which] ... delivered me from those scenes of wickedness and woe'.[6] Having been spared death, he described himself as conscience-bound to expose the evils of transatlantic slavery (although he continued to trade in slaves for a few years after the storm).

'Perhaps what I have said of myself may be applicable to the nation at large', wrote Newton.[7] His testimonies would indeed be incorporated into abolition discourses that conceived of the slave trade as a national sin.[8] The divinely ordained wrecking of the slave trader figured in abolitionist texts such as William Cowper's 'The Negro's Complaint' (1788) and James Montgomery's 'The Voyage of the Blind' (1824), as well as in J. W. M. Turner's famous *Slavers throwing overboard the Dead and Dying – Typhon [sic] coming on* (1840). As Newton put it, 'It is Righteousness that exalteth a nation; and Wickedness is the present reproach'.[9] The path away from wickedness was lit by the anti-slavery torch, and Marcus Wood observes in his study of visual representations of slavery that depictions of the anti-slave-trade ships' recapture and apparent emancipation of slaves bound for the Americas were readily incorporated into providential interpretations of Britain's abolitionist policies as evidence of the nation's rediscovered righteousness and its fitness for imperial supremacy. Such imagery fed into 'the implementation of an abolition myth' that pardoned Britons for their past participation in the slave trade by pointing to the self-sacrificing benevolence and moral superiority of their efforts against it.[10] Having been wrecked against the rocks of the slave trade, in other words, many Britons saw their nation's celestially decreed rescue in the work of the Africa Squadron. I will proceed to identify how this belief shaped representations of enslaved Africans, naval sailors and officers, before complicating the picture by examining writings that interpret the death of slaves and naval personnel at sea as evidence of the absence of divine favour for naval elimination of the slave trade.

One narrative that exemplifies what Wood sees as the propensity of British abolitionist discourse to spin self-affirming stories out of the miseries of Atlantic slavery is Mary Sherwood's *Dazee; or, the Recaptured Slave* (1821). A writer of didactic Christian fiction, Sherwood's first-hand experience of Africa was limited to an excursion at Cape Colony in 1816 during a stopover on a journey to England from India, where she lived with her soldier husband for eleven years.[11] Apparently the earliest fictionalisation of slave-trade suppression, *Dazee* was published at a time when detailed information about the Africa Squadron was confined to the little-known *Sierra Leone Gazette* and the annual reports of the African Institution. These contextual details are important in understanding *Dazee*. A patrician body with strong ties to government that acted 'almost a de facto slave-trade department' until an official Slave Trade Department was established in 1819, the African Institution abandoned the grass-roots campaigning strategies that were used effectively by the anti-slavery bodies in favour of 'gentlemanly politics' at the European Congresses held between 1814 and 1820.[12] Under the supervision of the African Institution, then the Slave Trade Department, naval suppression, above all other anti-slavery causes, was institutionalised and bureaucratised, absorbed into the 'official mind' of the nation, and thus distanced from public support and understanding.[13]

Dazee's uncomplicated plot spanning the enslavement, recapture and Christianisation of an African youth is said to derive from a Sierra Leone Co. report of 1794, which features a real case of family reunion similar to that of Dazee and his mother.[14] As such, it reflects the reading public's insulation, in the 1810s and 1820s, from the difficulties faced by naval crews in rescuing and 'repatriating' enslaved Africans. The passage describing the rescue of Dazee and his fellow captives is overloaded with religious imperatives as the liberator calls down into the slave hold, without fear of his auditors' inter-linguistic or inter-cultural incomprehension: 'My brethren, thank God, your deliverance is effected, your enemies and secured, and you shall now be made happy.'[15] Dazee's later reunion with his mother – also enslaved and redeemed at sea – is similarly dominated by the need to convert her from the 'abominations and absurdities of heathenism'.[16] Srinivas Aravamudan claims that 'Sherwood conflates deliverance from slavery with spiritual rebirth into Christ. The theme of "Christian son saving superstitious mother" expresses clearly ideological motives of "civilising" the old Africa according to newer evangelical imperatives.'[17] *Dazee* imparts the religious belief 'that spiritual salvation was the paramount concern of all humans, that worldly affairs were inconsequential', in the words of Moira Ferguson.[18] Importantly, whereas Newton claimed that his spiritual shipwrecking had enabled his direct communion with God, in *Dazee* the British naval rescuer stands in as the agent or representative of divine intervention. The hierarchical positioning of humankind beneath God is stratified along lines of race.

Christian redemption is the keynote in numerous missionary reports on naval suppression, including Elizabeth Melville's, which asserts:

> A feeling of patriotic pride always mingles with my pity on seeing a slaver brought in, to think that – thanks to Britain above all other kingdoms on the face of the globe – how soon these, our so unjustifiably oppressed fellow-mortals, will be blessed with a happier freedom than they ever knew in their heathen homes of the far interior.[19]

For Melville, naval suppression enabled nationalistic pride as it affirmed her belief in the heathenism of the peoples of West Africa. Christianised liberated Africans similarly conceived of their rescue as a spiritual release from heathenism. The Yoruba Methodist missionary Joseph Wright's short narrative begins with the following extraordinary sentence:

> I was born a heathen in a heathen land, and was trained up in my youth to the fashion and customs of that heathenish Country, but the Lord,

who would not have me to live to be old in that unhappy Country, brought among us war and confusion as the wages of our sins.[20]

Writings by and about the Yoruba Samuel Ajayi Crowther likewise re-inscribe pre-Christian life with Christian convictions. In a similar manner to Wright, Crowther recalls his enslavement as painful, yet 'blessed', for 'Providence had marked out for me to set out on my journey from the land of heathenism, superstition, and vices to a place where His Gospel is preached'.[21] Recent studies have emphasised the agency of Yoruba-speaking peoples such as the Egba, Ijesha and Awori who forged a collective 'Yoruba' identity for themselves amid the cultural diversity of Sierra Leone, partly by embracing Christianity.[22] At the time of publication, however, few readers in Britain were attuned to that diversity. Because his early life bore superficial similarities to that of the fictional Dazee – both, for example, were reunited with mothers who were yet to embrace Christianity following their rescue from the Atlantic crossing and repatriation to Sierra Leone – and despite his giving eloquent testimony as to the fear and confusion of the Atlantic crossing even after it had been reversed by naval intervention, Crowther and his biographers were able to draw clear Christian symbolism from his narrative of redemption, understanding it in straightforward terms as a journey from darkness into light – a case of 'good out of evil'.[23]

The flipside of the narrative of the liberated African's conversion to Christianity was its moralising effects upon naval rescuers. Even at the height of the anti-slavery movement in Britain, some commentators believed that common sailors on the anti-slave-trade patrols were not motivated by humanitarian concerns but monetary rewards, or even a simple love of adventure.[24] Perceiving conflict between financial gain and spiritual health, some questioned whether pecuniary incentives should be necessary in motivating sailors to rescue slaves.[25] The positive impact upon sailors of service in the Africa Squadron was nonetheless claimed in popular fictions of the nineteenth century. Conversion generally took the secular form of characters' maturation into readiness for leadership and service in the armed forces. In J. T. Haines's popular Napoleonic 'tar drama' *My Poll and My Partner Joe* (first performed 1835), for instance, service aboard a Man-of-War during its chase and capture of a slave ship, and contact with black slaves, reconciles a press-ganged sailor, Harry Hallyard, to his duty to king and country. In its first and second acts, until Hallyard rescues the slaves Zinga and Zanga, *My Poll and My Partner Joe* touches provocatively upon the comparison of the British labourer to the African slave, which, as Catherine Gallagher and others have shown, pervades in much writing by and about the working classes in the early Victorian period, and which prompted some of the more critical representations of naval suppression studied in the following section of this chapter.[26] Upon being press-ganged, Hallyard declares: 'What! force a man from his happy home, to defend a country whose laws deprive him of his liberty? But I must submit; yet … I shall strike for the hearts I leave weeping for my absence, without one thought of the green hills or the flowing rivers of a country that treats me as a slave!'[27] Yet Hallyard is led to reconsider his self-identification as 'a slave' upon his encounter with the 'real' victims of Atlantic slavery. At this point he identifies 'the British flag' as the insignia of freedom, telling the slaves: 'Dance, you black angels, no more captivity, the British flag flies over your head, and the very rustling of its folds knocks every fetter from the limbs of the poor slave.'[28] In awakening Hallyard to his imperial duty, and placing the British sailor in a position of kindly but clearly demar-cated authority over Africans, *My Poll and My Partner Joe* prefigures the several boys' own adventures about naval suppression published in the three decades or so following the disintegration of the Atlantic slave trade in the 1860s.[29]

The credentials of the gentleman-officer too were established in fictions of slave-trade suppression. In Charlotte M. Yonge's family saga *The Daisy Chain* (1856), one of the main romantic heroes is an officer of the anti-slave-trade squadron, Lieutenant Alan Ernestcliffe. The reader is first introduced to Ernestcliffe from the perspective of his 10-year-old brother, Hector, during the latter's interview with the physician who helps the officer recover from tropical fever. When Dr May asks Hector if his brother served in the navy, the boy volunteers the following profile:

> 'Lieutenant Ernestcliffe. He got his promotion last week. My father was in the battle of Trafalgar; and Alan has been three years in the West Indies, and then he was in the Mediterranean, and now on the coast of Africa, in the *Atlantis*. You must have heard about him, for it was in the newspaper, how, when he was mate, he had command of the *Santa Isabel*, the slaver they captured.'
>
> The boy would have gone on for ever, if Dr. May had not recalled him to his brother's present condition.[30]

The superfluous mention of Trafalgar connects its heroes to those in West Africa, as if a mantle has been passed from father to eldest son. The young Ernestcliffe's inability to conceal his pride at his brother's efforts is testimony to the emotive part that naval suppression could play in shaping the identities of apparently distant men, women and children – in this case filling an orphaned child with pride in his elder sibling and surrogate father. Pride indeed momentarily transports Hector from his present problems as he forgets his brother's illness. And while Dr May recalls the boy to the here and now by interrupting him, *The Daisy Chain* nonetheless fills in the picture of Alan Ernestcliffe's heroics, as the doctor subsequently learns from 'other sources' of his patient's distinguished conduct:

> in encounters with slave ships, and in command of a prize that he had had to conduct to Sierra Leone, [during which] he had shown great coolness and seamanship, in several perilous conjunctures, such as a sudden storm, and an encounter with another slaver, when his Portuguese prisoners became mutinous, and nothing but his steadiness and intrepidity had saved the lives of himself and his few English compatriots. He was, in fact, as Dr. May reported, pretty much of a hero. He had not, at that time, felt the effects of the climate but, owing to sickness and death among other officers, he had suffered much fatigue ... Immediately on his return, had followed his examination, and though he had passed with great credit, and it had been at once followed by well-earned promotion, his nervous excitable frame had been overtasked, and the consequence was a long and severe illness.[31]

As with the Hector's report to the doctor, the detail of Yonge's account of Lt Ernestcliffe's heroics presumes familiarity with the subject among her audience. Within the parameters of Yonge's domestic novel, service in the Africa Station serves as a short-hand guide to a character's moral trustworthiness.

All of the narratives discussed in this section conceived of the contact zone where slaves met their rescuers as one of powerful moral transformation. Crowther vividly recalls the fear and confusion which attended his first meeting with a naval party (he feared they were cannibals),[32] but other authors with less personal experience overlooked such difficulties to represent contact in uncomplicated ways that legitimated naval suppression and the political, philosophical and religious imperatives that underlay it. In meeting its generic requirement to entertain and instruct social groups habitually deemed in the nineteenth century to be in need of morally clear-cut explanations rather than difficult truths (women, the working classes and children), popular and juvenile fiction was particularly amenable to these ends. But the affirmative moralistic interpretation of naval suppression also exists, perhaps more subtly, in non-fictional texts by commentators attributed the cultural capital of high social rank, authority and seriousness. Lt Joseph Denman, the son of the Lord Chief Justice and abolitionist Thomas Denman, is one such commentator. As one of the principal agents of the aggressive, in-shore blockading tactics used in West Africa, Denman was a key witness in the parliamentary inquiries into naval suppression policy of the 1840s. Denman's defence of the squadron and his own strong-arm methods depended in part upon the memory of his first-hand experience of the evils of the Atlantic crossing during his service as prize-master of the *Maria de Gloria*, a barque captured by HMS *Curlew* off Rio de Janeiro in November 1833. Of his time in charge of the *Maria de Gloria*, Denman recalled: 'I was 46 days on that voyage, and altogether 4 months on board her, where I witnessed the most dreadful sufferings that human beings could endure.'[33] The implication, in his own testimony and in subsequent historical writing, is that Denman's experience aboard the prize *compelled* his later stance in favour of forcible abolitionism in West Africa and South America. 'Such an initiation into the horrors of the trade bit deep into the young man's mind', writes the naval historian Christopher Lloyd. 'The ruthless methods he subsequently adopted clearly owe their origin to that experience.'[34] Arguments of this kind emerge from the redemptive writings of Newton and subsequent evangelical writers as well as from the more complicated reality of officers' experiences of slave-trade suppression, as documented in this volume by Mary Wills.

The Africa Squadron under fire

The morally affirmative representations of naval suppression outlined above did not go unchallenged. Indeed, given that some of the busiest and most dramatic years of slave-trade suppression, in the 1830s and early 1840s, coincided with the popular ascent of the 'nautical novel' penned by the likes of Frederick Marryat, heroic depictions of the Africa Squadron are strikingly few and far between. Instead this genre tends towards cautionary and outright hostile depictions of the work of rescuing enslaved peoples on the high seas. At the height of the anti-slavery movement of the mid-1830s, abolitionist fanfare was opposed in two novels about the anti-slave-trade squadron written by Michael Scott, *Tom Cringle's Log* (1829–33) and *The Cruise of the 'Midge'* (1834–35). The son of a wealthy Glasgow merchant, Scott spent much of his career as a trader in Jamaica. He maintained personal and business ties to the island's 'white creole' elite after returning to found his own business in Glasgow in 1822.[35] The two novels he completed before his death in 1835 at the age of 46 were serialised in the anti-abolitionist *Blackwood's Magazine*, with *Tom Cringle's Log* appearing during the passage of the Emancipation Act.

Despite its setting in and immediately after the Napoleonic Wars, *Tom Cringle's Log* addresses contemporary controversies by opposing emancipation and defending the West Indian planters' way of life. Scott places polemical defences of the planters' rights into the mouths of the novel's most sympathetic characters, and in Chapter XIV, by means of extraordinary prolepsis, he inserts in the narrative a letter sent to the eponymous hero by another main character, the West Indian proprietor Aaron Bang, which criticises abolitionists and outlines a scheme for gradual emancipation of the most able slaves.[36] Detailed descriptions of post-revolutionary Haiti in ruins and unrest in the Spanish islands forebode of the destruction of Britain's colonies, while, in his Byronic soliloquies, Bang portrays himself and his fellow white creoles as romantic castaways of an empire that has abandoned them.[37] On a trip to Haiti, Bang and Cringle escape the island's ruined ports and towns in favour of the untouched forest. There, 'amidst the loneliness of the earth', Bang 'look[s] forward without a shudder, to set up my everlasting rest, to lay my weary bones in the earth, and to mingle my clay with that whereout it was moulded', before likening himself to 'a barbarian' and 'an aboriginal of the land'.[38] Barbara Lalla interprets passages such as this as Scott's Romantic celebration of individual choice, which is forever constrained and contradicted by his dogmatic belief in the racial superiority of whites.[39] Yet Lalla's argument equates anti-slavery values with autonomy in a way that Scott, and other pro-slavery voices of the 1830s, would have queried. Scott is concerned by the suffocation of the individual who blindly takes up the anti-slavery cause. However distasteful it is to modern-day readers, Scott's Romanticism claims bonds of belonging between the white planters and the West Indian soil. It declares the stoic nobility of the West Indian land-owning classes just as these peoples' humanity was questioned by abolitionists and enslaved peoples in Britain and the West Indies.

Other chapters of Tom Cringle's Log dramatise the human costs of slave-trade suppression. Chapter XV features a violent fight between a naval ship and a Spanish slave ship. The battle is won by the former, but not before its gunner fires into the enemy's hold, where the slave traders have taken refuge among their captives. The slave traders then blow up their own vessel in an attempt to kill the raiding naval party on board. All of the slave traders, numerous slaves and some naval personnel go down with the ship. Of the estimated one hundred and fifty slaves who escape into the water, only eighty-four are rescued; the rest are fired upon by their rescuers in an act of mercy killing:

Soon all was quiet; a wounded black here and there was shrieking in his great agony, and struggling for a moment before he sank into his watery grave for ever; a few pieces of wreck were floating and sparking on the surface of the deep in the blood-red sunbeams, which streamed in a flood of glorious light on the bloody deck, shattered hull, and torn rigging of the Wave, and on the dead bodies of and mangled limbs of those who

[134]

had fallen; while some heavy scattering drops of rain fell sparkling from a passing cloud, as if Nature had wept in pity over the dismal scene; or as if they had been blessed tears, shed by an angel, in his heavenward course ... as he hovered for a moment, and looked down in pity on the fantastic tricks played by ... weak man, in his little moment of power and ferocity.[40]

In the aftermath of the skirmish, bloated black corpses resurface and float alongside the *Wave* as sea-birds and fishes pick at their flesh. The scene seems designed to meet with William Blackwood's taste for tales of brutality and sensation (as famously lampooned by Edgar Allan Poe).[41] It also shares in the Romantic fixation on death at sea, which in turn derives from Shakespeare's 'rich and strange' sea-changes that befall the drowned human body.[42] The graphic intensity of the shipwreck, with its corporeal gore bathed in an incongruously 'glorious light', anticipates Turner's *Slave Ship*. Yet whereas Turner's artwork defies reductive decoding,[43] Cringle and Bang interpret the scene as evidence of the futility of the *Wave*'s attack on the slaver.[44] Their explanation seems to be shared by the imagined weeping of 'Nature', or the passing angel, which registers a lack of providential support for the cause. Scott's description of the flotsam and jetsam of the sinking slave ship connotes the misguided morality of naval suppression; it is an image to which writers would return amid the attack on naval suppression in 1840s.

The extent of Scott's first-hand knowledge of his subject is uncertain.[45] It may be that his stories are based on eyewitness reportage of the difficulties of naval suppression that first became available in the annual reports of the African Institution, and which appeared with increasing regularity in a variety of forums in the 1830s. A number of these were assembled by Thomas Fowell Buxton in *The African Slave Trade and Its Remedy* (1839). As it is based on numerous eyewitness accounts, including ones gathered by Buxton in personal correspondence, *The African Slave Trade and Its Remedy* is probably the most comprehensive mid-nineteenth-century analysis of the slave trade and its eradication. It asserts that naval suppression is failing, and it proposes not only the strengthening of the Africa Squadron but the extension of Britain's commercial and Christian influence into the West African interior. These civilising forces alone could sever the slave trade at the root, its argument ran.[46] Recent studies have noted the importance of Buxton's tome in constructing the West African interior as a place of primitive and barbaric rites, reversing the logic of earlier abolitionists such as Thomas Clarkson who believed that inland communities would be more 'civilised' than coastal ones because they were less degraded by contact with Europeans.[47]

[135]

As Eltis notes, Buxton also helped solidify a certain image of the post-1808 Atlantic crossing.[48] He exaggerates the scale of the traffic by claiming that in excess of 150,000 Africans were annually embarked for the Americas, with one-quarter dying at sea, and by underlining that atrocities during the oceanic transit of slaves – not least the jettisoning of living cargoes – had been exacerbated as British withdrawal from, then policing of, the traffic had forced it into the hands of mercenaries.[49] Economic and demographic historians have since corrected Buxton's calculations as to the volume of the ongoing traffic,[50] but in the 1840s his work was regarded as authoritative, and the government implemented Buxton's scheme in the form of the naval-led expedition up the River Niger in 1841–42.[51] One of the ironic outcomes of this disastrous mission was a new batch of narratives detailing the gloomy prospects of current anti-slave-trade measures. These reports would be enlisted in the parliamentary appeals of the early and mid-1840s in favour of terminating the West Africa Squadron.

Buxton's tome and the Niger travel narratives that followed it are cautious, sometimes gloomy, on the prospects of slave-trade suppression. But seldom if at all do they call into question justifications of the campaign as a righteous cause. Around the late 1840s, however, new accounts on the difficulties and ironies of the Africa Squadron undermined the idealism of authors who viewed it in Manichean terms as a question of good and evil, in which the conversion of liberated Africans to Christianity and 'civilisation' made 'good out of evil'. Some writers, in pointing to instances of social deprivation in Britain that the abolitionists overlooked in favour of redeeming Africans bound for the Americas, doubted the exigency of anti-slave-trade policy. This is the tenor of commentaries on the slave trade issued by two intellectual heavyweights of the mid-Victorian era, Thomas Carlyle and Charles Dickens. Carlyle's satirical attack on West Indian emancipation and his deployment of crude racial stereotypes in the 'Occasional Discourse on the Negro Question', which first appeared in *Fraser's Magazine* in 1849, have been frequently discussed in recent literary and cultural studies and need no introduction here. It suffices to note that in its often-overlooked final three paragraphs, Carlyle's speaker attacks the moral and religious argument that elimination of the slave trade is ordained by 'the laws of Heaven': if that is so, he asks, then why not 'go to Cuba and Brazil with a sufficiency of 74-gun ships, and signify to those nefarious countries, that their procedure on the negro question is too bad'? If 'this thing [is] done, the Heavens will prosper all other things with us! Not a doubt of it – provided your premise be not doubtful.' But Carlyle does doubt the premise: he points to the impoverished in Ireland and London to query whether

TELESCOPIC PHILANTHROPY.

Little London Arab. " PLEASE 'M, AIN'T WE BLACK ENOUGH TO BE CARED FOR ? "

(*With* Mr. Punch's *Compliments to* Lord Stanley.)

Figure 6.1 'Telescopic Philanthropy', *Punch*, 4 March 1865, p. 89.

'the buying of black war-captives in Africa, and bringing them over to the sugar-islands for sale again' is truly 'the most alarming contradiction to the said laws [of this universe] which is now witnessed on this earth'.[52]

Dickens's engagement with the slave trade is more sustained than Carlyle's. Having criticised slavery in the USA in *American Notes* (1842) and *Martin Chuzzlewit* (1843–44), in the early 1850s Dickens's attention was turned to Britain's anti-slave-trade actions. In late 1850 he published two short stories about the Africa Squadron in *Household Words*: Alfred Whaley Cole's 'Good Intentions: A Story of the African Blockade', and Franklin Fox and W. H. Wills's 'A Cape Coast Cargo'.[53] For Grace Moore, Dickens's publication of these stories 'reveal that he remained supportive of [abolitionism]'.[54] But Dickens saw slavery in the USA and the international slave trade as separate issues and, appalled as he no doubt was by the latter, the tales he published are at best ambiguous in their evaluation of the naval patrols. 'Good Intentions', which declares itself to be 'a true story in every-thing but names', describes the chase of a slave ship that ends with the jettisoning of its cargo.[55] The incident serves as an illustration of the narrator's introductory remark '[t]hat the horrors of the passage from Africa to Brazil are often frightfully aggravated by the dread of pursuit and capture by our cruisers'.[56] At the root of the problem was the increasing profitability of the trade, which led slave-ship captains to ever more mercenary tactics in shipping slaves. This was a widely recognised problem of naval suppression since Buxton had publicised it. More provocatively, the narrator of 'Good Intentions' also notes the parallel economic motivation of those who did the chasing: 'Visions of prize-money float before the eyes of every one of the pursuers, from the captain to the cabin boy.'[57] In noting the irony that human trafficking now afforded opportunities for profit to the naval crews that policed it, the story revisited a source of discomfort for onlookers who maintained that abolition was a moral and spiritual imperative regardless of the economic questions attached to it.

'A Cape Coast Cargo' is the tale of two sailors who unwittingly enlist on a slave ship, but realise their wrongs and help a British Man-of-War to capture their former crew-mates. Even this story of moral redemption stresses that when it comes to naval suppression 'good intentions' are in vain, as the slave traders successfully drown their captives *en masse* prior to their arrest. As with Scott's nautical novels, the spectacle of mass murder at sea is offered up reproachfully as evidence of the uselessness of naval suppression. In the same vein as 'Good Intentions', 'A Cape Coast Cargo' claims verisimilitude by referring its readers to actual cases to affirm that its plot is not simply 'romance'.[58] Lord Denman appears to have written to Dickens to question his motives for publishing these gloomy stories. Dickens responded by stating: 'I am not satisfied that the African Blockade advances the great end it is designed to promote.' The 'comparative indifference in the public mind' to the government's efforts against the slave trade he attributed to a mounting awareness of 'the many wrongs nearer home, that have to be set right'.[59] In one further, brief reference to the anti-slave-trade squadron in fiction first published by Dickens, the mutiny on HMS *Russell* that forms the main subplot of Elizabeth Gaskell's *North and South* (1854–55) is the consequence of cruelty by a captain whose overzealousness is explained by his having previously 'been nearly three years on the station, with nothing to do but keep slavers off, and work [his] men'.[60] The cost to British sailors' lives is weighed against the apparent unimportance of the patrol.

Dickens's next intervention in the debate was his lengthy review of the 'official narrative' of the Buxton-inspired, naval-led expedition up the Niger. The review is largely appreciative of the book and of the efforts of the crews involved. Indeed, the latter are portrayed as brave martyrs to a hopeless cause, for Dickens decried the scheme to eliminate slave trading by delivering European religion and trade into the Niger delta as far-fetched and vainglorious. He contributes to the feminisation of humanitarian sentiment in the 1850s and 1860s by ascribing the scheme to 'the weird old women' of 'the Exeter Hall platform'.[61] He calls the Africa Squadron 'inefficient and absurd' and, as in his letter to Denman, he concludes that humanitarian 'work at home must be completed' before Britain can hope to enlighten Africa.[62] Dickens pursued the same argument in chapter 4 of *Bleak House* (1852–53), 'Telescopic Philanthropy', in which Mrs Jellyby, the personification of 'the weird old women' of Exeter Hall, frets over the wellbeing of Africans yet is oblivious to the impoverishment of her own children. This satirical take on the anti-slavery movement was common around the middle of the nineteenth century; Dickens's allegation that the indifference of abolitionists to poverty and exploitation 'at home' amounted to moral hypocrisy is repeated in many forums, ranging from the *Times* to the Chartists' *Morning Star*, and from *Uncle Tom's Cabin* to some of the several hostile parodies of Harriet Beecher Stowe's novel. In a *Punch* cartoon of 1865 that takes its name from *Bleak House*, Britannia ignores the pleas of street urchins as she looks on at a ship of the Africa Squadron and an African coastal scene (Figure 6.1).

Equally if not more important is the commentary on racial difference in Dickens's Niger review. Much of the text recounts the anti-slave-trade treaty negotiations held between naval officers and three of the region's rulers, King Obi, King Boy and the Attah of Idah. Dickens portrays these as farcical encounters in which the African parties exploit the moral earnestness of their interlocutors to their own pecuniary advantage. To an extent, this was to read against the grain of the report of the encounter, and perhaps to undermine the quasi-authority that European travellers sometimes (though not always) attributed to themselves when making treaties on African soil. For Moore, the most telling aspect of Dickens's précis is that it 'does not make any generalizations on the subject of race ... [T]he evil of the attacks against the missionaries is attributed to King Boy and King Obi as individuals, rather than to a collective race.'[63] But Dickens's representations of African individuals are inescapably informed by his attitudes toward the 'collective race', which are made clear by his references to 'the barbarous African', 'ignorant and savage races' and 'these barbarians'.[64] Dickens credits the potentates with greater awareness of the hollowness of the ceremonial encounters and resultant treaties, yet in doing so he employs King Obi, in particular, in the role of *idiot savant* – 'a savage in a sergeant-major's coat' – whose efforts to enrich himself unveil the absurdity of the Niger mission as a whole.[65]

As with Carlyle's 'Occasional Discourse', Dickens's acerbic prose is illustrative of the new strain of racism that emerged from anthropological and other scientific studies to inform much European writing about people of African descent in the second half of the nineteenth century, and was itself both a symptom and cause of the recession in anti-slavery commitment in that period.[66] Indeed, it was in protest against a sentimental woodcut illustration of liberated Africans in Sierra Leone which appeared in *Transactions of the Ethnological Society* of 1863 that James Hunt founded the Anthropological Society of London.[67] In harnessing new theories of race actively to confront evangelical notions of the oneness of humankind by holding that Africans were of a different and inferior species to Europeans, the Anthropological Society attacked the evangelical and moral justifications of abolitionism in general, and the naval patrol – which its most famous member, the explorer Richard F. Burton, dubbed 'the Sentimental Squadron'[68] – in particular. Burton's attitude toward the anti-slavery movement is encapsulated in his assertion in *Mission to Gelele* (1864) that the 'kneeling negro' in the famous anti-slavery icon titled 'Am I Not a Man and a Brother?', 'properly speaking, should have been on all fours', such is his bestiality.[69] Burton proposed forced emigration of African 'recaptives' to the British West Indies: it 'is like sending a boy to school. It is his only chance of improvement.'[70] While Burton distinguished his plan from the pro-slavery arguments of old, it is nonetheless clear that the new racial sciences took debate on the slave trade almost entirely full circle, to a position from which a recapitulation of something akin to that traffic seemed, to a small and vocal minority, a reasonable solution.

Conclusion

The written representations surveyed in this chapter complicate Patrick Brantlinger's claim that '[i]n British literature from about 1830 to the 1870s, white heroes rarely doubt their ability to tame various geopolitical mistresses – Africa, the sea, the world – and to bring civilized order out of the chaos of savage life'.[71] They do so by demonstrating the diversity of perspectives on slave-trade suppression while it remained a burning issue in British political, social and humanitarian debates. As they imagined or recalled the work of the patrolling squadrons, one writer's evidence of absurd wastefulness and hypocrisy was another's proof of worthy sacrifice for a supreme cause. The religious and moralistic justifications of the campaign in particular were fiercely disputed, and this resulted in markedly different depictions of the chase and capture of slave ships, and the Africans they transported towards the Americas. Only in the latter decades of the nineteenth century, following the removal of the squadron and the eradication of the Atlantic slave trade, was consensus reached as to the moral righteousness of the campaign. Then writers of boys' own adventures such as W. H. G. Kingston and R. M. Ballantyne regaled new generations of readers with stories of young naval officers' daring conquest of slave-trading pirates and African savages.[72] Although some of these tales were ostensibly set at the height of the anti-slave-trade cruises in the 1830s, their bluster and bloodthirstiness betray that they are a product of the late Victorian desire for and confidence in Britain's right not only to end slavery but to rule in Africa. Between 1830 and 1860, few publications regarded the situation with such surety. In nineteenth-century Britain, the Africa Squadron's part in prolonging the culture of anti-slavery seemed at its most apparent in retrospect.

One thing that unites most of the writing about the anti-slave-trade patrols is its seeming lack of interest in the agency of enslaved Africans and liberated Africans. Shipboard insurrections continued to take place throughout the period of naval suppression, but seldom are they reported in detail, if at all, in British publications.[73] This is in contrast to the body of fictions of slave-ship rebellion produced by the US authors Herman Melville, Frederick Douglass, William Wells Brown, Lydia Maria Child and Martin Delaney.[74] Similarly, besides certain missionaries, the efforts of former slaves who made successful lives for themselves in Sierra Leone were little known outside of the colony. It is hard to disagree with Wood's verdict that abolitionists of the nineteenth century conceived of freedom for enslaved peoples as a boon when granted by kindly white patrons, under certain conditions, rather than autonomously seized by those peoples.[75]At the same time

it is important to understand this tendency to assert moral righteousness in the broader ideological and discursive context in which the
benefits of emancipation were contested, indeed openly questioned,
by writers of great influence and popularity.

Notes

1 J. Gallagher, 'Fowell Buxton and the New African Policy 1838–42', *Cambridge Historical Journal* 10 (1950), 36–58.
2 The focus of this chapter is upon written materials published in British media. Marcus Wood discusses visual representations in *Blind Memory: Visual Representations of Slavery in England and America, 1780–1865* (Manchester: Manchester University Press, 2000), pp. 7–8. Unpublished literary materials feature in chapter 4 of the present volume.
3 For a useful summary of first-hand, nonfictional accounts, see Philip D. Curtin, *The Image of Africa: British Ideas and Actions, 1780–1850* (Madison, WI: University of Wisconsin Press, 1964), p. 322.
4 Tim Fulford, 'Romanticizing the Empire: The Naval Heroes of Southey, Coleridge, Austen, and Marryat', *MLQ: Modern Language Quarterly* 60 (1999): 161–96.
5 Margarette Lincoln, 'Shipwreck Narratives of the Eighteenth and Early Nineteenth Century: Indicators of Culture and Identity', *Journal for Eighteenth-Century Studies*, 20 (1997), 155–72; Carl Thompson, *The Suffering Traveller and the Romantic Imagination* (Oxford: Oxford University Press, 2007); Matthew Rubery, *The Novelty of Newspapers: Victorian Fiction after the Invention of the News* (Oxford: Oxford University Press, 2009), pp. 23–45.
6 John Newton, *Thoughts on the Slave Trade* (1788), in *Slavery, Abolition and Emancipation: Writings in the British Romantic Period. Vol. 2: The Abolition Debate*, ed. Peter J. Kitson (London: Pickering and Chatto, 1999), pp. 77–117, at p. 79.
7 Newton, *Thoughts*, p. 83.
8 On the slave trade as national sin, see Linda Colley, *Britons: Forging the Nation, 1707–1837* [1992] (London: Pimlico, 2003), p. 353.
9 Newton, *Thoughts*, p. 82.
10 Wood, *Blind Memory*, pp. 7–8.
11 Moira Ferguson, 'Fictional Constructions of Liberated Africans: Mary Butt Sherwood', in Tim Fulford and Peter J. Kitson (eds), *Romanticism and Colonialism: Writing and Empire, 1780–1830* (Cambridge: Cambridge University Press, 1998), pp. 148–63, p. 151.
12 David Eltis, *Economic Growth and the Ending of the Transatlantic Slave Trade* (Oxford: Oxford University Press, 1987), p. 105. See Wayne Ackerson, *The African Institution (1807–1827) and the Antislavery Movement in Great Britain* (Lewiston, NY: Edwin Mellen Press, 2005), p. 105. Only in its petition campaign to compel the government to seek an immediate end to the French slave trade did the African Institution break with its own elitist approach. This appeal, which acquired three-quarters of a million men's and women's signatures over 800 petitions, played its part in the establishment of a permanent West Africa Squadron from 1818. According to Turley, it was the only occasion on which the continuing slave trade intruded into public debates until the end of the campaign for abolition of slavery in the British colonies in 1838. David Turley, *The Culture of English Antislavery, 1780–1860* (London: Routledge, 1991), p. 65.
13 Roger Anstey, 'The Pattern of British Abolitionism in the Eighteenth and Nineteenth Centuries', in Christine Bolt and Seymour Drescher (eds), *Anti-Slavery, Religion, and Reform: Essays in Memory of Roger Anstey* (Folkestone, Kent: Dawson, 1980), pp. 19–42, at p. 33.
14 Srinivas Aravamudan, 'Mary Sherwood, *Dazee; or, The Recaptured Slave* (1821)', in Srinivas Aravamudan (ed.), *Slavery, Abolition and Emancipation: Writing in the*

British Romantic Period. Vol. 6: Fiction (London: Pickering and Chatto, 1999), pp. 327–8, at p. 328.

15 Sherwood, *Dazee*, in *Slavery*, pp. 329–69, at p. 358.
16 Sherwood, *Dazee*, p. 363.
17 Aravamudan, 'Mary Sherwood', p. 328.
18 Ferguson, 'Fictional Constructions', p. 153.
19 Elizabeth Melville, *A Residence at Sierra Leone* (London: John Murray, 1849), pp. 135–6.
20 Joseph Wright, 'The Narrative of Joseph Wright' [Ms. 1839; 1841], in Philip D. Curtin, ed. *Africa Remembered: Narratives by West Africans from the Era of the Slave Trade* (Madison, WI: University of Wisconsin Press, 1968), pp. 322–33, at p. 322.
21 Samuel Ajayi Crowther, 'The Narrative of Samuel Ajayi Crowther' [1837], J. F. Ade Ajayi (ed.), in *Africa Remembered*, pp. 298–316, at p. 299.
22 J. D. Y. Peel, *Religious Encounter and the Making of the Yoruba* (Bloomington, IN: Indiana University Press, 2001); David Northrup, 'Becoming African: Identity Formation among Liberated Slaves in Nineteenth-Century Sierra Leone', *Slavery & Abolition* 27 (2006), 1–21.
23 'A. F. C.', *Good Out of Evil; or, The History of Adjai, The African Slave Boy* [1850] (London: Wertheim and Macintosh, 1852).
24 For example, Peter Leonard, *Records of a Voyage to the Western Coast of Africa, and of the Service on that Station for the Suppression of the Slave Trade, in the Years 1830, 1831, and 1832* (Edinburgh: William Tait, 1833), pp. 131–2.
25 Macgregor Laird and R. A. K. Oldfield, *Narrative of an Expedition in the Interior of Africa by the River Niger*, 2 vols (London: Richard Bentley, 1837), ii, 367–8; Anon., 'Prefatory Remarks to the Present Edition', in Thomas Clarkson, *History of the Rise, Progress, and Accomplishment of the Abolition of the African Slave Trade by the British Parliament* [1808] (London: John W. Parker, 1839), pp. 1–32, at pp. 4–7.
26 Catherine Gallagher, *The Industrial Reformation of English Fiction: Social Discourse and Narrative Form, 1832–1867* (Chicago, IL: University of Chicago Press, 1985), pp. 3–35.
27 John Thomas Haines, *My Poll and My Partner Joe: A Nautical Drama in Three Acts* (London: John Cumberland, n.d.), p. 23.
28 Haines, *My Poll and My Partner Joe*, p. 33. For further analysis, see Robert Burroughs, 'Sailors and Slaves: "The Poor Enslaved Tar" in Naval Reform and Nautical Melodrama', *Journal of Victorian Culture* 16 (2011), 305–23.
29 See Catherine Gallagher, 'Floating Signifiers of Britishness in the Novels of the Anti-Slave-Trade Squadron', in Wendy S. Jacobson, (ed.), *Dickens and the Children of Empire* (Basingstoke: Palgrave, 2000), pp. 78–93.
30 Charlotte M. Yonge, *The Daisy Chain; or, Aspirations* [1856] (London: Virago, 1988), p. 9.
31 Yonge, *The Daisy Chain*, pp. 9–10.
32 Crowther, 'Samuel Ajayi Crowther', p. 313.
33 Qtd in Christopher Lloyd, *The Navy and the Slave Trade* [1949] (London: Frank Cass, 1968), p. 93. See also Joseph Denman, *Practical Remarks on the Slave Trade* (London: J. Ridgway, 1839, 2nd edn), pp. 17–21.
34 Lloyd, *The Navy and the Slave Trade*, p. 93.
35 On 'white creole' culture and identity, see David Lambert, *White Creole Culture, Politics and Identity During the Age of Abolition* (Cambridge: Cambridge University Press, 2005); Christer Petley, 'Slavery, Emancipation and the Creole Worldview of Jamaican Colonists, 1800–1834', *Slavery & Abolition* 26 (2005), 93–114.
36 For examples of the explicit defence of planters' rights, see Michael Scott, *Tom Cringle's Log* [1829–33] (New York: Henry Holt, 1999), pp. 132, 148, 255, 399, 422; for the letter from Bang, pp. 354–8.
37 Scott, *Tom Cringle's Log*, pp. 278–9.
38 Scott, *Tom Cringle's Log*, p. 460.
39 Barbara Lalla, 'Dungeons of the Soul: Frustrated Romanticism in Eighteenth and Nineteenth Century Literature of Jamaica', *MELUS* 21, 3 (1996), 2–23.

40 Scott, *Tom Cringle's Log*, pp. 387–8.
41 Edgar Allan Poe, 'How to Write a Blackwood Article' [1838], in Poe, *Complete Tales and Poems* (Ljubljana: Mladinska Knjiga, 1966), pp. 302–12.
42 William Shakespeare, *The Tempest*, Virginia Mason Vaughan and Alden T. Vaughan (eds) (London: Arden Shakespeare, 2003), p. 178 (Act 1, Scene 2, lines 397–402). On Romanticism and suffering at sea, see Thompson, *The Suffering Traveller*.
43 Wood, *Blind Memory*, pp. 41–68.
44 Scott, *Tom Cringle's Log*, pp. 391–3.
45 See Eugene A. Nolte, 'Michael Scott and *Blackwood's Magazine*: Some Unpublished Letters', *Library* 8 (1953), 188–96.
46 Thomas Fowell Buxton, *African Slave Trade and its Remedy* (London: John Murray, 2nd edn, 1840).
47 Patrick Brantlinger, *Rule of Darkness: British Literature and Imperialism, 1830–1914* [1988] (London: Cornell University Press, 1990), p. 177; William Pietz, 'The Fetish of Civilization: Sacrificial Blood and Monetary Debt', in Peter Pels and Oscar Salemnick (eds), *Colonial Subjects: Essays on the Practical History of Anthropology* (Ann Arbor, MI: University of Michigan Press, 1999), pp. 53–81.Thomas Clarkson, *Cries of Africa, to the Inhabitants of Europe* (London: Harvey and Darton, 1822), p. 18.
48 Eltis, *Economic Growth*, p. 126.
49 Gallagher, 'Fowell Buxton', p. 41. The geographer James MacQueen, who advised Buxton on his 'remedy', likewise claimed with hyperbole that since abolition the slave trade had tripled 'in amount, and besides in horrors tenfold!!'. *A Geographical Survey of Africa* (London: B. Fellowes, 1840), p. xxiii.
50 David Eltis, 'The Volume and Structure of the Transatlantic Slave Trade: A Reassessment', *The William and Mary Quarterly* 58 (2001), 17–46.
51 See Howard Temperley, *White Dreams, Black Africa: The Antislavery Expedition to the Niger* (London: Yale University Press, 1991).
52 Carlyle's article was republished as a pamphlet in 1853 under the new and more provocative title 'Occasional Discourse on the Nigger Question'. It is reproduced under this title in *The Works of Thomas Carlyle*, 30 vols (London: Chapman and Hall, 1899), pp. xxix, 348–83. Quotations at pp. 381–3.
53 Alfred Whaley Cole, 'Good Intentions: A Story of the African Blockade', *Household Words*, 5 October 1850, 45–7; Franklin Fox and W.H. Wills, 'A Cape Coast Cargo', *Household Words*, 7 December 1850, 252–7.
54 Grace Moore, *Dickens and Empire: Discourses of Class, Race and Colonialism in the Works of Charles Dickens* (Aldershot, Hampshire: Ashgate, 2004), p. 55.
55 Cole, 'Good Intentions', p. 45. The tale is set in the Mozambique Channel, in the Indian Ocean, but this had been a subsidiary source for slaves in the Atlantic slave trade since the 1810s, and the narrator frames the tale with references to the Atlantic trade.
56 Cole, 'Good Intentions', p. 45.
57 Cole, 'Good Intentions', p. 45.
58 Fox and Wills, 'Cape Coast Cargo', p. 256.
59 Dickens to Denman, 16 December 1850, in Graham Storey, Kathleen Tillotson and Nina Burgis (eds), *The Letters of Charles Dickens*, 12 vols (Oxford: Clarendon, 1987), pp. vi, 236–7.
60 Elizabeth Gaskell, *North and South* (London: Penguin Classics, 2007), pp. 124–5.
61 Charles Dickens, 'The Niger Expedition', *Examiner*, 19 August 1848, 45–63, at p. 45. On the mid-Victorian attack on humanitarian sentiment, see Douglas A. Lorimer, *Colour, Class and the Victorians: English Attitudes to the Negro in the Mid-Nineteenth Century* (Leicester: Leicester University Press, 1978), pp. 113–14, 121.
62 Dickens, 'Niger Expedition', pp. 55, 63.
63 Moore, *Dickens and Empire*, p. 69.
64 Dickens, 'Niger Expedition', pp. 62, 63.
65 Dickens, 'Niger Expedition', pp. 49–57, at p. 55.
66 See Lorimer, *Colour, Class and the Victorians*, pp. 131–61. On Dickens's later

embroilment in the controversies that surrounded publication of Harriet Beecher Stowe's best-selling anti-slavery novel *Uncle Tom's Cabin*, see Harry Stone, 'Charles Dickens and Harriet Beecher Stowe', *Nineteenth-Century Fiction* 12 (1957), 188–202; Sarah Meer, *Uncle Tom Mania: Slavery, Minstrelsy, and Transatlantic Culture in the 1850s* (Athens, GA: University of Georgia Press, 2005), pp. 204–7.

67 George W. Stocking, Jnr, *Victorian Anthropology* (New York: The Free Press, 1987), p. 376.
68 Richard F. Burton, *A Mission to Gelele, King of Dahome* [1864, 2 vols] (London: Tylson and Edwards, 1893), i, 5.
69 Burton, *Mission to Gelele*, ii, 122 n2.
70 Burton, *Mission to Gelele*, ii, 136.
71 Brantlinger, *Rule of Darkness*, p. 44.
72 For commentary and further references see Gallagher, 'Floating Signifiers'.
73 See Eric Robert Taylor, *If We Must Die: Shipboard Insurrections in the Era of the Atlantic Slave Trade* (Baton Rouge, LA: Louisiana State University Press, 2006), pp. 210–13.
74 See Maggie Montesinos Sale, *The Slumbering Volcano: American Slave Ship Revolts and the Production of Rebellious Masculinity* (Durham: Duke University Press, 1997); Celeste-Marie Bernier, '"Arms Like Polished Iron": The Black Slave Body in Narratives of a Slave Ship Revolt', in Thomas Wiedemann and Jane Gardner (eds), *Representing the Body of the Slave* (London: Frank Cass, 2002), pp. 91–106; Gesa Mackenthun, *Fictions of the Black Atlantic in American Foundational Literature* (New York: Routledge, 2004), pp. 89–102.
75 Marcus Wood, *Slavery, Empathy, and Pornography* (Oxford: Oxford University Press, 2002); Wood, 'Emancipation Art, Fanon and the Butchery of Freedom', in Brycchan Carey and Peter J. Kitson (eds), *Slavery and the Cultures of Abolition* (Cambridge: D.S. Brewer, 2007), pp. 11–41.

CHAPTER SEVEN

Slave-trade suppression and the image of West Africa in nineteenth-century Britain

David Lambert

Introduction

This chapter considers the role of British naval suppression in the production of the image of West Africa.[1] The published accounts produced by naval officers serving in the West Africa Squadron, or others who travelled on its ships, were not primarily intended to add to British understanding of West Africa and its peoples. As detailed by Robert Burroughs in the previous chapter, some were written to entertain their readers with tales of the danger and occasional excitement of life in the squadron. They mainly consisted of accounts of cruising the coast for slave ships, chases and captures, as well as descriptions of Sierra Leone and the liberated Africans settled there. Texts also recounted visits to other British and foreign stations on the coast. Some accounts had a more overtly political intention, aiming to shore up support for the squadron's activities or to reveal it as a terrible waste of British lives and money. Nevertheless, all the accounts contained at least some information about parts of the West African littoral and particular African groups. As a result, it is legitimate to consider the broader contribution that they made to British knowledge and understanding, or perhaps more accurately the British *impression*, of West Africa.

The question of how 'suppressionist texts' shaped the image of West Africa can be considered in three ways. The first is their contribution to knowledge in a formal, factual sense – at least as this was defined in such contemporary works as *A Manual of Scientific Enquiry*, which was edited by Britain's most eminent scientist of the 1840s, John Herschel. This is information in such fields as 'physical geography', defined as 'the form and configuration of the earth's surface as it issues from the hand of nature', as well as 'political geography', which related to 'all those facts which are the immediate consequences of the operations of man, exercised either on the raw materials of the earth, or on the means of his intercourse with his fellow creatures'. There was also the field of 'ethnology'. While sharing much overlap with political geography, the emphasis of ethnology was more detailed, including the 'physical description' of 'tribes' or 'races' in terms of complexion, features, figure and stature, as well as their 'social state', which included means of subsistence, agriculture, customs, moral regulations, spiritual beliefs and language.[2]

By the time the West Africa Squadron was operating, a number of fields of scientific knowledge had been, or were being, formally institutionalised in Britain. These included geography, as evident in the creation of the Geographical Society of London, later the Royal Geographical Society, in 1830. Africa had long been of great interest to British geographers; in 1831, the African Association, which had sponsored expeditions to the continent from the 1790s, was absorbed into the RGS. There were also strong links between the Royal Navy and British exploratory efforts in Africa, and naval officers played a prominent role in nineteenth-century British expeditions to Africa. John Barrow, Second Secretary of the Admiralty until his retirement in 1846, was the key promoter of British expeditionary activity to Africa (and the Antarctic) in the early nineteenth century and was later one of the founders of the RGS.[3] The Society itself sponsored expeditions and the travels of individuals. Among these was the author of a suppressionist text, Captain James Edward Alexander, a British military officer who was engaged to explore parts of East Africa in the mid-1830s. To make his way there, he travelled aboard the frigate HMS *Thalia*, which was going to the Cape of Good Hope, under Rear Admiral Patrick Campbell, commander on the West Africa Station. Although producing an account of West Africa was not the primary purpose of his mission, Alexander applied a geographical perspective to gather data on this region, his intention being to contribute to knowledge of Africa as well as to please his sponsors.[4]

The second perspective is to consider wider, popular understandings of Africa conveyed by suppressionist texts. These extended beyond institutions like the RGS, although the Society also played a role in fostering them, particularly through its famous 'African nights'. Much of the interest in this context was centred on East Africa, however, especially the search for the sources of the Nile and the travels of such explorers as David Livingstone, Richard Burton, John Hanning Speke, Samuel Baker and Henry Morton Stanley. Nevertheless, the accounts of West Africa did have a potential readership that was wider than geographers, cartographers and ethnologists. Their publication roughly coincided with the expansion in geographical publishing in

[147]

the mid-Victorian period, although it is hard to separate the impact of suppressionist texts from other – missionary, exploratory – accounts of the same time.[5] Indicating the wider networks of readership in which they circulated, the texts were reviewed in the periodical press for what they revealed about the policy of suppression and African 'customs'.[6] Reviews in the *Literary Gazette*, *Athenaeum*, *Spectator* and other periodicals served as a means through which these works became known to potential readers and provided another channel for the information they contained to reach wider audiences. Moreover, such reviews give some indication of how these accounts were received, or at least insight into the expectations that shaped their reception.

The third perspective is to locate the suppressionist texts within the wider cultures of empire, especially in terms of the representation of Africa. The relationship between texts and power has been a longstanding concern of scholars across many fields, much of it originating with the work of Edward Said.[7] Attention has been given to how texts imaginatively colonised non-European territories, surveying, emptying and evaluating these lands in order to render them as potential colonies, as well as how they justified the European presence by casting their African inhabitants as 'savage brutes' who failed to make use of resources properly and needed the civilising presence of European governance, commerce, religion and technology. Suppressionist texts preceded the New Imperialism and the 'Scramble for Africa', although they were associated with a British territorial presence on the African coast at such places as Sierra Leone and the Gambia. Those texts that sought to defend British expansion served to justify this presence and the forms of local involvement and intervention that it enabled. Moreover, these texts contributed to a longer-standing discourse through which Africa was constructed as the 'Dark Continent'.[8] The transformation of the slave trade from something that was central to Britain's relationship with Africa and from which it profited, into something that it was seeking to end, was central to this process. In this light, it is possible to consider the ideological work performed by suppressionist texts and the extent to which they might have contributed to the wider articulation of British colonial discourse about Africa.

The texts under consideration in this chapter were published in the 1830s, 1840s and 1850s.[9] Although most were mainly travel accounts, being generally episodic in character, they were also made up of maps, visual illustrations and tables of figures.[10] Their authors were white British men, who, in most cases, were naval officers, surgeons and ships' chaplains.[11] Others travelled, but did not serve, on naval vessels. Some, such as Lieutenant Frederick Forbes, who commanded the HMS *Bonetta*, and the military officer Alexander had prior experience of writing about their travels.[12] Sir Henry Huntley, who commanded a couple of ships in the squadron, had published *Peregrine Scramble* (1849), a partly fictionalised account of his earlier naval service, and his prose had a more literary style.[13] So too did that of Peter Leonard, surgeon on HMS *Dryad*, even though he claimed to offer nothing more than a 'simple record of observation'. The authors were drawn from different political perspectives: some supported the British abolitionist policy, while others did not. For example, Leonard was a strong advocate and his account was intended to 'make known the horrors which attend the Slave Trade on the western coast of Africa' and thus strengthen public revulsion.[14] In contrast, Pascoe Grenfell Hill, who was the chaplain on the frigate HMS *Winchester*, believed that while the British public remained committed to fighting the slave trade, victory would be achieved in Brazil and Cuba, not West Africa.[15] Huntley was strongly opposed to suppression, despite, or rather because of, his extended service in the squadron and later as lieutenant-governor of the British settlements on the Gambia.[16]

In considering the contribution these texts made to the British image of West Africa, the remainder of this chapter is divided into four parts. It next considers their limited contribution to formal knowledge of West Africa, before going on to show that these texts mainly provided superficial and impressionistic accounts, fixing especially on unfamiliar or 'savage' customs and practices. It then discusses certain exceptions to this argument, wherein suppressionist writers made more of an effort to understand and convey the complexities of the African societies they encountered. The final theme addressed relates to what is perhaps the abiding concern of visitors to West Africa, its unhealthiness, including the danger posed to the writers themselves. The conclusions consider how the literal and figurative position of suppressionist writers – termed here the 'view from the ship' – shaped both the impressions of West Africa conveyed by these texts and give clues as to the broader ideological work they performed in the context of Britain's relationship with Africa.

Surveying the continent

Some suppressionist accounts sought to make contributions to geographical knowledge writ large. To a considerable extent, however, the key questions about West Africa that had so exercised British geographers in the late eighteenth and early nineteenth centuries had been resolved by the 1830s. What Philip Curtin termed the 'classic age of West African exploration' from 1790 to 1830 was dominated by the River Niger and questions concerning its direction, course and, crucially, its termination. It was not until the expedition by Richard and John Lander in 1830 that it was proven to the satisfaction of the British geographical establishment that the Niger terminated in the Gulf of Guinea.[17] Although by solving the so-called 'Niger problem' this 'discovery' effectively brought an end to this phase of European exploratory activity, some questions remained. Leonard's *Records of a Voyage to the Western Coast of Africa*, which was based on a voyage of 1830–32 and thus just after Landers' expedition, sought to contribute to the continuing resolution of the Niger problem. Based on observations, Leonard argued that a host of rivers, from the Rio Formosa to the Old Calabar, were interconnected by cross rivers and, hence, could collectively be considered the mouths of the Niger.[18] Such theories and broader European knowledge about the Niger would be put to the test by the Niger expeditions of 1832–34 and 1840–41.

The desire to contribute to knowledge of West African geography was most explicit in Alexander's account, which was unsurprising given his RGS sponsorship. His original mission was to explore parts of East Africa and when he set out he was 'high in hope of being able to add to our present imperfect knowledge of the geography of Eastern Africa; of being able to find new tribes and people with whom advantageous trade might be opened; of having the *chance* to render some service to my country; and of seeing men and things altogether new to Europeans'.[19] He approached West Africa with a similar perspective, seeing himself as part of a tradition of explorers and travellers to that region, quoting their work and remarking on the achievements of those that had been before him. Moreover, according to the 'Abstracts of Meteorological Observations' at the end of each of his chapters, Alexander took readings using a barometer and thermometer, as well as of wind direction, at noon every other day, recording this data alongside latitude and longitude. He also gathered and reproduced economic data on imports and exports at particular African locations.[20] While the map of the west coast of Africa that accompanied his *Narrative of a Voyage* was inaccurate, failing to depict the course of the Niger as it had been correctly determined in recent geographical discoveries, Alexander's meteorological observations and economic data indicated his wish to gather the sort of systematic data that characterised the field of geography.[21]

Other suppressionist writers also sought to provide systematic ethnological information on Africa. Forbes's account, for example, included a series of appendices containing the numerals in what he understood to be the languages of four distinct African groups he had encountered (the 'Vahie', the 'Grunoo', the 'Kroo' and the 'Fishmen'), as well as a lengthy vocabulary of the Vahie language, 'the language spoken at Cape Mount', which he had arranged.[22] Most, however, combined topographic and ethological sketches with anecdotes and picturesque scenes. Alexander, despite his geographical pretensions and desire to be an explorer rather than a mere traveller, did likewise. Particular locations in the West African littoral that were visited were described, from Sierra Leone southwards as far as the Atlantic islands and on to St Helena. While there were some accounts of scenery and landscapes, mainly based on forays inland, there was generally little attempt to collect information systematically on African geography. Moreover, it was often the human 'customs' that were of most interest.

African anecdotes

Other than Forbes's linguistic appendices, none of the suppressionist accounts sought to make systematic contributions to ethnological knowledge about West Africa, many instead conveying almost random facts about different populations and their cultural practices. Some were derived from direct observations, others from anecdotes that stemmed from meetings with Europeans officials, merchants and others on the West African coast. Recurrent themes of interest included local modes of warfare,[23] forms of dance and music – depicted in Alexander's account by an illustration of a 'Fantee Dance'[24] – and various West African cultural practices, including the 'palaver'.[25] Lacking the trained eye and, in most cases, linguistic skills necessary to understand fully these practices, the writers tended to focus on dress and the embodied physicality of the African people that they encountered. Hence, during a meeting with King Tom Standey, the ruler of the island of Anno Bono, Leonard described the people as follows:

> his subjects in myriads surrounded the verandah, within three feet of us, shouldering each other, and almost suffocating us with heat, dust, and the peculiar offensive odour proceeding from their filthy carcasses, and stunning us with the incessant, loud, and discordant clatter of their tongues.[26]

Alexander described a Fantee funeral he had witnessed at Accra in similar terms:

> Next, half a dozen wild-looking men appeared, who seemed to be under the excitement of liquor, and their waist-cloths trailing in the dust. They roared out songs; rushed madly ten or a dozen yards up the street, twisting violently their shoulders, arms, and legs; then wheeled round and returned, stooping and circling on their hams; whilst musicians beat drums and dry sticks, and loudly joined in the chorus.[27]

[151]

Unsurprisingly, it was those aspects of local African cultures that appeared to be furthest from the bourgeois Victorian culture of the observers and their readers that attracted the most attention, including the treatment of women and African religious and spiritual practices.[28] Indeed, descriptions of 'fetish' (or 'fetishe') objects, fetish men (priests) and fetish objects of worship, including animals, recurred in suppressionist texts.[29]

Overall, accounts of Africa produced in the context of naval suppression were free from the horrific savagery more common in later writing and that was a significant theme in the representation of the 'Dark Continent'. A striking exception was Huntley's *Seven Years' Service*, which recounted several scenes of native 'custom' intended to horrify (and titillate) its readers. One scene, which took place in Bonny on the Bight of Biafra, involved a public execution, in which the criminal was bludgeoned to death and his body fed to sharks. Another took place nearby in Calabar, where the approaching death of a local ruler prompted the 'fattening' of seven wives who were to accompany him to his grave, while Huntley also described in gory detail the practice of sacrificing enslaved people on the death of a Cameroon chief.[30] Perhaps the most dramatic anecdote occurred at the end of the first volume, involving the 'annual sacrifice of a young female child to the deity of the country, which was no other than the shark'.[31] This affecting scene was recounted by Huntley in great detail from the apparent perspective of a first-hand witness. It reached a terrifying climax:

> She attempted to jump back into the canoe, before the raft was quite launched, but she was bound to it – madly she tore from her head the wreath, and from her limbs the ribbons with which they were decorated – all was useless, her screams were drowned by the noises already described, and the inhuman cheers of the assemblage, in which the mother and relations were the most prominently partaking; the sacrifice was now on the water only waiting to be seized by the monster deity of the Calabar.[32]

Such scenes of 'native customs' were picked up by reviewers, not least because of Huntley's earlier (semi-)fictional writing. For example, the *Spectator* commented that he had 'more style and skill in composition than is generally possessed by men who visit the coast of Africa', though also noted that this might lead to 'over-detail and give rise to a little "colouring"'.[33]

Although this 'colouring' might have undermined Huntley's credibility as an objective witness, it gave his writing dramatic impact. Many of the features of later imperial discourse on Africa were present in his text. His intention in conveying such scenes was clear: Huntley ended the volume with an attack on British philanthropy and asserted that the various claims made for the potential of introducing civilisation to Africa were misplaced. In so doing, he sought to break apart the supposedly mutually reinforcing fields of commerce and civilisation, arguing that contact with Europeans had done nothing to modify 'paganism and barbarism' in Africa and that the only consequence had been to promote 'their adoption of drunkenness, and as much of the low trickery of business as they have capacity to acquire'.[34] Huntley's indictment can be read, in part, as an acknowledgement of the failure of British policy and humanitarian aims. It was also a call for a supposedly more pragmatic posture in Africa in which imperial strength was made manifest when necessary through means of force, the capacities of African groups were realistically evaluated, and any civilising 'humbug' was abandoned.[35] At the same time, his account, and especially its focus on disturbing and horrific scenes also chimed with a broader mid-century hardening of racial attitudes in British imperial culture. In this regard, Huntley's *Seven Years' Service* represents a mid-point between earlier suppressionist accounts that were shaped by the culture of early nineteenth-century British anti-slavery and those that would contribute to the 'darkening' of Africa in the second half of the century.[36]

Comprehending Africa

Among all the anecdotes and general observations about Africa, some suppressionist writers did seek to probe deeper into the societies they encountered to provide more detailed understanding of historical events, political structures and economic systems. Forbes stood out here. Much of his *Six Months' Service* focused on Cape Mount, a territory just north of Liberia, and considered the rise and fall of a particular local chief, King George Cain. Personally known to Forbes and described by him as 'my friend', Cain was depicted as an individual with a personal history:

> King Cain, so called by English visitors, was a man about eight-and-twenty, tall, well-built, and for a black handsome. At this birth he had been called Zeñäh. Becoming a member of the secret society called the Pourra (of which in its place) he took the name of Bahi, by a contraction of Bahi-zenah, which might be called his country name ... He was a clever man, and had he lived his family might have been the means of spreading civilization over that part of Africa.[37]

According to Forbes, the British had signed an anti-slave trade treaty with King Fano-Toro in 1846. The monarch faced a series of military threats, some stirred up by those who favoured the continuation of slave trading. Fano-Toro abdicated in favour of a military leader, Prince

George Cain, who was resented by his neighbours as an upstart and for his continuing adherence to the treaty. Although Cain defeated his enemies through force of arms, he was unable to establish a legit-imate replacement to slave trading, which had been central to the local economic system and had played a vital role in the distribu-tion of wealth and resources in the traditional political structure. In consequence, it appeared that only Cain, who had been rewarded with British gifts to secure his adherence to the treaty, had actually benefitted from the abandonment of slave trading. His people revolted and Cain was killed, wiping out the progress that had been made by the 1846 treaty.[38] The story of King Cain was a major preoccupation in *Six Months' Service*: a third of the substantive chapters focus on it and the politics of Cape Mount. Forbes used it to explain how the authority of African rulers was limited by 'custom' and the power of tradition,[39] as well as the political and economic contexts in which suppression was pursued and the countervailing forces that worked against the British. Such accounts were picked up by reviewers, who were dismayed to discover that the success of the policy apparently rested on individuals like Cain, who even Forbes described as a thief.[40]

Most African people did not receive the same attention as Cain. However, particular African groups were recurrent presences in a number of suppressionist accounts. Some were picked out because they were known to the authors themselves, others because of their presumed familiarity to the readers. The 'Kroomen' (Kru) were an example of the former and the Ashanti the latter. As John Rankin details in chapter 5 of this volume, Kru were a familiar presence on British naval vessels, which would often hire them on arrival at Sierra Leone to replace European crew members. Suppressionist accounts explained how individual Kru were engaged by Royal Navy ships on the basis of records of their previous service and the testimony of a head Kruman.[41] Although their self-adopted English names often provided a source of amusement for British authors (and presumably their audiences), while their oft-quoted description as the 'Scotchmen of Africa' articulated a patronising English perspective, Kru were generally held in consid-erable respect as hardworking and obedient.[42] Within a social-racial hierarchy that was topped by white, bourgeois Englishmen, the Kru were far below, yet superior to other Africans, including the liberated Africans settled at Sierra Leone and elsewhere. As Forbes put it, the Kru were 'the most useful of all the African tribes' and 'are generally fine athletic men'.[43] According to observers, the excellence of the Kru in comparison with other Africans was apparent in their physiognomy. As Huntley wrote about two Kru men he encountered: 'neither … partook of the heavy unintelligent feature of the true born negro, and

this is a difference enjoyed by the tribe, indeed the high nose and prominent forehead is more or less exhibited throughout it'.[44] The generally
positive accounts that writers like Huntley gave of the Kru, portraying
them as ideal servants and adjuncts to the squadron, paralleled the
records and testimony that were the basis for their individual recruitment to naval vessels. Moreover, by understanding the character,
customs and 'nature' of this people, it was possible to ensure that they
were managed most effectively. '[P]erfect confidence may be placed in
them,' Huntley wrote, 'if they are treated with kindness, firmness, and
above all, with a just and impartial regard to their rights and comforts,
as part of the ship's company; a consideration which has sometimes
been forgotten, and they then become sullen, shuffling, and discon-
tented, as naturally they may.'[45] Such comments give a clue as to the
broader ideological purpose of these accounts of African groups: by
fully understanding them, Britons were better placed to manage and
master them.[46]

Another group that attracted the attention of the suppressionist
writers was the 'Ashantee' (Ashanti) inland from the Gold Coast.
Britain's war with the Ashanti in the mid-1820s had impacted on the
British public due to the defeat suffered at Bonsaso in 1824 and death
of Charles MacCarthy, who had then been in charge of Britain's West
Africa possessions. Given this history, writers presumed that accounts
of this group would be of interest to their readers. They offered potted
histories of MacCarthy's death and the subsequent defeat of the Ashanti
by British reinforcements.[47] Moreover, in the light of the more recent
improvement in relations, the Ashanti came to serve as a barometer
for the success of British policy in West Africa more generally. As
Alexander put it:

> if the Ashantees could only be persuaded to substitute brute for human
> sacrifices, on the death of their relatives, it would be another great step
> towards civilization. The people here are a fine, brave, and muscular
> race, of a deep brown colour, – some with broad noses, and others with
> very good features; and it is distressing to see the prevalence of customs,
> which tend to annihilate them, by staining with human blood the graves
> of their ancestors.[48]

Overall, accounts of this group offered little new knowledge and instead
responded to the existing interest and expectations of the public.

While the Kru and Ashanti would have been somewhat familiar
to the readers of suppressionist accounts, rather different were the
populations of Atlantic islands such as Fernando Po and Anno Bono
(today Bioko and Annobón, respectively, in Equatorial Guinea). These
islands were visited by Leonard and Huntley in the early 1830s and
their inhabitants perhaps came closest in Africa's Atlantic littoral to

the unknown 'tribes' that Alexander had hoped to encounter in East Africa.[49] Their location on islands regularly visited by the ships of the squadron meant that this was one area where suppressionist writers could contribute to the British public's understanding. Indeed, the texts did convey some information about these populations, including their appearance and character as well as particular customs. One which attracted considerable interest from British visitors and metropolitan reviewers was the peculiar nature of kingship in Anno Bono. Leonard explained that the king was elected for a year by his people and obtained his revenue by securing gifts from passing European ships.[50] The writers also speculated on the origins of these insular populations. According to Huntley, for example, the Bubi of Fernando Po were a simple people and a 'species separate' from the coastal peoples.[51]

More significant than any ethnological information conveyed, however, and providing further evidence of the generally impressionistic character of most suppressionist texts, were how these encounters with Atlantic island populations were used to articulate broader themes about Europe's encounter with Africa. These encounters provided suppressionist writers with humorous episodes at the expense of African people, often turning on European technology. For example, accounts described the apprehension in which European visitors to Anno Bono were held, due to their previous experience of slaving raids. Thus, Leonard wrote of the 'distrust and fear with which many of them, particularly the women and children, received us' and of their 'innate horror of weapons of any sort, particularly fire-arms'. His party 'took advantage this terror to keep the people a distance' and even to provide themselves with amusement. For example, while being followed by a large group of local people, one of Leonard's colleagues 'suddenly stopped, and fixed an angry look on the nearest of the dense mass':

> They likewise stopped, looked at each other and at him, and shrank back a little, while he continued his look of displeasure, and gradually raised his hand to his pocket as if in search of a weapon; they then fairly took to their heels, made one desperate rush, and tumbled over each other in their haste to get out of the way, when he withdrew his snuff-box from his pocket, and, laughing at the success of his exploit, took a hearty pinch.[52]

Similarly, Huntley recounted a meeting with the king of Anno Bono in which a trick was played upon him:

> The next exhibition for the royal visitor was the Lucifer match; playing a piece of sandpaper between the folds of an old newspaper, the match was suddenly lighted, but nothing less than touching the flame, could

convince the royal mind that he saw actual fire; he requested a repetition of the performance, which was of course complied with; then asking in his best English, to be allowed a trial himself, the newspaper was given to him without the sand-paper, this having been secretly withdrawn; His Majesty drew the match through the paper time after time, but of course failed to produce fire, at which, the royal mind became much incensed, and he declared white man to be 'devils,' who could do what they liked with black man, and every thing else.[53]

In the narration of such encounters, there was little pretence of a civilising mission. The only lesson taught concerned the superiority of what the king called the white 'devils' – a term that reinforced the notion that superstition made Africans inferior to the 'scientific' British – while amusement at the expense of local people was the main aim. Yet it would be mistaken to overemphasise the strength of this ridicule. Consider, for instance, what Leonard and Huntley had to say about religious practice at Anno Bono, which had once been a Portuguese possession. Both described a poor 'imitation' and a 'mockery' even of what they considered to be 'Roman Catholic absurdities'.[54] Yet despite such comments, Leonard was not able to feel straightforwardly superior (there was 'a smile – certainly not a sneer', he wrote, about local forms of religious observance), while even Huntley saw the potential for religious advancement among the population.[55] If the accounts of the Atlantic island were certainly characterised by British disdain for their populations, then this was tempered by some continuing confidence in the transformative power of a European civilising presence.

A white man's grave?

Accounts of West African customs attracted much interest from reviewers, especially if deemed novel, strange or shocking, but the most abiding aspect of the image of the region concerned its supposedly deadly climate and reputation as 'the white man's grave'.[56] Debates about the British presence in West Africa had long turned on questions related to its human cost. Sierra Leone, established by humanitarians in the late eighteenth century, had often been subjected to criticisms on this basis. Such attacks peaked in the 1820s and were bound up with questions about the colony's role as the headquarters for the West Africa Squadron and site for the Courts of Mixed Commission. Following the publicity elicited by an intense pamphlet war, a Royal Commission was sent in 1825 to investigate the healthiness of Britain's West African settlements, including Sierra Leone and the Gambia. Partly generated by such attention, arguments were made for the establishment of a British presence at Fernando Po, which was envisioned as a new, healthier site for both the squadron's headquarters and the courts. Such a policy was based on the belief that Fernando Po's elevated topography kept it clear of the 'miasmas' that bedevilled low-lying terrain, while its insular status meant that it was distant from the unhealthy coast.[57] Yet in the context of general ignorance about the underlying causes of African diseases, such claims were contested. Moreover, after a British base was established at Fernando Po in 1827, questions were soon raised about whether it was really healthier than Sierra Leone, especially when yellow fever ravaged Fernando Po and other parts of the West African coast in 1829.[58] These problems did not lead to a rehabilitation of Sierra Leone's reputation, however, but to a general 'darkening' of the region as a 'white man's grave'.[59] Such perspectives continued to resonate across suppressionist accounts, often in personal ways for those serving in the squadron. As Forbes put it: '[t]he coast of Africa is (and, doubtless, with good reason) looked upon with great horror by members of public services, whose turn of duty may take them there'.[60] Indeed, West Africa was an unpopular station for those serving on it due to threats to health, at least until the widespread adoption of quinine in the mid-1850s.[61]

There was little scientific understanding of the causes of disease at this time and although 'intermittent' and 'remittent' fevers were recognised as distinct, there was no appreciation of the causes of malaria and yellow fever respectively. Instead, most accounts repeated the same ideas about the causes of ill-health in West Africa. On the one hand, particular productions of environments were to blame, such as the 'pestilential effluvia' exhaled from stagnant water and swamps, and the 'decomposed luxuriance of the vegetation, rank grass, and fallen foliage' that rendered 'this land so fatal to European life'.[62] In consequence, authors called for the improvement of the landscape of British settlements through clearance, drainage and cultivation.[63] At the same time, this environmental understanding was combined with an emphasis on the importance of behaviour in making Europeans vulnerable. For example, Alexander recalled what had happened at the Danish settlement at Accra in 1833: 'the men ate and drank, even for days together, till nothing was left in the castle of Christianborg; also smoked furiously; and danced with one another, overflowing with wine and friendship. These debauches were naturally succeeded by fevers, so violent to new comers, that they could not recover them.'[64] This perspective was moral as much as it was medical, of course, explaining ill-health and mortality in terms of excessive behaviour as well as exposure to dangerous places.[65] Such perspectives were not unique to West Africa and characterised much of the understanding of the European encounter with the tropical world at this time.[66]

Some suppressionist writers tried to move beyond such generalities. The naval surgeon Leonard hoped to bring some order to discussions. He was dismissive of the 'local prejudices' often to be found among those living in West Africa against environmental explanations of ill-health: 'The idea of climatorial or local insalubrity could not for a moment be entertained', he complained.[67] Whereas many blamed excessive lifestyles, a view repeated by Alexander, Leonard placed greater understanding on geography. He tended to generalise, however, dismissing the vaunted claims that had been made for the salubriousness of Fernando Po, and seeing it and Sierra Leone as 'both bad enough in that respect'.[68] Yet even Leonard, with his supposedly more objective perspective on the causes of West African unhealthiness, laid much store on the role of bodily practice in securing health. 'Temperance in this climate is imperatively necessary', he wrote, '[a]bstemiousness and excess are alike injurious'.[69] Recommending exactly three glasses of wine with dinner and food that was 'as little complicated as possible' as variety 'only aids the undertaker by driving so many nails in his coffin', Leonard also offered other advice for securing one's health in West Africa: '[t]emperance, regularity of the bowels, and a cold shower bath, – to wit, two or three buckets of salt water thrown over the body, morning and evening – will do more to preserve health in this climate than all other precautions put together.'[70] With its didactic tone and quantification of the amount of wine to be consumed and water to be used, Leonard's account was intended as a self-help manual for others serving on the West African coast. It was also an attempt to impose health-preserving order on a genuinely dangerous and poorly understood disease environment. To this extent, it was similar to Alexander's meteorological observations, which he hoped would foster an understanding of the sickliest times in the region given his belief that the production of dangerous 'effluvia' peaked with the hottest periods of the year.[71] Similarly, Forbes sought to chart the most dangerous parts of the coast.[72] Overall, however, the suppressionist accounts were not works of medical topography that sought to establish systematic links between health and particular environments.[73] Instead, their primary consequence was to convey the dangers of West Africa to European constitutions, including those of the authors themselves, and in so doing they reinforced the general impression of the region as a 'white man's grave'.

Conclusion: the view from the ship

Half a century ago, Philip Curtin wrote that the authors of suppressionist travel writing 'rarely had any real interest in Africa as such'. Instead, they wrote 'to give their fellow countrymen a vicarious enjoyment of their adventurers – laced with occasional political recommendations about the blockade or other timely subjects'.[74] Is Curtin's summation a fair one? Certainly, as Burroughs has shown, these accounts spent a lot of time focusing on the pursuit of slave ships – or complaining about the lack of action. Yet as Emma Christopher finds in her chapter, and as I have also shown, the liberated Africans at Sierra Leone (and Fernando Po) attracted attention, as did various African peoples and places, albeit to a lesser extent. To focus less on the particular objects of suppressionist texts and more on the general structuring of these accounts, however, does support Curtin's contention about the absence of 'real interest'.

It has already been noted that most of the suppressionist writers lacked the expertise, time or inclination to produce detailed, meaningful accounts of West Africa and its peoples. This perspective partly stemmed from the writers' location literally – but especially *figuratively* – aboard the ships of the squadron, which did much to shape their encounters with the region. Indeed, the 'view from the ship' is an apt meta-trope for the representation of African societies in most suppressionst accounts, stemming as it did from a particular political and cultural location. As other chapters in this volume have demonstrated, these ships could be sites of complex intercultural exchange with African peoples. Indeed, this cultural diversity might have made for more varied and perhaps penetrating accounts of West Africa. Yet suppressionist writers generally overlooked this complexity as they cast an ideologically blinkered gaze at the coast. Their perspective was almost universally superficial, with little time or effort spent understanding cultural forms and social structures. Instead, preconceptions and long-established clichés were usually repeated with little critical reflection. Even the landfalls that the suppressionist writers occasionally made permitted little more than brief rambles or dashes on horseback. Their encounters were largely with British officials, from whom they gleaned anecdotes, 'common-sense' and local 'wisdom'. The distanced and constrained perspective of suppressionist texts also reflected European anxieties about the West African environment, anxieties that were evident in advice on how to avoid the effects of the local climate, such as by not sleeping onshore. Although the threat to European health was real, the view from the ship resonates figuratively with how these texts sought to avoid potentially deadly entanglements with West Africa, while also paralleling the reading experience of those back in Britain: safely distant – in physical, cultural and moral terms – from getting too close to the coast.

The view from the ship structured how suppressionist texts produced a particular image of West Africa. Alexander's *Narrative of a Voyage* is exemplary here; he even wrote his account aboard the HMS *Thalia*, a point which he used to explain (perhaps excuse) the absence of deep reflection.[75] More broadly, his remarks on African cultures usually drew on superficial, surface observations of the societies he encountered, focusing on dress and physical appearance, and often based on short rambles and jaunts. While Alexander sought to persuade his readers that he was interested in getting beyond the supposedly shallow knowledge of coastal merchants – 'Surely a pilgrim's sketch is better than none at all!', he insisted – reviewers found his account 'unsubstantial'.[76] Moreover, Alexander's practice of sketching the landscapes and people he encountered during his travels is a useful metaphor not only for the power dynamics at play in the suppressionist encounter, with Africans as objects to be captured (and liberated) by the European gaze, but also his general failure to get below the surface.[77] Lacking the time, knowledge or willingness to engage with local societies, many of the places and practices that he and other writers described were cast in Eurocentric terms, remaining 'confused', 'strange', 'wretched' and 'rude'.[78]

In conclusion, and to return to the three ways in which suppressionist texts produced knowledge about West Africa, the contribution to formal geographical knowledge was limited. Other than the meteorological data gathered by Alexander, none of the writers discussed sought to gather data systematically, while the various descriptions of landscapes and places added little. In terms of wider, popular understandings of Africa, the periodical reviews of the suppressionist texts give helpful insights into what was deemed to be important at the time. Most of the reviewers were more concerned with what the accounts revealed about the success or otherwise of the policy of suppression, as evident in the number of slave ships captured and seized, as well as the 'progress' at Sierra Leone and among the liberated Africans. While the overall impression garnered was a familiar one about the failure of suppression, Africa itself remained less well-known: 'few go there willingly, and of those who go few return', as one reviewer put it.[79] To fill this gap, reviewers highlighted and repeated a 'few scattered observations' and anecdotes, such as Leonard's account of the nature of kingship at Anno Bono,[80] or Huntley's sensationalist descriptions of the practices associated with chiefly death. Overall, the impression engendered by the suppressionist accounts was of a 'country little known, and a people only partially understood'.[81]

Finally, the wider ideological work performed by these texts was somewhat limited with regard to the descriptions of West Africa itself (rather than encounters with slaves, liberated Africans and slave traders). To some extent, the suppressionist texts were 'anti-conquest' in character, seeking to 'secure their innocence in the same moment as they assert European hegemony' and thus articulating 'a utopian, innocent vision of European global hegemony'.[82] In this regard, suppressionist discourse could be seen to serve as a kind of vanguard for a later, more clearly colonising discourse, legitimising British intervention in Africa by simultaneously washing away the 'sins' of British involvement in slave trading and 'darkening' the continent. Yet, with regard to the production of the image of West Africa more narrowly, this ideological work was much less pronounced. Although there was a territorial aspect to the actions of the West Africa Squadron, as well as diplomatic engagement and commercial penetration in West African societies, this was very different from the later expansionism of the 'Scramble for Africa'. The view from the ship may have bequeathed suppressionist texts a largely superficial comprehension of African societies, but it also meant that these accounts did not become opportunities for imaginatively projecting British territorial power and presence onto the region. Nor should the precariousness of the British presence in West Africa be underestimated, both in the face of African polities as well as the poorly understood and greatly feared disease environment. Overall, this precariousness meant that the suppressionist texts were less confidently colonialistic. Ultimately, though, the apparent failure of suppressionist policy would contribute to the mid-to-late Victorian view of Africans as 'unredeemable' and to the 'darkening' of the image of West Africa, thus helping the lay of path toward a more nakedly imperialistic posture.[83]

Notes

1 The classic work on the development of British ideas about Africa from the late eighteenth to mid-nineteenth century is Philip D. Curtin, *The Image of Africa: British Ideas and Actions, 1780–1850* (London: Macmillan, 1965).
2 W. J. Hamilton, 'Geography', in John F. W. Herschel (ed.), *A Manual of Scientific Enquiry; Prepared for the Use of Her Majesty's Navy: And Adapted for Travellers in General* (London: John Murray, 1849), pp. 127–55, at p. 129; J. C. Prichard, 'Ethnology', in *Manual of Scientific Enquiry*, pp. 424–40.
3 J. M. R. Cameron, 'John Barrow, the *Quarterly*'s Imperial Reviewer', in Jonathan Cutmore (ed.), *Conservatism and the Quarterly Review* (London: Pickering and Chatto, 2007), pp. 133–49; Elizabeth Baigent, 'Founders of the Royal Geographical Society of London', in Lawrence Goldman (ed.), *Oxford Dictionary of National Biography* (Oxford: Oxford University Press, 2004 – present), http://www/oxforddnb.com/view/theme/95334. Accessed 18 June 2013.
4 Alexander arrived in southern Africa in 1835 as war had broken out with the Xhosa, serving there instead of undertaking his planned expedition.

5 L. C. Henderson, 'Geography, Travel and Publishing in Mid-Victorian Britain' (PhD dissertation, Royal Holloway, University of London, 2012); Curtin, *Image of Africa*, p. 341.
6 Compare Janice Cavell, *Tracing the Connected Narrative: Arctic Exploration in British Print Culture, 1818–1860* (Toronto, Buffalo, London: University of Toronto Press, 2008).
7 Edward W. Said, *Orientalism: Western Conceptions of the Orient* (London: Penguin, 1978); Edward Said, *Culture and Imperialism* (London: Chatto and Windus, 1993).
8 Patrick Brantlinger, 'Victorians and Africans: The Geneaology of the Myth of the Dark Continent', in Henry L. Gates Jr. (ed.), *'Race', Writing, and Difference* (London: University of Chicago Press, 1985), pp. 185–222.
9 While readerships can be very difficult to determine, none of the texts considered in this chapter went to more than a single edition, suggesting that sales were limited.
10 Alexander, who was not serving on the ship in which he travelled, had more time on his hands than other observers. During his travels, he produced sketches of the people and places he encountered and also gathered meteorological data. Examples of both appear in his text.
11 A few testimonies by liberated Africans were also published. See, for example, the 'Information obtained from Thomas Wogga, an African' in James MacQueen, 'Notes on African Geography', *Journal of the Royal Geographical Society* 15 (1845), 374–6. For discussion, see David Lambert, *Mastering the Niger: James MacQueen's African Geography and the Struggle over Atlantic Slavery* (Chicago, IL: University of Chicago Press, 2013), p. 249, fn 61. Other testimonies can be found in Philip D. Curtin (ed.), *Africa Remembered: Narratives by West Africans from the Era of the Slave Trade* (Madison, WI: University of Wisconsin Press, 1967).
12 Frederick Edwyn Forbes, *Five Years in China; from 1842 to 1847: With an Account of the Occupation of Labuan and Borneo by Her Majesty's Forces* (London: Richard Bentley, 1848); James Edward Alexander, *Travels to the Seat of War in the East, through Russia and the Crimea, in 1829, etc.* (Henry Colburn & Richard Bentley: London, 1830); James Edward Alexander, *Transatlantic Sketches, Comprising Visits to the Most Interesting Scenes in North and South America, and the West Indies; with Notes on Negro Slavery and Canadian Emigration* (London: Richard Bentley, 1833).
13 Henry Huntley, *Peregrine Scramble; or Thirty Years Adventures of a Blue Jacket* (Paris: A. and W. Galignanai and Co., 1849).
14 Peter Leonard, *Records of a Voyage to the Western Coast of Africa, in His Majesty's Ship* Dryad, *and of the Service on that Station for the Suppression of the Slave Trade, in the Years 1830, 1831, and 1832* (Edinburgh: William Tait, 1833), pp. iii, iv.
15 Pascoe Grenfell Hill, *A Voyage to the Slave Coasts of West and East Africa* (London: C. Gilpin, 1849), p. 18.
16 Henry Huntley, *Seven Years' Service on the Slave Coast of Western Africa*, 2 vols (London: Thomas Cautley Newby, 1850), i, 29.
17 Curtin, *Image of Africa*, p. 206.
18 Leonard, *Records of a Voyage*, pp. 210–11. See also Huntley's comments about African soils in *Seven Years' Service*, i, 164.
19 James Edward Alexander, *Narrative of a Voyage of Observation among the Colonies of Western Africa, in the Flag-ship* Thalia, *and of a Campaign in Kaffir-Land on the Staff of the Commander-in-Chief, in 1835*, 2 vols (London: Henry Colburn, 1837), i, 2.
20 Alexander, *Narrative of a Voyage*, i, 175–6.
21 Alexander, *Narrative of a Voyage*, opposite p. 1. Forbes also included a map of the West African coast between the Bullam shore and Liberia, including both nautical and political information. Frederick E. Forbes, *Six Months' Service in the African Blockade, from April to October 1848, in Command of HMS* Bonetta (London: Richard Bentley, 1849), opposite frontispiece.
22 Forbes, *Six Months' Service*, pp. 129–41. Forbes also compiled tables of data relating to the extent of the transatlantic slave trade on pp. 142–5. Forbes's interest and faculty with West African languages, especially the Vai language of Sierra Leone, was

demonstrated by his later work: Frederick E. Forbes, *Dahomey and the Dahomans: Being the Journals of Two Missions to the King of Dahomey, and Residence at his Capital, in the Years 1849 and 1850*, 2 vols (London: Longmans, 1851). See Myron J. Echenberg, '[Review of] Frederick E. Forbes, *Six Months' Service in the African Blockade: from April to October, 1848, in Command of H. M. S.* Bonetta', *Journal of Asian and African Studies* 7 (1972), 236–9.

23 Alexander, *Narrative of a Voyage*, i, 15; Forbes, *Six Months' Service*, pp. 102–3.
24 Alexander, *Narrative of a Voyage*, i, 171–2. The image appears opposite p. 177.
25 Forbes, *Six Months' Service*, p. 28.
26 Leonard, *Records of a Voyage*, p. 181.
27 Alexander, *Narrative of a Voyage*, i, 188.
28 Huntley, *Seven Years' Service*, i, 166.
29 Leonard, *Records of a Voyage*, p. 57; Huntley, *Seven Years' Service*, i, 364–5, 98–9.
30 Huntley, *Seven Years' Service*, ii, 7.
31 Huntley, *Seven Years' Service*, i, 396.
32 Huntley, *Seven Years' Service*, i, 399.
33 'Sir Henry Huntley's *Seven Years' Service on the Slave Coast of Africa*', *Spectator* 23, 1154 (1850), 759.
34 Huntley, *Seven Years' Service*, i, 400.
35 Christopher Lloyd attributes Huntley's views to his political perspective, describing him as a 'disgruntled Tory who had no use for the Whig crotchet of civilising Africa'. Christopher Lloyd, *The Navy and the Slave Trade* (London: Longmans, Green & Co., 1949), p. 72.
36 See Brantlinger, 'Victorians and Africans'.
37 Forbes, *Six Months' Service*, pp. 44, 46.
38 Forbes, *Six Months' Service*, pp. 70–2. For a very different account of these events, see Brantz Mayer, (ed.) *Captain Canot: or, Twenty Years of an African Slaver* (London George Routledge & Co., 1855), pp. 285–8.
39 Forbes, *Six Months' Service*, p. 29. For an example of more recent scholarship on these themes, see Svend E. Holsoe, 'The Manipulation of Traditional Political Structures among Coastal Peoples in Western Liberia during the Nineteenth Century', *Ethnohistory* 21 (1974), 158–67.
40 '*Six Months' Service in the African Blockade, from April to October 1848, in Command of H. M. S.* Bonetta', *Athenaeum* 1114 (1849), 219–20.
41 Huntley, *Seven Years' Service*, i, 21–3.
42 Alexander, *Narrative of a Voyage*, i, 108–9. See Jane Martin, *Krumen Down the Coast: Liberian Migrants in the West African Coast in the Nineteentth Century* (Boston, MA: African Studies Center, 1982).
43 Forbes, *Six Months' Service*, pp. 18, 20.
44 Huntley, *Seven Years' Service*, i, 20–1.
45 Huntley, *Seven Years' Service*, i, 18–19.
46 See also Robert Burroughs, '"[T]he true sailors of Western Africa": Kru Seafaring Identity in British Travellers' Accounts of the 1830s and 1840s', *Journal of Maritime Research* 11 (2009), 51–67. On the provision of medical care for Africans, see chapter 5 in this volume.
47 Huntley, *Seven Years' Service*, i, 71–4; Alexander, *Narrative of a Voyage*, i, 154, 58.
48 Alexander, *Narrative of a Voyage*, i, 158.
49 Alexander, *Narrative of a Voyage*, i, 2. While Fernando Po had an indigenous population, the Bubi, Anno Bono's population, were the descendants of enslaved people who had run away.
50 Leonard, *Records of a Voyage*, pp. 181–2. See Huntley, *Seven Years' Service*, i, 285–6.
51 Huntley, *Seven Years' Service*, i, 165.
52 Leonard, *Records of a Voyage*, 183.
53 Huntley, *Seven Years' Service*, i, 288.
54 Leonard, *Records of a Voyage*, pp. 176, 77; Huntley, *Seven Years' Service*, i, 284.
55 Leonard, *Records of a Voyage*, p. 185; Huntley, *Seven Years' Service*, i, 284.
56 See, for example, Anon., 'Reminiscences of the Gold Coast, being Extracts from Notes

Taken during a Tour of Service in 1847–8', *Colburn's United Service Magazine*, part 3 (1850), 67.

57 For discussion, see David Lambert, 'Sierra Leone and Other Sites in the War of Representation over Slavery', *History Workshop Journal* 64 (2007), 103–32; Martin Lynn, 'Britain's West African Policy and the Island of Fernando Po, 1821–43', *Journal of Imperial and Commonwealth History* 18 (1990), 191–207.

58 Robert T. Brown, 'Fernando Po and the Anti-Sierra Leonean Campaign: 1826–1834', *The International Journal of African Historical Studies* 6 (1973), 249–64.

59 László Máthé-Shires, 'Imperial Nightmares: The British Image of "the deadly climate" of West Africa, c.1840–74', *European Review of History* 8 (2001), 137–56.

60 Forbes, *Six Months' Service*, p. 123.

61 For detailed discussion of health in the naval and armed forces in this region, see chapter 5 in this volume.

62 Alexander, *Narrative of a Voyage*, i, 69; Huntley, *Seven Years' Service*, i, 12.

63 Leonard, *Records of a Voyage*, p. 173; Alexander, *Narrative of a Voyage*, i, 69.

64 Alexander, *Narrative of a Voyage*, i, 195–6.

65 Alexander, *Narrative of a Voyage*, i, 148–9.

66 David Arnold, *The Problem of Nature: Environment, Culture and European Expansion* (Oxford: Blackwell, 1996).

67 Leonard, *Records of a Voyage*, p. 20.

68 Leonard, *Records of a Voyage*, p. 173.

69 Leonard, *Records of a Voyage*, p. 76.

70 Leonard, *Records of a Voyage*, p. 76.

71 Alexander, *Narrative of a Voyage*, i, 149.

72 Forbes, *Six Months' Service*, p. 123.

73 Mark Harrison, 'Differences of Degree: Representations of India in British Medical topography, 1820–c.1870', in Nicolaas A. Rupke (ed.), *Medical Geography in Historical Perspective* (London: Wellcome Trust Centre for the History of Medicine at UCL, 2000), pp. 51–69.

74 Curtin, *Image of Africa*, p. 322.

75 Alexander, *Narrative of a Voyage*, i, xiv.

76 Alexander, *Narrative of a Voyage*, i, 159–60, 70, 93; 'Narrative of a Voyage of Observation among the Colonies of Western Africa, in the Flag Ship *Thalia*; and of a Campaign in Kaffirland, &c.,' *Athenaeum* 499 (1837), 355.

77 Alexander, *Narrative of a Voyage*, i, 169.

78 Alexander, *Narrative of a Voyage* , i, 161, 72; Leonard, *Records of a Voyage*, p. 180.

79 'Sir Henry Huntley's *Seven Years' Service*', p. 759.

80 See, for example, '*Records of a Voyage to the Western Coast of Africa*', *Athenaeum* 281 (1833), 164.

81 '*Seven Years' Service on the Slave Coast of Western Africa*', *Critic* 9, 227 (1850), 444.

82 Mary Louise Pratt, *Imperial Eyes: Travel Writing and Transculturation* (London: Routledge, 1992), pp. 7, 39.

83 Gill Gott, 'Imperial Humanitarianism: History of an Arrested Dialectic', in Berta Esperanza Hernández-Truyo (ed.), *Moral Imperialism: A Critical Anthology* (New York: New York University Press, 2002), pp. 19–38, at p. 23.

CHAPTER EIGHT

History, memory and commemoration of Atlantic slave-trade suppression

Richard Huzzey and John McAleer

In 1832, a small envelope was sent to the Admiralty in London from the coast of West Africa. Contained inside it was a handful of brown dust, described as the 'testings' taken from the timbers of HMS *Black Joke*. These powdered remnants were all that survived of one of the most famous and successful slave catchers in the history of the Royal Navy. According to one contemporary exaggeration, *Black Joke* did 'more towards putting an end to the vile traffic in slaves than all the ships on the station put together'.[1] Its success was partially due to its own history as a slaving ship. The vessel was probably built in Baltimore in the 1820s, subsequently becoming the Brazilian slave ship *Henriquetta*. Following her capture by the Royal Navy in 1827, the renamed *Black Joke* was responsible for freeing many hundreds of Africans held captive on slave ships and intended for slavery in the Americas. But the warm waters of West Africa proved to be her ultimate undoing. After undergoing the testing that produced the contents of the envelope sent to the Admiralty in May 1832, her timbers were found to have rotted to such an extent that she was declared unfit for service. The ship was ordered to Sierra Leone where it was broken up – deliberately 'destroyed by fire' – leaving only a few traces of her actions in support of Britain's campaign against the transatlantic slave trade.[2] The surveyors who reported on *Black Joke* attached specimens of the timbers to verify their report and, as Christopher Lloyd remarks, 'all that remains of that famous slave chaser is an envelope filled with brown dust in the Public Record Office'.[3]

The evanescent existence of this nondescript packet of dust symbolises public engagement with, and commemoration of, the British involvement in this aspect of the transatlantic slave trade. The envelope, and its contents, is a tangible reminder of the role played by the navy in promulgating Britain's nineteenth-century anti-slavery policies. But by virtue of the fact that the envelope contains all that remains of the *Black Joke*, it also acts as a potent symbol of the way in which much of the rest of the navy's suppression activities off the west coast of Africa in the first half of the nineteenth century fell from the public gaze. Relegated to a footnote in the history of the transatlantic slave trade, the Atlantic naval suppression squadrons have generally suffered one of three fates: they have been ignored by the general public; they have been seen by historians as precursors to greater successes in the Indian Ocean arena; or they have been deployed as a moral prophylactic against imperial guilt or an exemplar of sailors' martial virtue.

The most significant problem presented by the dusty remains of the *Black Joke* – for those eager to set the story of naval suppression within the broader history of the transatlantic slave trade – is the fact that the ship's history and career is divorced from the contexts in which the ship and its crew served. This deters a more rounded interpretation of slave-trade suppression activities. The difficulty of recreating the circumstances of Atlantic slave-trade suppression is not confined to the example of the *Black Joke* alone, however. This separation of objects related to the suppression of the slave trade from the wider contexts of what they are intended to commemorate was evident as late as 2009. In that year, Gordon Brown, the then British Prime Minister, visited the White House. As a gift to his host, Brown presented a desk tidy to the recently elected Barack Obama. The object was no ordinary desk tidy, as it was made from the timbers of HMS *Gannet*. Reuters reported that this ship 'served for a time on anti-slavery missions off Africa'.[4] But it was laden with much more potential meaning than this suggests. Presumably the object was intended to underpin the message that Britain was a key player in bringing the slave trade, and by extension slavery, to an end. The presentation of the desk tidy seemed to suggest that, while both countries were historically implicated in the slave trade, by the early nineteenth century they had rectified this aberration and were part of an anti-slavery alliance. It could also be seen as an attempt to reinforce the 'special relationship', founded on shared values of personal liberty and democracy, between the two countries. However, like many objects related to the suppression of the slave trade, the desk tidy was capable of sustaining multiple interpretations and conveying several messages, many of which are at odds with the presumed intention of its giver. For example, in relation to the transatlantic slave trade, and quite apart from the rhetoric of its liberty-professing founding fathers, Britain found the USA particularly intransigent when it came to patrolling the ocean for slave ships.[5] Highlighting Britain's involvement in slave-trade suppression could be seen as drawing attention to the ambiguous status of the USA in relation to anti-slavery operations. The ultimate irony was the fact that *Gannet* never patrolled the transatlantic traffic. It was launched in 1878, after the last of the Atlantic suppression squadrons had been recalled, and served in a squadron detailed to suppress the traffic in the Indian Ocean later in the century – a key driver behind British colonisation in East Africa.[6]

In both of these examples, objects are potent, albeit slippery and ambiguous, symbols of Britain's suppression of the slave trade. They also offer insights into the way in which this anti-slavery activity has been commemorated over the course of time. In both cases, the symbolic power of material culture was harnessed in an effort to reinforce the idea of Britain's fight against the nefarious activities of 'piratical' slave traders on the high seas. But these objects also illustrate the ways in which the memory of suppression activity has been channelled in particular directions or sublimated altogether. The material evidence of this episode is either almost entirely missing (the dust of HMS *Black Joke*) or is so decontextualised that it is capable of multiple and conflicted interpretations (the *Gannet* desk tidy). This chapter seeks to chart the ways in which slave-trade suppression in the Atlantic Ocean was represented in material culture, and the legacy of this commemoration for historical writing and public memory in the subsequent 200 years. It attempts to show how a partial, limited and decontextualised representation of slave-trade suppression has separated it from the broader history of the transatlantic slave trade. Furthermore, an examination of memorials, historiography and commemorations reveals the Royal Navy's anti-slavery duties as a crucial and under-represented episode of wider imperial history.

Contemporary commemoration, 1807–65

One of the key problems in representing suppression activities is that they were very quickly subsumed into a broader naval narrative of British history. In this interpretation, the suppression of the slave trade was just another, peculiarly nineteenth-century, activity engaged in by a navy which unswervingly defended Britain and British interests. Focusing on the role of the navy in executing the will of Parliament, or in contributing to a broader culture of anti-slavery in Britain, was less important than confirming its mettle as an anti-French fighting force or offering young men the opportunity to prove their physical and moral qualities. Well before material commemorations appeared in museums and exhibitions, this trend can be seen in memoirs and accounts derived from suppression activities.

This theme of setting suppression firmly in a naval context can be seen in the account of Peter Leonard, a surgeon serving on HMS

Dryad in the early 1830s. Leonard's account evinces two of the most common motifs running through naval representations from the eighteenth century: anti-French rhetoric and the idea of the unthinking sailor, happy to fight all-comers merely for the sake of it.[7] Much of Leonard's account is spent decrying the 'perfect idleness and inactivity of the Gallic squadron', which is in direct contrast to the operations of the Royal Navy.[8] Leonard continues to reinforce widely circulated naval stereotypes by affirming the fighting spirit of the British sailor in describing the encounter of the *Black Joke* with the Spanish slaver, *Marinerito*:

> It is gratifying to think that *Jack* is still the same – that he fights for the love of it just as he was wont to do – for it is not to be supposed that any notions concerning the inhumanity of slave-dealing, or the boon of emancipation which he is about to confer on so many hundreds of his fellow-creatures, enter his thoughtless head, when he begins the conflict.[9]

In highlighting the transferability of this characteristic, Leonard specifically denies any conscious sympathy among the sailors for the Africans they are liberating. It is as if the suppression activities of the navy are merely a testing ground for Jolly Jack Tars where they reassert their superior pluck.

As Leonard's account attests, suppression was seen essentially as a naval activity; it remained within the purview of the navy, responding to, and drawing on, other naval traditions. In material terms, this can be seen most obviously in church memorials commemorating naval personnel who took part in Britain's fight against the slave trade. The inscriptions on these memorials give an indication of the ways in which suppression activities were represented in the mid-nineteenth century. In some instances, these physical objects, generally inscribed and wall-mounted tablets in churches, clearly list and record the activities and successes of the navy's operations against the slave trade off the coast of West Africa. The memorial to Commodore William Jones, commander of HMS *Penelope*, is a case in point.[10] He is commemorated by a wall tablet in St Luke's Church at the Royal Hospital Haslar, in Gosport. *Penelope* served on the west coast of Africa and the inscription on Jones's memorial records that 'by His Judicious Arrangements / 115 Slave Vessels Were captured / And 6738 Human Beings Were Released From Slavery / Between 1st April 1844 And 12th March 1846 /'.[11]

Most memorials were concerned with emphasising the personal qualities of the individuals they were erected to commemorate. In these instances, the deceased person's involvement in slave-trade suppression is often cited as evidence of broader public and private virtues. Lieutenant James Still, for example, is commemorated in the church of Church of St Mary the Virgin, in High Pavement, Nottingham, after falling 'victim to the ravages of the Yellow Fever' during service on HMS *Pheasant* at the age of 21. The inscription on the memorial notes that for four years he had been 'employed in the fatal service of enforcing obedience to that sacred Law, which to the honour of his Country and in the spirit of Christian Love, forbade the Traffick in Human Blood'.[12] John Lodwick, who is commemorated by a wall tablet in St Andrew's Church, Rochford, perished at the age of 35. The inscription on his memorial drew attention to his promotion for 'gallantry in an encounter with a slave ship' in early 1845 before Lodwick shortly later fell 'victim to the pestilential fever of the coast of Africa'. The 'admiration and respect for his gallant and truly estimable character' encouraged his friends to have the memorial erected.[13] Both Still's and Lodwick's naval service, and specifically the young men's anti-slavery duties, were used to make broader points about their character and commitment.

A more elaborate memorial than either of these two is found at St Mary's Church, in Tenby, Pembrokeshire. Captain Bird Allen died at Fernando Po on 25 October 1841 while in command of HMS *Soudan* on Thomas Buxton's Niger Expedition.[14] In Bird's case, the memorial also includes a figural element. The sculpture shows a seated classical male figure, head on hand in a suitably dejected attitude. He holds a flagpole and a flag drapes across his right shoulder. His last voyage, the inscription informs us, was part of an effort 'to promote the introduction of Christianity and civilisation / Into that country'. Like the other memorials to individuals, the stress is on the deceased's personal virtues, with Allen's friends keen 'to record their strong sense of his Christian excellence and / Professional talents, and to testify their deep regret for his loss / and that of his brave companions who with him / fell victims to the climate of the River Niger.' The impression of a godly man dying in a just and noble cause is reinforced by the quoting of scripture: 'Mark the perfect man and behold the upright: For the end of that man is peace. Ps 37 v 37.'[15] These memorials illustrate one of the ways in which the navy's role in slave-trade suppression activities was represented to people back in Britain. But, by situating anti-slavery endeavours in the context of naval service and operations, suppression is less connected to the transatlantic slave trade and Britain's varying attitudes towards it, and rather more connected with traditional forms of naval commemoration.

Memorials were not the only physical artefacts that represented Britain's involvement in suppression in the Atlantic. From the mid-nineteenth century onwards, as the focus of the navy's suppression activities moved to the Indian Ocean and as the number of surviving personnel involved in the Atlantic operations dwindled, the commemoration of suppression was increasingly channelled through material culture derived from particular incidents or specific ships. As noted above, there is a certain ambiguity in commemorating the suppression of the slave trade through physical remains. Many of the material objects with connections to the suppression of the slave trade follow a similar pattern in being ostensibly removed from the context of slavery and the slave trade. There are several examples in the National Maritime Museum, which has one of the largest collections of material relating to the British involvement in the slave trade in the world.[16] The commemoration of suppression activities often followed the same traditions as other naval commemorations in retaining a ship-based, service-centred focus.

For example, in addition to the envelope of dust sent to the Admiralty, the rotting timbers of the *Black Joke* yielded enough wood to make a snuff box, which is now in the collection of the National Maritime Museum (Figure 8.1). The lid of the box shows a view of the ship, fully rigged; the back and sides are carved in deep relief with representations of 'African life'; the front is similarly carved with a scene copied from a medal commemorating the abolition of the slave trade in 1807. Although this object is directly related to the suppres-

Figure 8.1 Snuff box made from timbers of *Black Joke.*
(© National Maritime Museum, Greenwich, London, ZBA2435)

Figure 8.2 Wine cooler made from timbers of *El Almirante* by Thomas Walker, *c.* 1840. (© National Maritime Museum, Greenwich, London, ZBA3083)

sion campaign off the coast of West Africa, it incorporates imagery and symbolism from the earlier abolition campaign in Britain. There is no recognisable iconography of suppression here to compare to the image of the *Brooks* or the kneeling and supplicant slave of Wedgwood's medallions, which instantly evoke earlier abolition campaigns. Indeed, even the documentary evidence associated with the object emphasises abolition. It suggests that the European shown shaking hands with the African man on the front panel is 'probably Fox', further foregrounding the political activity surrounding abolition rather than the suppression activities of the ship from which the box itself was made.[17]

Many of the other objects relating to suppression are also divorced from the context of anti-slavery. A wine cooler made from the timbers of the slave ship *El Almirante* gives little away in terms of its ultimate provenance, for example (Figure 8.2). *El Almirante* was captured by the *Black Joke* on 1 February 1829, but the gilded plate on the front merely alludes to the fact that it is 'a tribute of admiration and respect from Commodore Collier CB to Lieutenant Henry Downes for his gallant conduct in command of HM Tender Black Joke'.[18] Like the snuff box, this example highlights the fact that the commemoration of naval suppression activity was often calibrated in terms of individual ships. The production of mementoes from timbers, the distribution of shreds of flags and so on, derive from long-standing maritime and, specifically, naval traditions.[19] As a result, objects were frequently decontextualised and abstracted from the activities and politics of suppression, turning them into relics associated with specific vessels and encouraging their omission from the larger story of Britain's involvement in the transatlantic slave trade and its suppression.

Even objects that seem directly to illustrate suppression activities are often less than helpful in providing the wider context for these naval operations. The action of the *Black Joke* against *El Almirante*, for example, is depicted in an aquatint by William John Huggins (Figure 8.3). Huggins was one of the best-known maritime artists in early-nineteenth-century London. He had served as a steward and assistant purser on East India Company ships. Later, he had a studio close to the Company's headquarters in London's Leadenhall Street and was a prolific painter of East Indiamen for Company officers. In this image, however, the depiction of the suppression squadron in action shows little more than two ships engaged in close-range action.[20] Huggins's *The Capture of the Slaver 'Formidable' by HMS 'Buzzard', 17 December 1834* is another one of many images that were produced by British marine artists in the decades after the 1807 Act made British involvement in the slave trade illegal (Figure 8.4). Again,

Figure 8.3 Edward Duncan, after William John Huggins, *H.M. Brig* Black Joke ... *engaging the Spanish Slave Brig* El Almirante *in the Bight of Benin, Feby. 1st 1829*, 1830, engraving. (© National Maritime Museum, Greenwich, London, PAH8175)

Huggins followed a familiar pattern to other artists, showing navy vessels in action against Spanish and Portuguese vessels still engaged in the Atlantic slave trade. In this image, the Spanish slaving brig *Formidable* is taken by the naval brigantine *Buzzard* (10 guns).[21] These images serve to decontextualise the actions from the specific Atlantic circumstances of these suppression activities and place them within the orbit of naval operations more generally.[22]

Perhaps the most extreme example of decontextualisation is found in a hand-sewn flag in the collection. The flag is charged with the stylised figure of an African holding a staff, appliquéd in brown fabric. His garments and the ribbons on the staff flutter in a notional breeze that coruscates across the considerable surface of the flag, which measures over twelve metres square.[23] The paper label attached to the hoist describes it as a 'Flag taken from a slaver captured off the east coast of Africa & sent to my father (W. H. Wylde of the Foreign Office) by Commodore Eardley Wilmot'.[24] Whatever the purported provenance, visual evidence, as well as the fact that Commodore Wilmot's

Figure 8.4 William John Huggins, *The Capture of the Slaver* Formidable *by H.M.S.* Buzzard, *17 December 1834, c.* 1834, oil on canvas
(© National Maritime Museum, Greenwich, London, BHC0625)

anti-slavery naval career was spent on the west coast of Africa, casts doubt on whether this artefact relates to the east coast slave trade of the later nineteenth century. The flag is an example of how subsequent anti-slavery activities in the Indian Ocean, and the later Victorian public's relationship with these operations, served to obfuscate many representations of suppression in the Atlantic. These material commemorations have parallels in the ways in which suppression has, until recently, been written about by historians.

Histories of suppression, 1865–2000

In the later nineteenth century, naval suppression in the Atlantic was quickly subsumed by a more general narrative of national consistency. As Britain engaged in East African suppression and the formal expansion of empire, both abolitionists and the Liberal–Imperialist Prime Minister Lord Rosebery could agree on the importance of Britain's 'heroic self-denying exertions, which she has made to put down this iniquitous traffic'.[25] For as long as historians shared a simple faith in the moral motives for slave-trade abolition, the navy's role could represent an inevitable and incontrovertible force for good in the world. The eminent historian W. E. H. Lecky, for example, pronounced in 1869 that,

[t]he unweary, unostentatious and inglorious crusade of England against slavery may probably be regarded as among the three or four perfectly virtuous pages comprised in the history of nations.[26]

His reticence about the expense and frustrations of naval suppression demonstrated a lack of interest in its details or consequences. Into the early twentieth century, such sentiments served the purposes of anti-slavery activists looking back on Britain's efforts for slave-trade suppression. On occasions such as the 1933–34 centenaries of emancipation and Wilberforce's death, campaigners hoped that Britain would feel attached to their country's abolitionist heritage and contribute to a twentieth-century attack on slavery.[27] In these contexts, the meanings or realities of naval suppression mattered less than the patriotic consistency the tradition represented. Produced to celebrate the inter-war anniversaries, Sir Reginald Coupland's history *The British Anti-Slavery Movement* (1933) concluded that 'the average Englishman' considered the transatlantic slave trade 'so damnable a business that any decent person was obliged to do what he could to stop it'. The impact of suppression on West Africa was wholly ignored, appearing only briefly in a final chapter on the post-1880 European scramble for empire. Instead, Coupland favoured a diplomatic and political narrative of the naval campaign.[28]

This patriotic satisfaction was shared by historians of the navy, though they had rather different interests at heart. Geoffrey Callender, Professor of History at the Royal Naval College, Greenwich, and subsequently first director of the National Maritime Museum, accorded a noble and uncomplicated role to Britain's naval activities in the nineteenth century. His 1924 paean to Britain's naval past, *The Naval Side of British History*, declared simply that '[t]he "Pax Britannica" has changed the outlook of all who plough the sea; and many a weary soul, broken by servitude, has clutched the hem of the Union Jack in childlike faith that under that emblem no man need remain a slave'.[29]

What united the accounts of naval scholars such as Callender with those of imperial historians such as Coupland was an interest in naval suppression as the microcosm of some larger heroic project, be it abolitionism or naval mastery. Writing before the Second World War, they unsurprisingly showed little interest in the consequences of naval suppression for African sovereignty or racist attitudes. For Coupland, indeed, naval operations were part of an anti-slavery tradition of moral trusteeship, which he hoped the British Empire of his day would emulate.[30] For Callender, like those stone memorials commemorating fallen sailors of the West Africa Squadron in the nineteenth century, suppression was simply one context for the virtues he found in Britain's naval past.

This pattern was not wholly abandoned in post-war accounts, though some did focus on the story of the West Africa Squadron as a subject in its own right. In his study, Christopher Lloyd – one of Callender's successors at Greenwich – sought to give the campaign 'the attention it deserves' and so demonstrate that the sailors involved 'deserve to be commemorated' for 'remarkable examples of fortitude' equal to those of Britain's greatest naval heroes.[31] While this meant a fuller interest in the experiences of serving officers and the economic context for West African slave trading, Lloyd's work sought to be a tribute to the navy, as well as an analysis of its work. W. E. F. Ward similarly set out to reveal the hidden history of the Royal Navy's valour.[32]

Such nods to hagiography contrast starkly with the work of Eric Williams, whose views became influential from the 1960s.[33] His *Capitalism and Slavery* condemned British abolition as a beneficent side-effect of industrial capitalist development. His Marxist interpretation of British anti-slavery looked more to macro-economic factors than individual motives, but Williams did incorporate suppression into his narrative. He took care to dismiss naval suppression as a weapon of economic terrorism, used against British producers' rivals and opposed by capitalists with overseas interests.[34] While it is quite reasonable to question the government's blindness towards curbing the importation of slave-grown goods or ending the investment of capital in slave industries, manuscript sources and quantitative analyses cast doubt on any interpretation of the West Africa Squadron as an intended distraction.[35] Williams's argument has, however, been developed by Johnson U. J. Asiegbu, who sees Britain's forced settlement of Africans 'liberated' from slave vessels as the malevolent motive for the naval blockade of West Africa. While British authorities undoubtedly made the most of such opportunities to strengthen their tremulous free-labour experiment, such a conspiracy is not supported by any documentary proof.[36]

As the broader field of anti-slavery history moves beyond the stark alternatives of patriotic pride and calculating self-interest, so too have scholars specifically examining Atlantic slave-trade suppression. The defining modern study in the sub-field is a book by David Eltis, somewhat mis-marketed as *Economic Growth and the Ending of the Transatlantic Slave Trade* (1987).[37] Shying away from generalisations, the book provides great narrative and quantitative detail alongside astute analysis of the cost and impact of naval interdiction.

Moreover, it supports a broader trend amongst historians of slavery and abolition to emphasise the thriving, exploitative robustness of the slave system, rather than painting it as a declining, archaic institution. Such nuanced questions have guided studies of individual diplomatic relationships surrounding Anglo-French or Anglo-Spanish suppression by Paul-Michael Kielstra and David Murray.[38] These take the lead from the work done in the national context of Brazilian politics by Leslie Bethell, in his influential account of local and foreign factors in abolitionism.[39]

The diplomatic system surrounding Mixed Commission Courts has attracted attention, in recent decades, from legal scholars and specialists in the new discipline of 'international relations'.[40] Some of this interest is perhaps misplaced, given the relative insignificance of the Mixed Commissions to naval suppression. Regardless, these directions in research have complicated the pictures proffered by either hagiographers or economic determinists. Specialisation did not help to produce any new master-narratives to replace the old alternatives. The past decade has started to see one emerge, as scholars consider the general phenomenon of naval suppression, focusing on its relationship to imperialism.

Following early work by Suzanne Miers, historians of slave-trade suppression have taken a greater interest in the imperial context and implications of naval suppression.[41] Far from diverting attention from the specific to the general, this approach has elevated suppression as a subject in its own right, rather than a maritime episode in anti-slavery histories or a humanitarian diversion in naval histories.[42] Two major volumes of essays have considered the links between suppression and empire since the bicentenary. One was a semi-official publication by the UK Foreign and Commonwealth Office, emerging from its 2007 workshop on suppression, which placed 'empire' alongside 'diplomacy' in the title. The other, edited by Derek Peterson, focused on the broader connections between imperialism and abolitionism, allowing Seymour Drescher and Robin Law to consider aspects of slave-trade suppression.[43] Law spells out the erosion of African sovereignty resulting from the navy's forward policies in West Africa.[44] Although the present volume considers the Atlantic, interest in East African and Indian Ocean naval suppression has also flourished. Besides active research projects from contributors to this volume, a range of new scholars are developing work in this field.[45]

Commemoration and history today

The issue of how slavery, and Britain's involvement in the transatlantic slave trade in particular, has been represented and commemorated has been the subject of scholarly attention for some time.[46] This debate has generally focused around how these issues are explored and acknowledged in museums.[47] Recently, more attention has been paid to other forms of cultural commemoration.[48] Since the bicentenary commemorations of the passing of the Slave Trade Abolition Act in 2007, remembering and commemorating the history of the British involvement in the transatlantic slave trade have acquired new relevance and controversy. Discussions often revolve around the ways in which material culture, and the museums in which it is housed, should represent this history to a diverse range of audiences.[49] On the rare occasions they engage with the navy's crusade, museums and heritage sites have struggled to incorporate developing scholarly debates about morality and self-interest. In Plymouth's Ford Park Cemetery, for example, a Victorian monument to the crew of HMS *Rattlesnake*, who died serving on the West Africa Station in the late 1860s, illustrates exactly this difficulty at a local level. Visitors are advised that 'it is true that it was in Britain's commercial interest that the slave trade to foreign countries was ended' but that 'it would be wrong not to acknowledge also the humanitarian cause for which these men died'.[50]

The 200th anniversary of this parliamentary and legal milestone inspired a range of public events, exhibitions, publications, academic conferences and even a special edition of commemorative stamps.[51] 'Abolition 200' – the umbrella term for the commemoration activities in 2007 – was not just about commemorating the parliamentary act of 1807. In fact, most of the public consultation conducted by government, funding bodies and cultural institutions sent a very clear signal that the focus should not just be on the perceived triumph of the abolition moment in 1807, but on the context of this triumph. How and why had Britain become the leading slave-trading country in the eighteenth century? What are the legacies of that involvement today? Some people were fearful that the anniversary would be used as an excuse to indulge in self-congratulatory rhetoric, rather than as an opportunity to reflect on broader historical issues.[52] And, as a result, many of the public exhibitions and events in 2007 attempted to paint a broader picture of Britain's involvement in the transatlantic slave trade. In doing so, this approach laid bare the contradictions at the heart of the abolition story, demythologising many of its heroes in the process.

As many events and activities surrounding the bicentenary were careful to concentrate on Britain's involvement in the slave trade at the eighteenth-century height of the traffic, the suppression of the slave trade by the Royal Navy often played only a minor part. The Royal Naval Museum and the National Maritime Museum were two museums whose collections and remit perhaps best supported a focus on the navy's role in suppressing the slave trade. However, in the case of the latter, the suppression squadron was subsumed within a wider narrative point about British and naval activity in the Atlantic Ocean over the course of two centuries. Within such a broad time-frame, the navy's role was complex and ambivalent: until 1807, it had protected the transatlantic slave trade as any other branch of British commerce. The decision to tell a wider story – of economic, migratory, political and military connections and exchanges across the Atlantic – led to a permanent exhibition, 'Atlantic Worlds'. In this large sweep of history, suppression activities and their material remains comprised just one display case.

The Royal Naval Museum in Portsmouth was perhaps the only museum in the country that dedicated a special exhibition to the suppression of the transatlantic trade. The exhibition used diaries and ships' logs from the period to relay the experiences of life onboard, such as that of Cheesman Henry Binstead, an officer on the HMS *Owen Glendower*.[53] It presented the Royal Navy's role in combatting the slave trade, but also emphasised the continuing work of the Royal Navy 'in defending human rights across the world today'.[54] Reporting such links to 'the task begun in 1808', a BBC report thus concluded that 'although the Navy's initial 50-year campaign ended, its interception and destruction of human trafficking has not'.[55]

This important bicentennial year was one in which Britain (partially) re-engaged with its slave-trade past. But, for all that, the role played by the navy's suppression squadrons was bit-part, at best. In some respects, this air-brushing from the historical narrative was to be expected. The apparent dearth of material culture is one practical challenge for curators. However, the apparent absence of naval suppression from the general narrative also betokens another, potentially more serious, problem in the representation of Britain's slave-trading and slave-trade-suppressing past. By focusing almost exclusively on the slave-trading activities of Britain in the eighteenth century, rather than the complex Victorian politics of nineteenth-century anti-slavery, a number of important issues are left unconsidered. For example, the problem of why, and to what extent, many Britons saw slave-trade suppression as so integral to their nation's global dominance, economic success and self-identity is largely brushed over.

Public representations of British slavery and anti-slavery have, therefore, found naval suppression difficult to incorporate. There are no easy routes for curators in navigating between the Scylla of patriotic self-vindication and the Charybdis of summary dismissal. In the last decade, however, historians have begun to give the topic sustained attention, avoiding these fates and focusing on the complexities of the motives, choices and consequences of West African suppression. The final section of this chapter considers current interpretations of the squadron's activities and suggests future directions for historians and curators engaging with the public understanding of the past.

Conclusion

In many ways, the commemorations surrounding the 2007 bicentenary have had little effect on public awareness or interpretations of the naval campaigns. When acknowledged, suppression activities are often still recognised as a heroic episode in the history of the nation or its naval service. Like his abolitionist predecessors, Aidan McQuade, director of the British-based charity Anti-Slavery International, understandably invokes suppression as a national sacrifice that modern Britons should be proud to emulate. He suggests that suppression represented an 'inexplicably forgotten campaign of the Royal Navy', where 'the scale of the achievement and the suffering endured for the sake of others cannot but fill one with a profound sense of admiration'.[56] In a book published in the year of commemorations, Marika Sherwood took a contrary approach, seeking to puncture pride in abolition with evidence of continuing financial investment and unprosecuted participation in Atlantic slavery. To do this, she follows Eric Williams in doubting the significance or sincerity of the naval suppression campaigns.[57]

Politicians have shown greater interest than the general public in interpreting the legacies of slave-trade abolition. It is not the place of a scholarly essay such as this chapter to condone or condemn particular policies facing Britain today on the basis of historical evidence. However, it is instructive to compare politicians' references to slave-trade suppression with the direction of recent academic research. From a twenty-first-century vantage point, some commentators have found it hard to resist viewing the navy's actions through contemporary debates about humanitarian intervention, particularly following the 2004 invasion of Iraq. Since the bicentenary, Labour peer Clive Soley has been particularly vocal in drawing parallels between the West Africa Squadron and modern security questions, arguing against fidelity to international law in at least six parliamentary debates along the lines that 'the Royal Navy's intervention to stop the slave trade throughout the 19th century was unlawful'.[58] In a 2011 paper claiming that proactive action in Iraq and Libya was on 'the right side of history', Soley invoked British suppression of the slave trade as 'the first liberal intervention'. Discussing the mid-Victorian campaign to abandon naval force against the slave trade, he concluded that critical 'commentators and lawyers are using the same arguments against intervention today' by objecting to violations of international law.[59] Meanwhile, in his 2010 plans to see that 'history is taught as a proper subject' in British schools, Conservative Education Secretary Michael Gove named 'the role of the Royal Navy in putting down the slave trade' as one reason pupils 'can celebrate the distinguished role of these islands in the history of the world'.[60]

Besides promoting faith in Britain's moral purpose as a nation, politicians have also used suppression for its other traditional purpose: reflecting and reinforcing the virtues of the naval service. In the House of Commons, Conservative MP Andrew Robathan suggested in 2007 that 'we should remember with pride the role of the Royal Navy in suppressing the transatlantic slave trade' at a time when 'this country's naval capability risks being turned into that of Belgium'. In response, the Armed Forces Minister Adam Ingram assured members that '[t]he bravery of the Royal Navy should be marked, alongside all the other events that are taking place in respect of the abolition of the slave trade', though he did not show the same sympathy to Robathan's Belgian comparison.[61] Such attitudes – reflecting traditional interests in the symbolism of the suppression campaign, rather than its intricacies or consequences – are more in keeping with the accounts of Lecky, Callendar or Coupland than those from Eltis, Law or Peterson.

These readings of suppression therefore place legislators at odds with recent historical investigation. While this could be judged as a difference between hard-headed, realist politicians and squeamish, lily-livered academics, such a summary dismissal would signal a squandered opportunity. Whatever personal views scholars hold about modern political questions, their historical research highlights the complicated problems and unintended consequences that muddy Lord Soley's simple narrative. His party colleague David Miliband, then Foreign Secretary and heir presumptive to Gordon Brown, wrote in a 2009 preface to Hamilton and Salmon's collection that '[h]umanitarian intervention in Africa, aimed initially at suppressing the trade at source, would likewise serve eventually as a mask for imperial expansion'.[62] Such sensitivity to the complexities emerging from anti-slavery operations is unusual in political appropriations of the historical example.[63] Back in 1995, one of Miliband's predecessors as Foreign Secretary, Douglas Hurd, explained his reticence to intervene in Bosnia, noting the dangers of 'the imperial principle of the international community imposing from outside a particular solution and form of government – as we did with the slave trade, for example'. Whether or not the civil conflicts of the former Yugoslavia bore out his remark that '[i]t is much easier to make choices if one believes that there is nothing but virtue on one side and nothing but vice on the other', he revealed a concern for the imperial consequences of Britain's anti-slave-trade activities.[64] In their willingness to consider the imperial context of British slave-trade suppression, Miliband and Hurd differed from other politicians. Whatever the differences between the elevated chambers of the Palace of Westminster and the distinguished pages of scholarly journals, however, popular interest in suppression of the slave trade remains low.

The difficulty of reconciling humanitarian commitment with imperial consequences has proved equally challenging to authors targeting the general reading public. In a self-described 'swashbuckling naval adventure' of 2009, Siân Rees acknowledges British sailors as 'unthinkingly racist yet dying in their thousands to save individuals with whom they had nothing in common but humanity'.[65] Though wary of violent episodes which punctuated the 'arduous campaign', Rees concludes in the final page of her book that the navy placed 'armed intervention, whatever its benevolent intentions, second to due process'.[66] Lord Soley would disagree, but there is a far greater significance to Rees's conclusions. In many ways, this tension in her treatment reflects the struggles between moral and imperial perspectives on the motives or effects of naval suppression in all attempts at the public history of suppression.

The evidence of many public consultations and much academic research has highlighted that the history of the suppression of the slave trade cannot be interpreted through the single prism of naval squadrons, much less the careers of individual ships and crew. As Robert Blyth has reminded us, the wider historical context in which suppression activities took place must be taken into account.[67] First, naval anti-slavery operations took place after centuries of British participation in the transatlantic slave trade. Second, even when Britain turned its attention to eradicating the trade in the nineteenth century, this was low down on the Royal Navy's list of priorities. And, finally, it is important for future public commemoration to situate the suppression of the slave trade within the broader context of nineteenth-century British imperialism, rather than ignoring it, dismissing it or celebrating it: 'the undoubtedly high ideals of abolition and the promotion of legitimate trade were also among the precursors of partition and colonial rule in Africa'.[68] Complexity is often a hard course for public history to follow, but suppression or celebration of naval anti-slavery operations are no longer viable strategies for historians or curators of Britain's imperial past. While further debate should only be welcomed, global and imperial perspectives on slave-trade suppression seem to offer fruitful directions for both historical research and its dissemination in the heritage sector.

Notes

1 Peter Leonard, *Records of a Voyage to the Western Coast of Africa in His Majesty's Ship* Dryad, *and of the Service on that Station for the Suppression of the Slave Trade in the Years 1830, 1831 and 1832* (Edinburgh: William Tait, 1833), p. 259.
2 Leonard, *Records of a Voyage*, p. 265.
3 Christopher Lloyd, *The Navy and the Slave Trade* (London: Routledge, 1968), p. 72.
4 'British PM Brown Goes to DC Bearing Gifts for Obama', Reuters, 2 March 2009, http://blogs.reuters.com/frontrow/2009/03/02/british-pm-brown-goes-to-dc-bearing-gifts-for-obama/. Accessed 18 September 2011.
5 See chapter 2 in this volume.
6 See Richard Huzzey, *Freedom Burning: The British Empire's Struggle with Slavery* (Ithaca, NY: Cornell University Press, 2012).
7 There is an increasingly rich literature on the representation of the Royal Navy, and its sailors, in eighteenth-century Britain. See Margarette Lincoln, *Representing the Royal Navy: British Sea Power, 1750–1815* (Aldershot: Ashgate, 2002); Isaac Land, *War, Nationalism and the British Sailor, 1750–1850* (Basingstoke: Palgrave Macmillan, 2009).
8 Leonard, *Records of a Voyage*, p. 132.
9 Leonard, *Records of a Voyage*, pp. 131–2. There are a number of images depicting this encounter, on 26 April 1834, in the collection of the National Maritime Museum. These include R. A. Graham, *The capture of the Spanish slave brig* Marinereita, *by H. Majesty's brig* Black Joke, watercolour, 1834. Item PAD8684; Charles Philip Reinagle, *H. M. Brig* Black Joke *Lieut Wm Ramsay, Tender to H. M. S.* Dryad *engaging the Spanish Slave Brig* Maranerito *in the Bight of Biafra*, hand-coloured aquatint, n.d. Item PAG9099. See Douglas Hamilton and Robert J. Blyth (eds), *Representing Slavery: Art, Artefacts and Archives in the Collections of the National Maritime Museum* (Aldershot: Lund Humphries, 2007), p. 308. For further discussion of this passage, see Robert Burroughs, 'Sailors and Slaves: "The Poor Enslaved Tar" in Naval Reform and Nautical Melodrama', *Journal of Victorian Culture* 16 (2011), 305–23.
10 On Jones's activities, see Huzzey, *Freedom Burning*, pp. 3–4, 146–7.
11 Memorial number: M5163. See http://www.nmm.ac.uk/memorials/Memorial. cfm?Topic=27&MemorialPage=3&MemorialID=M5163&Full=Transcript. Accessed 18 September 2011. More information about all of the memorials discussed here can be found on the online maritime memorial database, which contains records of over 5,000 church, cemetery and public memorials to seafarers and victims of maritime disasters.
12 Memorial number: M2630. See http://www.nmm.ac.uk/memorials/Memorial. cfm?Topic=27&MemorialPage=2&MemorialID=M2630&Full=Transcript. Accessed 18 September 2011.
13 Memorial number: M3725. See http://www.nmm.ac.uk/memorials/Memorial. cfm?Topic=27&MemorialPage=2&MemorialID=M3725&Full=Transcript. Accessed 18 September 2011.
14 See Howard Temperley, *White Dreams, Black Africa: The Antislavery Expedition to the Niger, 1841–1842* (New Haven and London: Yale University Press, 1992).
15 Memorial number: M4347. See http://www.nmm.ac.uk/memorials/Memorial. cfm?EventGroup=15&MemorialPage=2&MemorialID=M4347&Full=Transcript. Accessed 18 September 2011.
16 A grant from the Heritage Lottery Fund enabled the acquisition of the Michael

Graham-Stewart collection, a major collection of slavery-related material which forms the core of Museum's displays on slavery. See Hamilton and Blyth (eds), *Representing Slavery*.

17 Object accession number: ZBA2435. See Hamilton and Blyth (eds), *Representing Slavery*, p. 201.
18 Object accession number: ZBA3083–4. See Hamilton and Blyth (eds), *Representing Slavery*, p. 205.
19 See Rina Prentice, *A Celebration of the Sea* (London: HMSO, 1994).
20 Object accession number: PAH8175. See Hamilton and Blyth (eds), *Representing Slavery*, p. 308.
21 The *Buzzard* intercepted the Spanish ship, loaded with slaves for the Middle Passage, in the Bight of Benin, off the west coast of Africa. After 45 minutes, the *Formidable* surrendered with the loss of seven men. Two of the *Buzzard*'s crew were killed. The captured ship was taken to Freetown, Sierra Leone, but not before 307 of the cargo of 707 enslaved Africans perished.
22 For other examples, see Hamilton and Blyth (eds), *Representing Slavery*, pp. 308–9.
23 Object accession number: AAA2003. For further information, see Hamilton and Blyth (eds), *Representing Slavery*, p. 172.
24 Arthur Parry Eardley Wilmot (1815–86) was employed in anti-slavery operations off West Africa in HMS *Harlequin* (1850–53) and as Commodore in HMS *Rattlesnake* (1862–66). William Wylde's involvement with anti-slavery operations continued into the 1870s when the British moved to suppress the trade off Zanzibar.
25 As quoted, approvingly, in the *Anti-Slavery Reporter*, October 1932, p. 92.
26 W. E. H. Lecky, *The History of European Morals*, 2 vols (London: Longmans, 1869), i, 161. On the context of this statement, see David Brion Davis, *Inhuman Bondage: The Rise and Fall of Slavery in the New World* (Oxford and New York: Oxford University Press, 2006), p. 234.
27 *Anti-Slavery Reporter*, October 1932, p. 92; see also John Oldfield, *'Chords of Freedom': Commemoration, Ritual and British Transatlantic Slavery* (Manchester: Manchester University Press, 2007).
28 R. Coupland, *The British Anti-Slavery Movement* (London, T. Butterworth, 1933), p. 188.
29 Geoffrey Callender, *The Naval Side of British History* (London: Christophers, 1925), p. 234.
30 Alex May, 'Reginald Coupland', *Oxford Dictionary of National Biography*, ed. by L. Goldman (Oxford: Oxford University Press, 2004 – present), http://www.oxforddnb.com/view/article/32585. Accessed 22 October 2011.
31 Lloyd, *The Navy and the Slave Trade*, pp. ix–xii.
32 William E. F. Ward, *The Royal Navy and the Slavers* (New York: Schocken Books, 1969). On Ward's interpretation, see John Beeler, 'Maritime Policing and the Pax Britannica: The Royal Navy's Anti-Slavery Patrol in the Caribbean, 1828–1848', *The Northern Mariner/Le marin du nord* 16, 1 (2006), 1–20.
33 Regarding scholars' delay in responding to Williams, see Seymour Drescher, 'Antislavery Debates: Tides of Historiography in Slavery and Antislavery', *European Review* 19 (2011), 131–48. As one of Williams's principal critics, Drescher also summarises subsequent challenges to economic determinism in the study of abolition.
34 Eric Williams, *Capitalism and Slavery* [1944] (London, 1964), pp. 170–6.
35 David Eltis, 'The British Contribution to the Nineteenth-Century Transatlantic Slave Trade', *Economic History Review* 32 (1979), 211–27.
36 Johnson U. J. Asiegbu, *Slavery and the Politics of Liberation: A Study of Liberated African Emigration and British Anti-Slavery Policy* (London: Longman, 1969); Johnson U. J. Asiegbu, 'The Dynamics of Freedom: A Study of Liberated African Emigration and British Antislavery Policy', *Journal of Black Studies* 7 (1976), 95–106. For objections, see H. J. Fisher, 'Review of Johnson U. J. Asiegbu, *Slavery and the Politics of Liberation* (London, 1969)', *Bulletin of the School of Oriental and African Studies, University of London* 34 (1971), 188–90.

37 David Eltis, *Economic Growth and the Ending of the Transatlantic Slave Trade* (Oxford: Oxford University Press, 1987). While the title reflects Eltis's roots as an econometrician, it has probably misled some historians from other fields about its broader significance to research on the transatlantic slave trade.

38 Paul-Michael Kielstra, *The Politics of Slave Trade Suppression in Britain and France* (Basingstoke: Routledge, 2000); David R. Murray, *Odious Commerce: Britain, Spain and the Abolition of the Cuban Slave Trade* (Cambridge: Cambridge University Press, 2002).

39 Leslie Bethell, *The Abolition of the Brazilian Slave Trade* (Cambridge: Cambridge University Press, 1970). On subsequent debates see Jeffrey D. Needell, 'The Abolition of the Brazilian Slave Trade in 1850: Historiography, Slave Agency and Statesmanship', *Journal of Latin American Studies* 33 (2001), 681–711.

40 For legal aspects, see Holger L. Kern, 'Strategies of Legal Change: Great Britain, International Law, and the Abolition of the Transatlantic Slave Trade', *Journal of the History of International Law* 6 (2004), 233–58; Tara Helfman, 'The Court of Vice Admiralty at Sierra Leone and the Abolition of the West African Slave Trade', *Yale Law Journal* 115 (2006), 1122–56. For International Relations approaches, see Edward Keene, 'A Case Study of the Construction of International Hierarchy: British Treaty-Making against the Slave Trade in the Early Nineteenth Century,' *International Organization* 61 (2007), 311–39; Robert A. Pape and Chaim D. Kaufman, 'Explaining Costly International Moral Action: Britain's Sixty-year Campaign against the Atlantic Slave Trade', *International Organization* 53 (1999), 631–68. For an historian's treatment, see Leslie Bethell, 'The Mixed Commissions for the Suppression of the Transatlantic Slave Trade in the Nineteenth Century', *Journal of African History* 7 (1966), 79–93.

41 See, for example, Suzanne Miers, *Britain and the Ending of the Slave Trade* (London: Longman, 1975); Suzanne Miers and Richard Roberts (eds), *The End of Slavery in Africa* (Madison, WI: University of Wisconsin Press, 1988); Suzanne Miers, 'Slavery and the Slave Trade as International Issues, 1890–1939', *Slavery & Abolition* 19 (1998), 16–37; Suzanne Miers and Martin A. Klein (eds), *Slavery and Colonial Rule in Africa* (London: Frank Cass, 1999).

42 For example, Kristin Mann, *Slavery and the Birth of an African City: Lagos, 1760–1900* (Bloomington, IN: Indiana University Press, 2007) develops the existing historiographical debate surrounding suppression and the annexation of Lagos, 1851–61, while Lauren Benton, 'Abolition and Imperial Law, 1790–1820', *Journal of Imperial and Commonwealth History* 39 (2011), 355–74, uses suppression to reinterpret questions of imperial sovereignty.

43 Keith Hamilton and Patrick Salmon (eds), *Slavery, Diplomacy and Empire: Britain and the Suppression of the Slave Trade, 1807–1975* (Brighton: Sussex Academic Press, 2010); Derek R. Peterson (ed.), *Abolitionism and Imperialism in Britain, Africa, and the Atlantic* (Athens, OH: Ohio University Press, 2010).

44 Robin Law, 'Abolition and Imperialism: International Law and the British Suppression of the Atlantic Slave Trade', in *Abolitionism and Imperialism*, pp. 150–74.

45 See, for example, Robert Harms, Bernard K. Freamon and David W. Blight, *Indian Ocean Slavery in the Age of Abolition* (New Haven, CT: Yale University Press, 2013).

46 For an overview, see Catherine Hall, 'Remembering 1807: Histories of the slave trade, slavery and abolition', *History Workshop Journal* 64 (2007), 1–5.

47 The subjects of slavery and its abolition have been displayed in Britain since 1906, when Wilberforce House opened as a museum in Hull. Widespread museum engagement with the subject, however, did not manifest itself until the end of the twentieth century. Major new exhibitions in Liverpool and Bristol, two British ports with significant involvement in the slave trade, set the trend. 'Against Human Dignity' at Merseyside Maritime Museum in 1994 and, in 1999, 'A Respectable Trade?' at Bristol City Museum and Art Gallery and then the Bristol Industrial Museum laid the groundwork for commemorations in 2007. The Liverpool and Bristol displays are critiqued in Elizabeth Kowaleski-Wallace, *The British Slave Trade and Public Memory* (New York: Columbia University Press, 2006), pp. 25–64. On the represen-

tation of slavery in museums in the 1990s, see Moira Simpson, *Making Representations: Museums in the Post-colonial Era* (London: Routledge, 1996), pp. 17–20.

48 For examples of how slavery, the slave trade and their abolition have been commemorated in physical monuments, see James Walvin and Alex Tyrrell, 'Whose History is it? Memorializing Britain's Involvement in Slavery', in Paul Pickering and Alex Tyrrell (eds), *Contested Sites: Commemoration, Memorial and Popular Politics in Nineteenth-Century Britain* (Ashgate: Aldershot, 2004), pp. 147–69; Madge Dresser, 'Set in Stone? Statues and Slavery in London', *History Workshop Journal* 64 (2007), 162–99; Andy Green, 'Remembering Slavery in Birmingham: Sculpture, Paintings and Installations', *Slavery & Abolition* 29 (2008),189–201.

49 Katherine Prior, 'Commemorating Slavery 2007: A Personal View from Inside the Museums', *History Workshop Journal* 64 (2007), 200–11; Douglas Hamilton, 'Representing Slavery in British Museums: The Challenges of 2007', in Cora Kaplan and John Oldfield (eds), *Imagining Transatlantic Slavery and Abolition* (Basingstoke: Palgrave Macmillan, 2009), pp. 127–44. See also Marcus Wood, *Blind Memory: Visual Representations of Slavery in England and America, 1780–1865* (Manchester: Manchester University Press, 2000); Diana Paton and Jane Webster, 'Remembering Slave Trade Abolitions: Reflections on 2007 in International Perspective', *Slavery & Abolition* 30 (2009), 161–7; John McAleer, '"That infamous commerce in human blood": Reflections on Representing Slavery and Empire in British Museums", *Museum History Journal* 13 (2013), 72–86. For responses to the commemorations, see Jefferey R. Kerr-Ritchie, 'Reflections on the Bicentennial of the Abolition of the British Slave Trade', *Journal of African American History* 93 (2008), 532–42; '1807 Commemorated', Institute for the Public Understanding of the Past, University of York, http://www.history.ac.uk/1807commemorated. Accessed 25 October 2011.

50 Ford Park Cemetery, Plymouth: A Heritage Trail (Plymouth: Ford Park Cemetery Trust, 2004), p. 13.

51 See HM Government, *Bicentenary of the Abolition of the Slave Trade Act, 1807–2007* (Wetherby: Department of Communities and Local Government, 2007).

52 See Oldfield, 'Chords of Freedom', pp. 117–20.

53 Review of Chasing Freedom, '1807 Commemorated', Institute for the Public Understanding of the Past, University of York, http://www.history.ac.uk/ 1807commem orated/exhibitions/museums/chasing.html. Accessed 18 September 2011.

54 See 'Chasing Freedom', National Museum of the Royal Navy, http://www.royalnaval museum.org/Visit_Tempexhibit_ChasingFreedom.htm. Accessed 18 September 2011.

55 'From Slave Trade to Humanitarian Aid', BBC News, 19 March 2007, http://news. bbc.co.uk/1/hi/england/hampshire/6430401.stm. Accessed 18 September 2011.

56 As quoted by Lord West, the Security Minister and former First Sea Lord: Hansard, 5 March 2010, c. 1738.

57 Marika Sherwood, *After Abolition: Britain and the Slave Trade since 1807* (London: I. B. Tauris, 2007).

58 Hansard, 21 June 2007, c. 352; see also Hansard, 15 November 2007, c. 606; Hansard, 18 June 2009, c. 1242; Hansard, 5 March 2010, c. 1724; Hansard, 12 November 2010, c. 421; Hansard, 1 April 2011, c. 1477.

59 Lord Soley, 'The Right Side of History', The Henry Jackson Society, http://www. henryjacksonsociety.org/cms/harriercollectionitems/The+Right+Side+of+History.pdf. Accessed 24 October 2011.

60 Hansard, 15 November 2010, c. 634

61 Hansard, 26 March 2007, c. 1151; see similar arguments during the 2010 strategic defence review: Hansard, 12 November 2010, c. 456.

62 David Miliband, 'Foreword', in Keith Hamilton and Patrick Salmon (eds), *Slavery, Diplomacy and Empire: Britain and the Suppression of the Slave Trade* (Eastbourne: Sussex University Press, 2009), pp. vii–viii. Material of this kind is typically drafted for ministers by civil servants or advisors, so the words probably reflect the sensitivities of the Foreign Office rather than the Foreign Secretary himself. For objections to anti-slavery serving as a 'mask' rather than a motive, see Huzzey, *Freedom*

Burning.

63 But see Hansard, 18 November 1999, c. 145; Hansard, 15 November 2007, c. 612.
64 Hansard, 6th series, 9 May 1995, cclix, c. 589.
65 Siân Rees, *Sweet Water and Bitter: The Ships that Stopped the Slave Trade* (London: Vintage, 2009), dust jacket and p. 6.
66 Rees, *Sweet Water*, p. 308.
67 Robert J. Blyth, 'Britain, the Royal Navy and the Suppression of Slave Trades in the Nineteenth Century', in Hamilton and Blyth (eds), *Representing Slavery*, pp. 78–91, p. 90
68 Blyth, 'Britain', p. 90.

Bibliography

Primary sources

Manuscripts

Arkwright family papers, Derbyshire Record Office

Cheesman Henry Binstead diaries, National Museum of the Royal Navy, Portsmouth

British Foreign and Anti-Slavery Society papers, Rhodes House Library, Oxford

Buckle papers, West Sussex Record Office

Fleetwood Buckle diaries, Wellcome Library

Church Missionary Society archives, Cadbury Research Library, University of Birmingham

George Collier report, National Museum of the Royal Navy

E. H. Columbine journal, Sierra Leone Collection, Richard Daley Library, University of Illinois at Chicago

Thomas Davies journal, National Maritime Museum

Hugh Dunlop remark book, Special Collections and Archives Department, Nimitz Library, United States Naval Academy

Robert Flockhart letters, National Archives of Scotland

William Hall journal, Cadbury Research Library, University of Birmingham

Hastings correspondence transcriptions, National Maritime Museum

Hotham family papers, Hull University Archives, Hull History Centre

HMS Thalia remark book, UK Hydrographic Office Archive

McIlroy letterbook, National Maritime Museum

Meynell papers, National Maritime Museum

Minto papers, National Library of Scotland

John M'Kie papers, National Library of Scotland

Murray Family of Murraythwaite papers, National Archives of Scotland

Arthur Onslow journal, Mitchell Library, State Library of New South Wales

Pasley papers, National Library of Scotland

Henry Rogers journal, private collection

Lord John Russell papers, National Archives, Kew

Sotherton-Estcourt papers, Gloucestershire Archives

Horace Waller papers, Yale Divinity School

Paintings

Graham, R. A., *The capture of the Spanish slave brig* Marinereita, *by H. Majesty's brig* Black Joke, watercolour, 1834, National Maritime Museum

Meynell, Francis, 'Slave deck of the *Albaroz*', watercolour, 1845, Album of Lt. Meynell's Watercolours, National Maritime Museum

——, 'Rescued Africans on Deck of British Ship *Albatross*', watercolour, 1845, Album of Lt. Meynell's Watercolours, National Maritime Museum

Reinagle, Charles Philip, *H.M. Brig* Black Joke *Lieut. Wm Ramsay, Tender to H.M.S.* Dryad *engaging the Spanish Slave Brig* Maranerito *in the Bight of Biafra*, hand-coloured aquatint, n.d., National Maritime Museum

Official papers

Admiralty records (ADM 1, 37, 38, and 101), National Archives, Kew
British and Foreign State Papers
Colonial Office records (CO 267), National Archives, Kew
Hansard's Parliamentary Debates
Parliamentary Papers
War Office records (WO 12 and 334), National Archives, Kew

Newspapers and periodicals

African Herald
Anti-Slavery Reporter
Athenaeum
Bell's Life in London and Sporting Chronicle
Birmingham Daily Post
Blackburn Standard
Bradford Observer
Caledonian Mercury
Chambers's Edinburgh Journal
Colburn's United Service Magazine
Daily News
Examiner
Glasgow Herald
Hampshire Advertiser & Salisbury Guardian
Household Words
Lancaster Gazette
Leeds Mercury
Liverpool Mercury
Lloyd's Weekly Newspaper
Missionary Register
Morning Chronicle
Morning Post
Northern Star
Punch
Royal Gazette and Sierra Leone Advertiser
Saturday Review
Sierra Leone Gazette
Times
York Herald

Published works

Alexander, James Edward, *Narrative of a Voyage of Observation among the Colonies of Western Africa, in the Flag-ship Thalia, and of a Campaign* in Kaffir-Land on the Staff of the Commander-in-Chief, in 1835, 2 vols (London: Henry Colburn, 1837)

——, Transatlantic Sketches, Comprising Visits to the Most Interesting Scenes in North and South America, and the West Indies; with Notes on Negro Slavery and Canadian Emigration (London: Richard Bentley, 1833)

——, Travels to the Seat of War in the East, through Russia and the Crimea, in 1829 (Henry Colburn & Richard Bentley: London, 1830)

Barnard, F. L., A Three Years Cruise in the Mozambique Channel [1848] (London: Dawsons, 1969)

British and Foreign Anti-Slavery Society, Twenty-Second Annual Report of the British and Foreign Anti-Slavery Society (London: British and Foreign Anti-Slavery Society, 1861)

Bryson, Alexander, Report on the Climate and Principal Diseases of the African Station (London: William Clowes and Sons, 1847)

Burton, Richard Francis, A Mission to Gelele, King of Dahome [1864; 2 vols] (London: Tylson and Edwards, 1893)

Buxton, Thomas Fowell, African Slave Trade and its Remedy (London: John Murray, 2nd edn, 1840)

'A. F. C.', Good Out of Evil; or, The History of Adjai, The African Slave Boy [1850] (London: Wertheim and Macintosh, 1852)

Canot, Theodore, Captain Canot: or, Twenty Years of an African Slaver, ed. Brantz Mayer (London: George Routledge & Co., 1855)

Carlyle, Thomas, 'Occasional Discourse on the Nigger Question', in The Works of Thomas Carlyle, 30 vols (London: Chapman and Hall, 1899), xxix, 348–83

Church, Mary, Sierra Leone: or, The Liberated Africans, in a Series of Letters from a Young Lady to her Sister in 1833 and 34 (London: Longman and Co., 1835)

Clarke, Robert, Sierra Leone. A Description of the Manners and Customs of the Liberated Africans: With Observations upon the Natural History of the Colony and a Notice of the Native Tribes (London: James Ridgway, 1846)

Clarkson, Thomas, History of the Rise, Progress, and Accomplishment of the Abolition of the African Slave Trade by the British Parliament [1808] (London: John W. Parker, 1839)

——, Cries of Africa, to the Inhabitants of Europe (London: Harvey And Darton, 1822)

Collier, G. R., and Charles MacCarthy, West African Sketches: Complied from the Reports of Sir G. R. Collier, Sir Charles MacCarthy and Other Official Sources (London: Seeley and Son, 1824)

Colvile, Andrew, Memorandum by the Acting Committee of West India Planters and Merchants (London: Macnin, Lewis and Böhm, 1853)

Denman, Joseph, The Slave Trade, The African Squadron and Mr. Hutt's Committee, 2 editions (London: John Mortimer, 1849 and 1850)

——, Instructions for the Guidance of Her Majesty's Naval Officers Employed in the Suppression of the Slave Trade (London: T. R. Harrison, 1844)

——, Practical Remarks on The Slave Trade and on the Existing Treaties with Portugal, 2 editions (London: J. Ridgway, 1839)

Denman, Lord Thomas, *A Letter from Lord Denman to Lord Brougham on the Final Extinction of the Slave Trade* (London: J. Hatchard and Son, 2nd edn, 1848)

Eardley-Wilmot, J. E., *Lord Brougham's Acts and Bills, From 1811 to the Present Time* (London: Longman, 1857)

Forbes, Frederick Edwyn, *Dahomey and the Dahomans: Being the Journals of Two Missions to the King of Dahomey, and Residence at his Capital, in the Years 1849 and 1850*, 2 vols (London: Longmans, 1851)

——, *Six Months' Service in the African Blockade, from April to October 1848, in Command of H.M.S. Bonetta* (London: Richard Bentley, 1849)

——, *Five years in China; from 1842 to 1847: With an Account of the Occupation of Labuan and Borneo by Her Majesty's Forces* (London: Richard Bentley, 1848)

Free Trade in Negroes (London: J. Ollivier, 1849)

Gaskell, Elizabeth, *North and South* [1855] (London: Penguin Classics, 2007)

Haines, John Thomas, *My Poll and My Partner Joe: A Nautical Drama in Three Acts* (London: John Cumberland, n.d.)

Hamilton, W. J., 'Geography', in John F. W. Herschel (ed.), *A Manual of Scientific Enquiry; Prepared for the Use of Her Majesty's Navy: And Adapted for Travellers in General* (London: John Murray, 1849), pp. 127–55

Herschel, John F. W. (ed.), *A Manual of Scientific Enquiry; Prepared for the Use of Her Majesty's Navy: And Adapted for Travellers in General* (London: John Murray, 1849)

Heyrick, Elizabeth, *Immediate Not Gradual Abolition* (London: Hatchard et al., 1824)

Hill, Pascoe Grenfell, *A Voyage to the Slave Coasts of West and East Africa* (London: C. Gilpin, 1849)

Holman, James, *Travels in Madeira, Sierra Leone, Teneriffe, St. Jago, Cape Coast Castle Fernando Po, Princes Island, etc.*(London: George Routledge, 2nd edn, 1840)

Huntley, Henry, *Seven Years' Service on the Slave Coast of Western Africa*, 2 vols (London: Thomas Cautley Newby, 1850)

——, *Peregrine Scramble; or Thirty Years Adventures of a Blue Jacket* (Paris: A. and W. Galignanai and Co., 1849)

Jackson, R. M., *Journal of a Voyage to Bonny River on the West Coast of Africa in the Ship Kingston from Liverpool*, ed. Roland Jackson [1826] (Letchworth: Garden City Press, 1934)

Johnson, W. A. B., *A Memoir of the Rev. W. A. B. Johnson, Missionary to the Church Missionary Society in Regent's Town, Sierra Leone*, ed. Stephen H. Tyng [1853] (Memphis, TN: General Books, 2010)

——, *A Memoir of W. A. B. Johnson, a Missionary at Sierra Leone, 1816–23, compiled by R.B. Seeley* (London: Thames Ditton, 1852)

Key, Sir Astley Cooper, *Memoirs of the Admiral the Right Honorable Sir Astley Cooper Key*, ed. P. H. Colomb (London, 1898)

Laird, Macgregor, and R. A. K. Oldfield, *Narrative of an Expedition in the Interior of Africa by the River Niger*, 2 vols (London: Richard Bentley, 1837)

Leonard, Peter, *Records of a Voyage to the Western Coast of Africa, in His*

Majesty's Ship Dryad, and of the Service on that Station for the Suppression of the Slave Trade, in the Years 1830, 1831 and 1832 (Edinburgh: William Tait, 1833)

Lind, James, *An Essay on Diseases Incidental to Europeans in Hot Climates: With the Method of Preventing their Fatal Consequences* (London: T. Becket and P. A. de Hondt, 1768)

Livingstone, David, *Narrative of an Expedition to the Zambesi and its Tributaries* (London: John Murray, 1865)

MacQueen, James, 'Notes on African Geography', *Journal of the Royal Geographical Society* 15 (1845), 374–76

——, *A Geographical Survey of Africa* (London: B. Fellowes, 1840)

Marryat, Captain Frederick, *Peter Simple* [1834], 2 vols (London: Macmillan, 1904)

Matson, Commander Henry James, *Remarks on the Slave Trade and African Squadron*, (London: James Ridgeway, 3rd edn, 1848)

Melville, Elizabeth H., *A Residence at Sierra Leone* (London: John Murray, 1849)

Napier Hewett, Captain J. F., *European Settlements on the West Coast of Africa* (London: Chapman and Hall, 1862)

Ouseley, William Gore, *Notes on the Slave Trade with Remarks on the Measure Adopted for its Suppression* (London: John Rodwell, 1850)

Peacock, Thomas Love, *Gryll Grange* (London: Parker, Son and Bourn, 1860)

Poe, Edgar Allan, 'How to Write a Blackwood Article' [1838] in Edgar Allan Poe, *Complete Tales and Poems* (Ljubjlana: MladinskaKnjiga, 1966), pp. 302–12

Prichard, J. C., 'Ethnology' in John F. W. Herschel (ed.), *A Manual of Scientific Enquiry; Prepared for the Use of Her Majesty's Navy: And Adapted for Travellers in General* (London: John Murray, 1849), pp. 424–40

Pritchett, Morris, *Some Account of the African Remittent Fever Which Occurred on Board Her Majesty's Steam-Ship Wilberforce in the River Niger and Whilst Engaged on the Western Coast of Africa: Comprising an Inquiry into the Causes of Disease in Tropical Climates* (London: John Churchill, 1843)

Rankin, F. Harrison, *The White Man's Grave*, 2 vols (London: Richard Bentley, 1836)

Scott, Michael, *Tom Cringle's Log* [1829–33] (New York: Henry Holt, 1999)

Shakespeare, William, *The Tempest*, Virginia Mason Vaughan and Alden T. Vaughan (eds) (London: Arden Shakespeare, 2003)

[Stephen, Sir George], 'A Barrister', *Analysis of the Evidence Given Before The Select Committee on the Slave Trade* (London: Partridge and Oakey, 1850)

[Stephen, James], *The Dangers of the Country* (London: J. Butterworth and J. Hatchard, 1807)

——, *War in Disguise, or, the Frauds of Neutral Flags* (London: J. Hatchard, 1805)

Stowe, Harriet Beecher, *Uncle Tom's Cabin* (Boston, MA: John P. Jewett, 1852)

Trotter, Thomas, *An Essay, Medical, Philosophical, and Chemical, on Drunkenness, and Its Effect on the Human Body* (London: Longman, 2nd edn, 1804)

Turnbull, David (ed.), *The Jamaica Movement, for Promoting the Enforcement of the Slave-Trade Treaties, and the Suppression of the Slave Trade* (London: Gilpin, 1850)

Walker, Samuel Abraham, *The Church of England Mission in Sierra Leone* (London: Seeley, Burnside and Seeley, 1847)

Wilberforce, Samuel, *Cheap Sugar Means Cheap Slaves* (London: Ridgway, 1848)

Yonge, Charlotte M., *The Daisy Chain; or, Aspirations* [1856] (London: Virago, 1988)

Collected primary sources and curated data sets

Bennett, Norman R. and George E. Brooks, Jr. (eds), *New England Merchants in Africa: A History Through Documents, 1802–1865* (Boston, MA: Boston University Press, 1965)

Church Missionary Society archive, Section IV: African Missions, Adam Matthews Publications

Curtin, Philip (ed.), *Africa Remembered: Narratives by West Africans from the Era of the Slave Trade* (Madison, WI: University of Wisconsin Press, 1968)

'Diary of Richard Carr McClement', Scottish Catholic Archives, www.scottishcatholicarchives.org.uk/Learning/DiaryofRichardCarrMcClement/DiaryExtracts/Empire/tabid/186/Default.aspx. Accessed 20 June 2011

Eltis, David (ed.), 'Voyages: The Transatlantic Slave Trade Voyages Database', Emory University, www.slavevoyages.org. Accessed 10 June 2014

——, and David Richardson, *Atlas of the Transatlantic Slave Trade* (London: Yale University Press, 2010)

Hall, Catherine, Nicholas Draper and Keith McClelland (eds), 'Legacies of British Slave-Ownership' database, UCL, http://www.ucl.ac.uk/lbs/. Accessed 10 June 2014

Hamilton, Douglas and Robert J. Blyth (eds), *Representing Slavery: Art, Artefacts and Archives in the Collections of the National Maritime Museum* (Aldershot: Lund Humphries, 2007)

Kitson, Peter J. and Debbie Lee (eds), *Slavery, Abolition and Emancipation: Writings in the British Romantic Period*, 8 vols (London: Pickering and Chatto, 1999)

Lloyd, Christopher, (ed.), *The Health of Seamen: Selections from the Works of Dr. James Lind, Sir Gilbert Blane and Dr. Thomas Trotter* (London: Navy Records Society, 1965)

'Maritime Memorials', National Maritime Museum, www.nmm.ac.uk/memorials/. Accessed 18 September 2011

'Project Canterbury', the Church of England, http://anglicanhistory.org. Accessed 9 June 2014

Storey, Graham, Kathleen Tillotson and Nina Burgis (eds), *The Letters of Charles Dickens*, 12 vols, (eds) (Oxford: Clarendon, 1987), vi

Secondary sources
Published works

Ackerson, Wayne, *The African Institution (1807–1827) and the Antislavery Movement in Great Britain* (Lewiston, NY: Edwin Mellen Press, 2005)

Adderley, Rosanne, *'New Negroes from Africa': Slave Trade Abolition and Free African Settlement in the Nineteenth-Century Caribbean* (Bloomington & Indianapolis, IN: Indiana University Press, 2006)

Alie, Joe A. D., *A New History of Sierra Leone* (London: Macmillan, 1990)

Allain, Jean, 'Nineteenth-Century Law of the Sea and the British Abolition of the Slave Trade', *British Yearbook of International Law* 78 (2008), 342–88

Anstey, Roger, 'The Pattern of British Abolitionism in the Eighteenth and Nineteenth Centuries', in Christine Bolt and Seymour Drescher (eds), *Anti-Slavery, Religion, and Reform: Essays in Memory of Roger Anstey* (Folkestone, Kent: Dawson, 1980), pp. 19–24

——, *The Atlantic Slave Trade and British Abolition, 1760–1810* (London: Macmillan Press, 1975)

Aravamudan, Srinivas, 'Mary Sherwood, *Dazee; or, The Recaptured Slave* (1821)', in Srinivas Aravamudan (ed.), *Slavery, Abolition and Emancipation: Writing in the British Romantic Period. Vol. 6: Fiction* (London: Pickering and Chatto, 1999), pp. 327–8

Arnold, David, *The Problem of Nature: Environment, Culture and European Expansion* (Oxford: Blackwell, 1996)

Asiegbu, Johnson U. J., 'The Dynamics of Freedom: A Study of Liberated African Emigration and British Antislavery Policy', *Journal of Black Studies* 7 (1976), 95–106

——, *Slavery and the Politics of Liberation, 1787–1861: A Study of Liberated African Emigration and British Anti-slavery Policy* (Harlow: Longmans, 1969)

Austen, Ralph A. and Woodruff D. Smith, 'Images of African and British Slave-Trade Abolition: The Transition to an Imperialist Ideology, 1787–1807', *African Historical Studies* 2, 1 (1969), 69–83

Baigent, Elizabeth, 'Founders of the Royal Geographical Society of London', in Lawrence Goldman (ed.), *Oxford Dictionary of National Biography* (Oxford: Oxford University Press, 2004 – present), http://www/oxforddnb.com/view/theme/95334. Accessed 18 June 2013

Beech, J. G., 'The Marketing of Slavery Heritage in the United Kingdom', *International Journal of Hospitality and Tourism Administration* 2, 3/4 (2001), 85–105

Beeler, John, 'Maritime Policing and the Pax Britannica: The Royal Navy's Anti-Slavery Patrol in the Caribbean, 1828–1848', *The Northern Mariner/ Le marin du nord* 16, 1 (2006), 1–20

Bender, Thomas (ed.), *The Antislavery Debate: Capitalism and Abolitionism as a Problem of Historical Interpretation* (Berkeley, CA: University of California Press, 1992)

Benton, Lauren, 'Abolition and Imperial Law, 1790–1820', *Journal of Imperial and Commonwealth History* 39 (2011), 355–74

Bernier, Celeste-Marie, '"Arms Like Polished Iron": The Black Slave Body in Narratives of a Slave Ship Revolt', in ThomasWiedemann and Jane Gardner (eds), *Representing the Body of the Slave* (London: Frank Cass, 2002), pp. 91–106

Bethell, Leslie, *The Abolition of the Brazilian Slave Trade: Britain, Brazil and the Slave Trade Question, 1807–1869* (Cambridge: Cambridge University Press, 1970)

——, 'The Mixed Commissions for the Suppression of the Transatlantic Slave Trade in the Nineteenth Century', *Journal of African Historical Studies* 7 (1966), 79–93

Blackett, Richard, *Divided Hearts: Britain and the American Civil War* (Baton Rouge, LA: Louisiana State University Press, 2001)

Blake, Richard, *Evangelicals in the Royal Navy 1775–1815: Blue Lights and Psalm-Singers* (Woodbridge: Boydell Press, 2008)

Blyth, Robert J., 'Britain, the Royal Navy and the Suppression of Slave Trades in the Nineteenth Century', in Douglas Hamilton and Robert J. Blyth (eds), *Representing Slavery: Art, Artefacts and Archives in the Collections of the National Maritime Museum* (Aldershot: Lund Humphries, 2007), pp. 78–91

Brantlinger, Patrick, *Rule of Darkness: British Literature and Imperialism, 1830–1914* [1988] (London: Cornell University Press, 1990)

——, 'Victorians and Africans: The Geneaology of the Myth of the Dark Continent', in Henry L. Gates Jr. (ed.), *'Race', Writing, and Difference* (London: University of Chicago Press, 1985), pp. 185–222

Brooks, George E., Jr., *The Kru Mariner in the Nineteenth Century* (Bloomington, IN: Indiana University Press, 1971)

——, 'A View of Sierra Leone ca. 1815', *Sierra Leone Studies* 13 (1960), 24–31

Brown, Christopher Leslie, *Moral Capital: Foundations of British Abolitionism* (Chapel Hill, NC: University of North Carolina Press, 2006)

Brown, David, *Palmerston and the Politics of Foreign Policy, 1846–55* (Manchester: Manchester University Press, 2002)

Brown, Robert T., 'Fernando Po and the Anti-Sierra Leonean Campaign: 1826-1834', *International Journal of African Historical Studies* 6 (1973), 249–64

Burroughs, Robert, 'Sailors and Slaves: "The Poor Enslaved Tar" in Naval Reform and Nautical Melodrama', *Journal of Victorian Culture* 16 (2011), 305–23

——, 'Eyes on the Prize: Journeys in Slave Ships Taken as Prizes by the Royal Navy', *Slavery & Abolition* 31 (2010), 99–115

——, '"[T]he true sailors of Western Africa": Kru Seafaring Identity in British Travellers' Accounts of the 1830s and 1840s', *Journal of Maritime Research* 11 (2009), 51–67

Burton, Gera, 'Liberty's Call: Richard Robert Madden's Voice in the Anti-Slavery Movement', *Irish Migration Studies in Latin America* 5 (2007), 199–207

Bynum, W. F., *Science and the Practice of Medicine in the Nineteenth Century* (Cambridge: Cambridge University Press, 1994)

Callender, Geoffrey, *The Naval Side of British History* (London: Christophers, 1925)

Cameron, J. M. R., 'John Barrow, the *Quarterly*'s Imperial Reviewer', in Jonathan Cutmore (ed.), *Conservatism and the Quarterly Review* (London: Pickering and Chatto, 2007), pp. 133–49

Campbell, Duncan A., *English Public Opinion and the American Civil War* (Woodbridge: Boydell, 2003)

Campbell, Gwyn (ed.), *Abolition and its Aftermath in the Indian Ocean, Africa and Asia* (Abingdon, Oxon: Routledge, 2005)

Canney, Donald L., *Africa Squadron: The US Navy and the Slave Trade* (Dulles, VA: Potomac Books, 2006)

Cavell, Janice, *Tracing the Connected Narrative: Arctic Exploration in British Print Culture, 1818–1860* (Toronto, Ontario: University of Toronto Press, 2008)

Chamberlain, Muriel, *Pax Britannica? British Foreign Policy, 1789–1914* (London: Longman, 1988)

Christopher, Emma, *Slave Ship Sailors and Their Captive Cargoes, 1730–1807* (Cambridge: Cambridge University Press, 2006)

——, Cassandra Pybus and Marcus Rediker (eds), *Many Middle Passages: Forced Migration and the Making of the Modern World* (Berkeley, CA: University of California Press, 2007)

Colley, Linda, *Britons: Forging the Nation, 1707–1837* (London: Yale University Press, 1992)

Coupland, Reginald, *The British Anti-Slavery Movement* (London: T. Butterworth, 1933)

Crooks, J. J., *A History of Sierra Leone* (London: Cass, 1972)

Curtin, Philip D., 'The End of the "White Man's Grave"? Nineteenth-Century Mortality in West Africa', *Journal of Interdisciplinary History* 21 (1990), 63–88

——, *Death by Migration* (Cambridge: Cambridge University Press, 1989)

——, 'African Health at Home and Abroad', *Social Science History* 10 (1986), 369–98

——, *The Image of Africa: British Ideas and Actions, 1780–1850* [Madison, WI: University of Wisconsin Press, 1964] (London: Macmillan, 1965)

——, 'White Man's Grave: Image and Reality, 1780–1850', *Journal of British Studies* 1 (1961), 94–110

Daget, Serge, 'France, Suppression of the Illegal Trade, and England, 1817–1850', in David Eltis and James Walvin (eds), *The Abolition of the Atlantic Slave Trade: Origins and Effects in Europe, Africa, and the Americas* (Madison, WI: University of Wisconsin Press, 1981), pp. 193–217

Darwin, John, 'Imperialism and the Victorians: The Dynamics of Territorial Expansion', *English Historical Review* 112 (1997), 614–42

Davis, David Brion, *Inhuman Bondage: The Rise and Fall of Slavery in the New World* (Oxford: Oxford University Press, 2006)

Davis, R. R., 'James Buchanan and the Suppression of the Slave Trade, 1858–1861', *Pennsylvania History* 33 (1966), 446–59

Delaporte, Francois, *The History of Yellow Fever: An Essay on the Birth of Tropical Medicine* (Cambridge, MA: MIT Press, 1991)

Dorsey, Joseph C., *Slave Traffic in the Age of Abolition: Puerto Rico, West Africa, and the Non-Hispanic Caribbean, 1815–59* (Gainesville, FL: University Press of Florida, 2003)

Drescher, Seymour, 'Antislavery Debates: Tides of Historiography in Slavery and Antislavery', *European Review* 19 (2011), 131–48

——, 'Emperors of the World: British Abolitionism and Imperialism', in D. R. Peterson (ed.), *Abolitionism and Imperialism in Britain, Africa, and the Atlantic* (Athens, OH: Ohio University Press, 2010), pp. 129–49

——, 'Public Opinion and Parliament in the Abolition of the British Slave Trade', in Stephen Farrell, Melanie Unwin and James Walvin (eds), *The British Slave Trade: Abolition, Parliament and People* (Edinburgh: Edinburgh University Press, 2007), pp. 42–65

——, *The Mighty Experiment: Free Labour versus Slavery in British Emancipation* (Oxford: Oxford University Press, 2004)

——, 'Whose Abolition? Popular Pressure and the Ending of the British Slave Trade', *Past and Present* 143 (1994), 136–66

——, Review of Thomas Bender (ed.), *The Antislavery Debate: Capitalism and Abolitionism as a Problem of Historical Interpretation* (Berkeley, CA: University of California Press, 1992), *History and Theory* 32 (1993), 311–29

——, 'The Ending of the Slave Trade and the Evolution of European Scientific Racism', *Social Science History* 14 (1990), 415–50

——, 'The Slaving Capital of the World: Liverpool and National Opinion in the Age of Abolition', *Slavery & Abolition* 9 (1988), 128–43

——, 'Public Opinion and the Destruction of British Colonial Slavery', in James Walvin (ed.), *Slavery and British Society 1776–1846* (London: Macmillan, 1982), pp. 22–48

——, *Econocide: British Slavery in the Era of Abolition* [1977] (Chapel Hill, NC: University of North Carolina Press, 2nd edn, 2010)

Dresser, Madge, 'Set in Stone? Statues and Slavery in London', *History Workshop Journal* 64 (2007), 162–99

Dyde, Brian, *The Empty Sleeve: The Story of the West India Regiments of the British Army* (London: Readers Book Club, 1997)

Echenberg, Myron J., Review of Frederick E. Forbes, *Six Months' Service in the African Blockade: from April to October, 1848, in Command of H. M. S. Bonetta*, *Journal of Asian and African Studies* 7 (1972), 236–9

Ellis, A. B., *History of the First West India Regiment* (London: Chapel and Hall, 1885)

Eltis, David, 'The Volume and Structure of the Transatlantic Slave Trade: A Reassessment', *The William and Mary Quarterly* 58 (2001), 17–46

——, *Economic Growth and the Ending of the Transatlantic Slave Trade* (Oxford: Oxford University Press, 1987)

——, 'The British Contribution to the Nineteenth-Century Transatlantic Slave Trade', *Economic History Review* 32 (1979), 211–27

——, and David Richardson, 'A New Assessment of the Transatlantic Slave Trade', in David Eltis and David Richardson (eds), *Extending the Frontiers: Essays on the New Transatlantic Slave Trade Database* (New Haven, CT: Yale University Press, 2008), pp. 1–60

Everill, Bronwen, 'Bridgeheads of Empire? Liberated African Missionaries in West Africa', *Journal of Imperial and Commonwealth History* 45 (2012), 789–805

Fehrenbacher, Don E., *The Slaveholding Republic: An Account of the United States Government's Relations to Slavery* (Oxford: Oxford University Press, 2001)

Ferguson, Moira, 'Fictional Constructions of Liberated Africans: Mary Butt Sherwood', in Tim Fulford and Peter J. Kitson (eds), *Romanticism and Colonialism: Writing and Empire, 1780–1830* (Cambridge: Cambridge University Press, 1998), pp. 148–63

Fisher, H. J., Review of Johnson U. J. Asiegbu, *Slavery and the Politics of Liberation* (Harlow: Longmans, 1969), *Bulletin of the School of Oriental and African Studies, University of London* 34 (1971), 188–90

Fladeland, Betty, 'Abolitionist Pressures on the Concert of Europe, 1814–1822', *Journal of Modern History* 38 (1966), 355–73

Ford Park Cemetery, Plymouth: A Heritage Trail (Plymouth: Ford Park Cemetery Trust, 2004)

Foreman, Amanda, *A World on Fire: An Epic History of Two Nations Divided* (London: Allen Lane, 2010)

Frost, Diana, 'Diasporan West African Communities: The Kru in Freetown and Liverpool', *Review of African Political Economy* 29 (2002), 285–300

Fryer, Peter, *Black People in the British Empire: An Introduction* (London: Pluto Press, 1988)

Fulford, Tim, 'Romanticizing the Empire: The Naval Heroes of Southey, Coleridge, Austen, and Marryat', *MLQ: Modern Language Quarterly* 60 (1999), 161–96

Fyfe, Christopher, *A History of Sierra Leone* (Oxford: Oxford University Press, 1962)

Gallagher, Catherine, 'Floating Signifiers of Britishness in the Novels of the Anti-Slave-Trade Squadron', in Wendy S. Jacobson (ed.), *Dickens and the Children of Empire* (Basingstoke: Palgrave, 2000), pp. 78–93

——, *The Industrial Reformation of English Fiction: Social Discourse and Narrative Form, 1832–1867* (Chicago: University of Chicago Press, 1985)

Gallagher, John, 'Fowell Buxton and the New African Policy 1838-42', *Cambridge Historical Journal* 10 (1950), 36–58

Gilroy, Paul, *The Black Atlantic: Modernity and Double Consciousness* (Cambridge, MA: Harvard University Press, 1993)

Goldman, Lawrence, '"A Total Misconception": Lincoln, the Civil War and the British, 1860–65', in Richard Carwardine and Jay Sexton (eds), *The Global Lincoln* (Oxford: Oxford University Press, 2011), pp. 107–22

Gott, Gill, 'Imperial Humanitarianism: History of an Arrested Dialectic', in Berta Esperanza Hernández-Truyo (ed.), *Moral Imperialism: A Critical Anthology* (New York: New York University Press, 2002), pp. 19–38

Green, Andy, 'Remembering Slavery in Birmingham: Sculpture, Paintings and Installations', *Slavery & Abolition*, 29 (2008), 189–201

Hall, Catherine, *Macaulay and Son: Architects of Imperial Britain* (London: Yale University Press, 2012)

——, 'An Empire of God or of Man? The Macaulays, Father and Son', in Hilary M. Carey (ed.), *Empires of Religion* (Basingstoke: Palgrave Macmillan, 2008), pp. 64–83

——, 'Remembering 1807: Histories of the Slave Trade, Slavery and Abolition', *History Workshop Journal* 64 (2007), 1–5

——, *Civilising Subjects: Metropole and Colony in the English Imagination, 1830–1867* (Oxford: Polity, 2002)

Hamilton, Douglas, 'Representing Slavery in British Museums: The Challenges of 2007', in Cora Kaplan and John Oldfield (eds), *Imagining Transatlantic Slavery and Abolition* (Basingstoke: Palgrave Macmillan, 2009), pp. 127–44

Hamilton, Keith, 'Zealots and Healots: The Slave Trade Department of the Nineteenth-Century Foreign Office', in Keith Hamilton and Patrick Salmon (eds), *Slavery, Diplomacy and Empire: Britain and the Suppression of the Slave Trade, 1807–1915* (Eastbourne: Sussex Academic Press, 2009), pp. 20–41

——, and Patrick Salmon (eds), *Slavery, Diplomacy and Empire: Britain and the Suppression of the Slave Trade, 1807–1915* (Eastbourne: Sussex Academic Press, 2009)

Harms, Robert, Bernard K. Freamon and David W. Blight (eds), *Indian Ocean Slavery in the Age of Abolition* (New Haven, CT: Yale University Press, 2013)

Harries, Patrick, 'The Hobgoblins of the Middle Passage: the Cape and the Trans-Atlantic Slave Trade', in Ulrike Schmieder, Katja Füllberg-Stolberg and Michael Zeuske (eds), *The End of Slavery in Africa and the Americas: A Comparative Approach* (Berlin: LIT Verlag, 2011), pp. 27–50

Harrison, Gordon, *Mosquitoes, Malaria, and Man: A Story of the Hostilities since 1880* (New York: Dutton, 1978)

Harrison, Mark, 'Differences of Degree: Representations of India in British Medical Topography, 1820–c.1870', in Nicolaas A. Rupke (ed.), *Medical Geography in Historical Perspective* (London: Wellcome Trust Centre for the History of Medicine at UCL, 2000), pp. 51–69

Helfman, Tara, 'The Court of Vice Admiralty at Sierra Leone and the Abolition of the West African Slave Trade', *Yale Law Journal* 115 (2006), 1122–56

HM Government, *Bicentenary of the Abolition of the Slave Trade Act, 1807–2007* (Wetherby: Department of Communities and Local Government, 2007)

Hogg, Peter C., *The African Slave Trade and its Suppression: A Classified and Annotated Bibliography* (Abingdon: Frank Cass, 1973)

Holsoe, Svend E., 'The Manipulation of Traditional Political Structures among Coastal Peoples in Western Liberia during the Nineteenth Century', *Ethnohistory* 21 (1974), 158–67

Hopkins, A. G., 'The "New International Economic Order" in the Nineteenth Century: Britain's First Development Plan for Africa', in Robin Law (ed.), *From Slave Trade to 'Legitimate' Commerce: The Commercial Transition in Nineteenth-Century West Africa* (Cambridge: Cambridge University Press, 1995), pp. 240–64

Howe, Anthony, 'Two Faces of British Power: Cobden versus Palmerston', in

David Brown and Miles Taylor (eds), *Palmerston Studies II* (Southampton: Hartley Institute, 2007), pp. 168–92

Howell, Raymond C., *The Royal Navy and the Slave Trade* (Beckenham: Croom Helm, 1987)

Hunter, Mark C., *Policing the Seas: Anglo-American Relations and the Equatorial Atlantic, 1819–1865* (St John's, Newfoundland: International Maritime Economic History Association, 2008)

Huzzey, Richard, 'Concepts of Liberty: Freedom, Laissez-Faire and the State after Britain's Abolition of Slavery', in Catherine Hall, Nick Draper and Keith McClelland (eds), *Emancipation and the Remaking of the British Imperial World* (Manchester: Manchester University Press, 2014), pp. 149–71

——, 'The Moral Geography of British Anti-Slavery Responsibilities', *Transactions of the Royal Historical Society*, sixth series, 22 (2012), 111–39

——, *Freedom Burning: Anti-Slavery and Empire in Victorian Britain* (Ithaca, NY: Cornell University Press, 2012)

——, 'Gladstone and the Suppression of the Slave Trade' in Roland Quinault, Roger Swift, and Ruth Clayton Windscheffel (eds), *William Gladstone: New Studies and Perspectives* (Farnham: Ashgate, 2012), pp. 253–66

——, 'Free Trade, Free Labour, and Slave Sugar in Victorian Britain', *Historical Journal* 53 (2010), 359–79

Jones, Howard, *Blue and Gray Diplomacy: A History of Union and Confederate Foreign Relations* (Chapel Hill, NC: University of North Carolina Press, 2010)

——, *Abraham Lincoln and a New Birth of Freedom: The Union and Slavery in the Diplomacy of the Civil War* (Lincoln, NE: University of Nebraska Press, 1999)

——— and Donald A. Rakestraw, *Prologue to Manifest Destiny: Anglo-American Relations in the 1840s* (Wilmington, DE: Scholarly Resources, 1997)

Kaufmann, Chaim D. and Robert A. Pape, 'Explaining Costly International Moral Action: Britain's Sixty-Year Campaign against the Atlantic Slave Trade', *International Organization* 53 (1999), 631–68

Keene, Edward, 'A Case Study of the Construction of International Hierarchy: British Treaty-Making against the Slave Trade in the Early Nineteenth Century,' *International Organization* 61 (2007), 311–39

Kennedy, Paul, *The Rise and Fall of British Naval Mastery* (London: Allen Lane, 1976)

Kern, Holger Lutz, 'Strategies of Legal Change: Great Britain, International Law, and the Abolition of the Transatlantic Slave Trade', *Journal of the History of International Law* 6 (2004), 233–58

Kerr-Ritchie, Jefferey R., 'Reflections on the Bicentennial of the Abolition of the British Slave Trade', *Journal of African American History* 93 (2008), 532–42

Kielstra, Paul-Michael, *The Politics of Slave Trade Suppression in Britain and France, 1814–48* (New York: St. Martin's Press, 2000)

King, James Ferguson, 'The Latin-American Republics and the Suppression of the Slave Trade', *Hispanic American Historical Review* 24 (1944), 387–411

Kiple, Kenneth, *The Caribbean Slave: A Biological History* (Cambridge: Cambridge University Press, 1984)

Klunder, W. C., *Lewis Cass and the Politics of Moderation* (Kent, OH: Kent State University Press, 1996)

Kowaleski-Wallace, Elizabeth, *The British Slave Trade and Public Memory* (New York: Columbia University Press, 2006)

Kup, A. P., *Sierra Leone: A Concise History* [Cambridge: Cambridge University Press, 1961] (Newton Abbot: David and Charles, 1975)

Lalla, Barbara, 'Dungeons of the Soul: Frustrated Romanticism in Eighteenth and Nineteenth-Century Literature of Jamaica', *MELUS* 21, 3 (1996), 2–23

Lambert, David, *Mastering the Niger: James MacQueen's African Geography and the Struggle over Atlantic Slavery* (Chicago, IL: University of Chicago Press, 2013)

——, 'Sierra Leone and Other Sites in the War of Representation over Slavery', *History Workshop Journal* 64 (2007), 103–32

——, *White Creole Culture, Politics and Identity During the Age of Abolition* (Cambridge: Cambridge University Press, 2005)

Land, Isaac, *War, Nationalism and the British Sailor, 1750–1850* (Basingstoke: Palgrave Macmillan, 2009)

Lavery, Brian, *Nelson's Navy: The Ships, Men and Organisation, 1793–1815* (London: Conway Maritime Press, 1989)

Law, Robin, 'Abolition and Imperialism: International Law and the British Suppression of the Atlantic Slave Trade', in Derek Peterson (ed.), *Abolition and Imperialism in Britain, Africa, and the Atlantic* (Athens, OH: Ohio University Press, 2010), pp. 150–74

——, *Ouidah: The Social History of a West African Slaving 'Port', 1727–1892* (Athens, OH: Ohio University Press, 2004)

____ (ed.), *From Slave Trade to 'Legitimate Commerce': The Commercial Transition in Nineteenth-Century West Africa* (Cambridge: Cambridge University Press, 1995)

Lecky, W. E. H., *The History of European Morals*, 2 vols (London: Longmans, 1869)

LeVeen, E. P., *British Slave Trade Suppression Policies, 1821–1868* (New York: Arno, 1977)

Lewis, Michael, *The Navy in Transition, 1814–1864: A Social History* (London: Hodder and Stoughton, 1965)

Lincoln, Margarette, *Representing the Royal Navy: British Sea Power, 1750–1815* (Aldershot: Ashgate, 2002)

——, 'Shipwreck Narratives of the Eighteenth and Early Nineteenth Century: Indicators of Culture and Identity', *Journal for Eighteenth-Century Studies* 20 (1997), 155–72

Lloyd, Christopher, *The Navy and the Slave Trade: The Suppression of the African Slave Trade in the Nineteenth Century* [London: Longman, 1949] (London: Frank Cass, 1968)

Lorimer, Douglas A., *Colour, Class and the Victorians: English Attitudes to the Negro in the Mid-Nineteenth Century* (Leicester: Leicester University Press, 1978)

Lynn, Martin, 'Britain's West African Policy and the Island of Fernando Po, 1821–43', *Journal of Imperial and Commonwealth History* 18 (1990), 191–207

Mackenthun, Gesa, *Fictions of the Black Atlantic in American Foundational Literature* (New York: Routledge, 2004)

Mann, Kristin, *Slavery and the Birth of an African City: Lagos, 1760–1900* (Bloomington, IN: Indiana University Press, 2007)

Mannix, Daniel P. and Malcolm Cowley, *Black Cargoes: A History of the Atlantic Slave Trade* [1962] (London: Longmans, 1963)

Marshall, P. J. and Glyndwr Williams, *The Great Map of Mankind: British Perceptions of the World in the Age of Enlightenment* (London: J. M. Dent & Sons, 1982)

Martin, Jane, *Krumen Down the Coast: Liberian Migrants in the West African Coast in the Nineteenth Century* (Boston, MA: African Studies Center, 1982)

Martinez, Jenny S., *The Slave Trade and the Origins of International Human Rights Law* (Oxford: Oxford University Press, 2012)

Máthé-Shires, László, 'Imperial Nightmares: The British Image of "the deadly climate" of West Africa, c.1840–74', *European Review of History* 8 (2001), 137–56

Mathieson, William Law, *Great Britain and the Slave Trade, 1839–1865* (London: Longmans, 1929)

May, Alex, 'Reginald Coupland', in Lawrence Goldman (ed.), *Oxford Dictionary of National Biography* (Oxford: Oxford University Press, 2004 – present), http://www.oxforddnb.com/view/article/32585. Accessed 22 October 2011

McAleer, John, '"That infamous commerce in human blood": Reflections on Representing Slavery and Empire in British Museums', *Museum History Journal* 13 (2013), 72–86

McCaskie, T. C., 'Cultural Encounters: Britain and Africa in the Nineteenth Century', in Andrew Porter (ed.), *The Oxford History of the British Empire: Volume III: The Nineteenth Century* (Oxford: Oxford University Press, 1999), pp. 665–89

McKenna, Joseph, *British Ships in the Confederate Navy* (Jefferson, NC: McFarland, 2010)

Meer, Sarah, *Uncle Tom Mania: Slavery, Minstrelsy, and Transatlantic Culture in the 1850s* (Athens, GA: University of Georgia Press, 2005)

Miers, Suzanne, 'Slavery and the Slave Trade as International Issues, 1890–1939', *Slavery & Abolition* 19 (1998), 16–37

——, *Britain and the Ending of the Slave Trade* (London: Longman, 1975)

——, and Martin A. Klein (eds), *Slavery and Colonial Rule in Africa* (London: Frank Cass, 1999)

——, and Richard Roberts (eds), *The End of Slavery in Africa* (Madison, WI: University of Wisconsin Press, 1988)

Miliband, David, 'Foreword', in Keith Hamilton and Patrick Salmon (eds), *Slavery, Diplomacy and Empire: Britain and the Suppression of the Slave Trade* (Eastbourne: Sussex Academic Press, 2009), pp. vii–viii

Milne, A. Taylor, 'The Lyons-Seward Treaty of 1862', *American Historical Review* 38 (1933), 511–25

Mishra, Amit Kumar, 'Indian Indentured Labourers in Mauritius: Reassessing the "New System of Slavery" vs. Free Labor Debate', *Studies in History* 25 (2009), 229–51

Moore, Grace, *Dickens and Empire: Discourses of Class, Race and Colonialism in the Works of Charles Dickens* (Aldershot: Ashgate, 2004)

Morgan, Philip D., 'Black Experiences in Britain's Maritime World', in David Cannadine (ed.), *Empire, the Sea and Global History: Britain's Maritime World, c.1760–c.1840* (Basingstoke: Palgrave Macmillan, 2007), pp. 105–33

Murray, David R., *Odious Commerce: Britain, Spain, and the Abolition of the Cuban Slave Trade* (Cambridge: Cambridge University Press, 1980)

——, 'Richard Robert Madden: His Career as a Slavery Abolitionist', *Studies: An Irish Quarterly Review* 61 (1972), 41–53

Needell, Jeffrey D., 'The Abolition of the Brazilian Slave Trade in 1850: Historiography, Slave Agency and Statesmanship', *Journal of Latin American Studies* 33 (2001), 681–711

Nolte, Eugene A., 'Michael Scott and *Blackwood's Magazine*: Some Unpublished Letters', *Library* 8 (1953), 188–96

Northrup, David, 'Becoming African: Identity Formation among Liberated Slaves in Nineteenth-Century Sierra Leone', *Slavery & Abolition* 27 (2006), 1–21

——, *Indentured Labor in the Age of Imperialism, 1834–1922* (Cambridge: Cambridge University Press, 1995)

Nwulia, Moses D.E., *Britain and Slavery in East Africa* (Washington, DC: Three Continents Press, 1975)

Oldfield, J. R., *'Chords of Freedom': Commemoration, Ritual and British Transatlantic Slavery* (Manchester: Manchester University Press, 2007)

——, *Popular Politics and British Anti-Slavery: The Mobilisation of Public Opinion against the Slave Trade 1787–1807* (Manchester: Manchester University Press, 1995)

Padfield, Peter, *Rule Britannia: The Victorian and Edwardian Navy* [1981] (London: Pimlico, 2002)

Paton, Diana, and Jane Webster, 'Remembering Slave Trade Abolitions: Reflections on 2007 in International Perspective', *Slavery & Abolition* 30 (2009), 161–7

Peel, J. D. Y., *Religious Encounter and the Making of the Yoruba* (Bloomington, IN: Indiana University Press, 2001)

Perreau-Saussine, Amanda, 'British Acts of State in English Courts', *British Yearbook of International Law* 78 (2007), 186–254

Peterson, John, *Province of Freedom: A History of Sierra Leone* (London: Faber and Faber, 1969)

Petley, Christer, 'Slavery, Emancipation and the Creole Worldview of Jamaican Colonists, 1800–1834', *Slavery & Abolition* 26 (2005), 93–114

Pietz, William, 'The Fetish of Civilization: Sacrificial Blood and Monetary Debt', in Peter Pels and Oscar Salemnick (eds), *Colonial Subjects: Essays on the Practical History of Anthropology* (Ann Arbor, MI: University of Michigan Press, 1999), pp. 53–81

Porter, Andrew, 'Trusteeship, Anti-Slavery, and Humanitarianism', in Andrew

Porter (ed.), *The Oxford History of the British Empire: Volume III: The Nineteenth Century* (Oxford: Oxford University Press, 1999), pp. 198–221

Porter, Arthur, *Creoledom: A Study of the Development of Freetown Society* (Oxford: Oxford University Press, 1963)

Pratt, Mary Louise, *Imperial Eyes: Travel Writing and Transculturation* (London: Routledge, 1992)

Prentice, Rina, *A Celebration of the Sea: The Decorative Art Collections of the National Maritime Museum* (London: HMSO, 1994)

Preston, Anthony and John Major, *Send a Gunboat: The Victorian Navy and Supremacy at Sea, 1854–1904* [1967] (London: Conway, 2007)

Prior, Katherine, 'Commemorating Slavery 2007: A Personal View from Inside the Museums', *History Workshop Journal* 64 (2007), 200–11

Rediker, Marcus, *The Slave Ship: A Human History* (London: John Murray, 2007)

Rees, Siân, *Sweet Water and Bitter: The Ships that Stopped the Slave Trade* (London: Chatto and Windus, 2008)

Richardson, David, 'Shipboard Revolts, African Authority and the Atlantic Slave Trade', *The William and Mary Quarterly* 58 (2001), 69–92

Ridley, Jasper, *Lord Palmerston* (London: Constable, 1970)

Rodger, N. A. M., *The Wooden World: An Anatomy of the Georgian Navy* (London: Fontana Press, 1986)

Rubery, Matthew, *The Novelty of Newspapers: Victorian Fiction after the Invention of the News* (Oxford: Oxford University Press, 2009)

Rubin, Alfred P., *Ethics and Authority in International Law* (Cambridge: Cambridge University Press, 1997)

Ryan, Maeve, 'The Price of Legitimacy in Humanitarian Intervention: Britain, the Right of Search, and the Abolition of the West Africa Slave Trade, 1807–1867', in Brendan Simms and D. J. B. Trim (eds), *Humanitarian Intervention: A History* (Cambridge: Cambridge University Press, 2011), pp. 231–56

Ryden, David Beck, *West Indian Slavery and British Abolition, 1783–1807* (Cambridge: Cambridge University Press, 2010)

Said, Edward W., *Culture and Imperialism* (London: Chatto and Windus, 1993)

——, *Orientalism: Western Conceptions of the Orient* (London: Penguin, 1978)

Sale, Maggie Montesinos, *The Slumbering Volcano: American Slave Ship Revolts and the Production of Rebellious Masculinity* (Durham, NC: Duke University Press, 1997)

Samson, Jane, 'Hero, Fool or Martyr? The Many Deaths of Commodore Goodenough', *Journal for Maritime Research* 10 (2008), 1–22

Schwarz, Suzanne, 'Commerce, Civilization and Christianity: The Development of the Sierra Leone Company', in David Richardson, Suzanne Schwarz and Anthony Tibbles (eds), *Liverpool and Transatlantic Slavery* (Liverpool: Liverpool University Press, 2007), pp. 255–76

Shaikh, Farida, 'Judicial Diplomacy: British Officials and the Mixed Commission Courts', in Keith Hamilton and Patrick Salmon (eds), *Slavery, Diplomacy and Empire: Britain and the Suppression of the Slave Trade, 1807–1975* (Eastbourne: Sussex Academic Press, 2009), pp. 42–64

Sheriff, Abdul, *Slaves, Spices and Ivory in Zanzibar* (London: James Currey, 1987)

Sherwood, Marika, *After Abolition: Britain and the Slave Trade Since 1807* (London: I. B. Tauris, 2007)

Sibthorpe, A. B. C., *The History of Sierra Leone* [1881] (London: Frank Cass, 1970)

Simpson, Moira, *Making Representations: Museums in the Post-colonial Era* (London: Routledge, 1996)

Spitzer, Leo, *The Creoles of Sierra Leone: Responses to Colonialism 1870–1945* (Madison, WI: University of Wisconsin Press, 1974)

Stanziani, Alessandro, 'Beyond Colonialism: Servants, Wage Earners and Indentured Migrants in Rural France and on Reunion Island (c. 1750–1900)', *Labor History* 54 (2013), 64–87

Stocking, George W., Jnr., *Victorian Anthropology* (New York: The Free Press, 1987)

Stone, Harry, 'Charles Dickens and Harriett Beecher Stowe', *Nineteenth-Century Fiction* 12 (1957), 188–202

Taylor, Robert, *If We Must Die: Shipboard Insurrections in the Era of the Atlantic Slave Trade* (Baton Rouge, LA: Louisiana State University Press, 2006)

Temperley, Howard, *White Dreams, Black Africa: The Antislavery Expedition to the Niger, 1841–42* (New Haven, CT: Yale University Press, 1991)

——, *British Anti-Slavery 1833–1870* (Longman: London, 1972)

Terrell, Christopher, 'Columbine, Edward Henry (1763–1811)', in Lawrence Goldman (ed.), *Oxford Dictionary of National Biography* (Oxford: Oxford University Press, 2004 – present), www.oxforddnb.com/view/article/64853. Accessed 9 March 2009

Thomas, Hugh, *The Slave Trade: The History of the Atlantic Slave Trade, 1440–1870* (London: Picador, 1997)

Thompson, Carl, *The Suffering Traveller and the Romantic Imagination* (Oxford: Oxford University Press, 2007)

Tinker, Hugh, *A New System of Slavery: The Export of Indian Labour Overseas, 1830–1920* (Oxford: Oxford University Press, 1974)

Trouillot, Michel-Rolph, *Silencing the Past: Power and the Production of History* (Boston, MA: Beacon Press, 1995)

Turley, David, 'Anti-Slavery Activists and Officials: "Influence", Lobbying and the Slave Trade, 1807–1850', in Keith Hamilton and Patrick Salmon (eds), *Slavery, Diplomacy and Empire: Britain and the Suppression of the Slave Trade, 1807–1915* (Eastbourne: Sussex Academic Press, 2009), pp. 81–92

——, *The Culture of English Antislavery, 1780–1860* (London: Routledge, 1991)

Turner, Michael J., 'The Limits of Abolition: Government, Saints and the "African Question", c. 1780–1820', *English Historical Review* 112 (1997), 319–57

Ukpabi, S. C., 'West Indian Troops and the Defence of British West Africa in the Nineteenth Century', *African Studies Review* 17 (1974), 133–50

Utting, Francis A. J., *The Story of Sierra Leone* (London: Longmans, 1931)

Waller, John, *The Discovery of the Germ* (London: Icon Books, 2002)

Walvin, James, *England, Slaves and Freedom, 1776–1838* (Basingstoke: Macmillan, 1986)

——, 'The Public Campaign in England against Slavery, 1787–1834', in David Eltis and James Walvin (eds), *The Abolition of the Atlantic Slave Trade: Origins and Effects in Europe, Africa and the Americas* (Madison, WI: University of Wisconsin Press, 1981), pp. 63–79

——, and Alex Tyrrell, 'Whose History is it? Memorializing Britain's Involvement in Slavery', in Paul Pickering and Alex Tyrrell (eds), *Contested Sites: Commemoration, Memorial and Popular Politics in Nineteenth-Century Britain* (Ashgate: Aldershot, 2004), pp. 147–69

Ward, William E. F., *The Royal Navy and the Slavers: The Suppression of the Atlantic Slave Trade* (London: George Allen and Unwin, 1969)

Williams, Eric, *Capitalism and Slavery* [1944] (London: André Deutsch, 1964)

Wilson, Warren E. and Gary L. McKay, *James D. Bullock: Secret Agent and Mastermind of the Confederate Navy* (Jefferson, NC: McFarland, 2012)

Wolffe, John, 'Lord Palmerston and Religion: A Reappraisal', *English Historical Review* 120 (2005), 907–36

Wood, Marcus, *The Horrible Gift of Freedom* (Athens, GA: University of Georgia Press, 2010)

——, 'Emancipation Art, Fanon and the Butchery of Freedom', in Brycchan Carey and Peter J. Kitson (eds), *Slavery and the Cultures of Abolition* (Cambridge: D.S. Brewer, 2007), pp. 11–41

——, *Slavery, Empathy, and Pornography* (Oxford: Oxford University Press, 2002)

——, *Blind Memory: Visual Representations of Slavery in England and America, 1780–1865* (New York: Routledge, 2000)

Wright, John, *The Trans-Saharan Slave Trade* (New York: Routledge, 2007)

Internet sources

'British PM Brown Goes to DC Bearing Gifts for Obama', Reuters, 2 March 2009, http://blogs.reuters.com/frontrow/2009/03/02/british-pm-brown-goes-to-dc-bearing-gifts-for-obama/. Accessed 18 September 2011

'Chasing Freedom', National Museum of the Royal Navy, www.royalnaval-museum.org/Visit_Tempexhibit_ChasingFreedom.htm. Accessed 18 September 2011

Cubitt, Geoff, Laurajane Smith and Helen Weinstein (eds), '1807 Commemorated', Institute for the Public Understanding of the Past, University of York, www.history.ac.uk/1807commemorated. Accessed 25 October 2011

'From Slave Trade to Humanitarian Aid', BBC News, 19 March 2007, http://news.bbc.co.uk/1/hi/england/hampshire/6430401.stm. Accessed 18 September 2011

Soley, Lord Clive, 'The Right Side of History', The Henry Jackson Society, www.henryjacksonsociety.org/cms/harriercollectionitems/The+Right+Side+of+History.pdf. Accessed 24 October 2011

Unpublished works

Churchill, Wendy, 'Female Complaints: The Medical Diagnosis and Treatment of British Women, 1590–1740' (PhD dissertation, McMaster University, 2005)

Doulton, Lindsay, 'The Royal Navy's Anti-Slavery Campaign in the Western Indian Ocean, c. 1860–1890: Race, Empire and Identity' (PhD dissertation, University of Hull, 2010)

Garber, Mrs Cassandra, of the Krio Descendants' Yunion, interview with Emma Christopher, Freetown, 2009

Henderson, L. C., 'Geography, Travel and Publishing in Mid-Victorian Britain' (PhD dissertation, Royal Holloway, University of London, 2012)

Huzzey, Richard, 'Faith in Free Labor'. Forthcoming

Jones, Peter, 'Palmerston and the Suppression of the Slave Trade'. Supplied in personal correspondence with Richard Huzzey

Morgan-Williams, Prince, interview with Emma Christopher, Regent, 2010

Index

INDEX

INDEX

Lightning Source UK Ltd.
Milton Keynes UK
UKHW022345110321
380086UK00011B/345